HOLLYWOOD OR BUST!

Copyright © 2022 by June Wilkinson.

All rights are reserved worldwide. No part of this publication may be replicated, redistributed, or given away in any form without the author's or publisher's prior written consent.

First Edition.
Published February 2023
by Indies United Publishing House

Available in E-Book, Paperback, and Hardcover.

ISBN: 978-1-64456-579-7 [Hardback]
ISBN: 978-1-64456-580-3 [Paperback]
ISBN: 978-1-64456-581-0 [ePub]

Library of Congress Control Number: 2022951633

INDIES UNITED PUBLISHING HOUSE, LLC
P.O. BOX 3071
QUINCY, IL 62305-3071
IndiesUnited.net

I dedicate this book to my daughter Brahna and my mother, Lily.

I also wish to thank my friends and supporters, Peter Hughes,

Richard Richard, Sue Spoley, Joyce Richards, and Robert and Sue Emery.

HOLLYWOOD OR BUST!

A MEMOIR

The life and times of the legendary actress, model, and Playboy phenominom

June Wilkinson

INDIES UNITED PUBLISHING HOUSE, LLC

Chapter 1

The first question one asks when writing a memoir is how to begin. I wrestled with that for a while. Where and when I was born struck me as boring. Although I have documented my childhood and career mostly chronologically, I wrote of many memories of people and events as they came to mind.

Stay with me as I roam freely through my life and career.

Except for a marriage that went sour, I've led a reasonably successful and happy life in show business. It began in 1952 at the early age of 12 in England, where I was born. During my career, I was blessed to work with many of the biggest talents in the entertainment industry. I consider myself fortunate to count many of them among my closest friends, including the late Hugh Hefner, who built the Playboy empire. He brought me to the American public's attention.

It's Sunday evening, and I'm on my way to the Playboy Mansion in Los Angeles. It was my favorite place to be on a Sunday night. I've been going there since I left Houston following my July 1978 separation from my husband, Dante "Dan" Pastorini. Sunday night at the Mansion meant great food, good friends, and, hopefully, a good movie.

My first movie night was in 1965 at the original Playboy Mansion in Chicago. Although I had graced the pages of Playboy magazine several times beginning in the September 1958 issue, I had never been to the Mansion and had only met Hefner briefly on a few occasions. I was 25 at the time and appearing in the stage play Pajama Tops at the Sheraton Theater in Chicago when I received a message from Hef inviting me to join him and his guests for dinner and a movie Sunday night. Unfortunately, the play didn't end until the movie was over. Still, I was curious to see the inside of that famous place—that flamboyant palace of hedonistic pleasure that was so talked about.

When I arrived, it was wall-to-wall people, many gorgeous ladies dressed and undressed. But, to my surprise—I'm not sure what I expected—despite the rumors, no orgies were going on that I could see. Everyone was on their best behavior—sorry to disappoint. Years later, when I visited the Los Angeles Playboy Mansion, I learned that if there was action, it took place quietly tucked away in the pool area hidden in the famous grotto. Maybe there was action in the indoor pool at the original Chicago Mansion, but I never witnessed it.

The Chicago club was very hip, cool, casual, and intellectual. Remember, this was the sixties, and Hef had created a level of sophistication for what was perceived—at least in his mind—to be the perfect playboy lifestyle. And then there were the sumptuous buffets, which have always been the signature of Sunday nights at the Mansion.

That was the 1960s; it was now the 1970s in Los Angeles, and my head was no longer in a carefree, happy place. After an intense whirlwind romance, I fell in love with and married Houston Oilers quarterback Dan Pastorini on June 1, 1973, at The Highlands Inn in Carmel, California. Dan was in his prime, considered one of the best NFL quarterbacks, and immensely popular on and off the playing field.

When we married, we made a deal: I wouldn't work during the football season, and when the season was over, we would move to my house in Los Angeles, and I would work during that period. My home, on almost three-quarters of an acre, was high above Sunset Boulevard, with one of the most incredible views in the city.

Like most superstars, Dan had an enormous ego fed by the constant fanatic fan adulation. In Houston, the fans treated him like a Greek God. It was always the best table at restaurants, tabs constantly being picked up by business people wanting to get close to him, and invitations to parties we would never have been invited to. You get the picture!

JUNE WILKINSON

The adoring ladies he never said no to brought down the house of cards because, let's face it, Dan was handsome and a sports superstar. When temptation presented itself, Dan didn't know how—or didn't care to—say no. The ladies of Houston and elsewhere threw themselves at him with abandon. If you think Tiger Woods had many affairs, I'm sure his numbers pale compared to Mr. Pastorini's. The fame and the attention it brought were too much for him to ignore.

To give you an example of how women brazenly approached Dan, we were having dinner in a nice restaurant after a football game when a classy-looking woman, around age 25, came to our table. She asked Dan for his autograph, and while he was signing her menu, she leaned over (trying to show as much cleavage as possible) and said, "Do you fuck as well as you throw the football?" She ignored me as if I wasn't there. I couldn't believe she had the gall to say such a rude, classless statement in front of the man's wife. Dan looked at her and said, *"I don't know; ask my wife."* I calmly looked at her and said, *"No, he throws the football better."* She never once looked at me, took the autographed menu, and walked away; so much for adult public behavior.

Being a major NFL superstar and keeping your missteps from becoming public is near impossible. There is little or no room for privacy thanks to probing sports writers, the press, the roaming paparazzi, and those who want to bring you down. I have never understood that. Your life becomes a glowing billboard on a busy freeway. In time, inklings of Dan's sexual indiscretions became known to me thanks to the probing press. Women, out to score a celebrity, just kept coming on to him like NFL linemen determined to knock the quarterback flat on his back—pun intended.

Although she certainly was not the sole reason for our split, the straw that finally broke the Camel's back arrived in the form of actress Farrah Fawcett. Farrah and Dan met at a tennis match, sparks flew, and a torrid affair followed. This was when Farrah was estranged from her then-husband, actor Lee Majors, TV's Six Million Dollar Man. Even though there had been many others, Dan's affair with Farrah hurt the most because of her high public profile. And, believe it or not, I had no idea the two had begun an affair until it hit TV news, newspapers, and radio as the affair started to play out in public, much to my dismay.

I finally decided I had to get out of a deteriorating situation. I bought a townhouse in Sherman Oaks, California, bid goodbye to Pastorini and Houston, Texas, packed my bags and young daughter, moved out, and resumed my acting career.

That was not the end of it by any stretch of the imagination. I did have a one-time delicious payback on the Farrah Fawcett affair. Dan and Lee Majors knew each other. They appeared in a very forgettable film in 1979 titled Killer Fish. They did not, however, become fast friends. Dan thought Majors was a real ass, and I assume Majors thought the same of Dan. Little love was lost between them.

The bad blood only deepened when Dan and Farrah's affair became public. So, now I'm living in Sherman Oaks, and Dan, still playing for the Oilers, remained in Houston. One Sunday, Dan decided to fly to Los Angeles on a Sunday to spend quality time with Farrah. But when he arrived, much to his dismay, Farrah told him she had scheduled a meeting with Lee that night to discuss some mutual business dealings, and she could not spend the evening with him.

I was off to my usual dinner and a movie at the Los Angeles Playboy Mansion on Sunday. I left Sherman Oaks, drove over the mountain via Beverly Glen to Sunset Boulevard, turned left, then right on Charing Cross Road, passing those street corner vendors who sell outdated maps to starry-eyed out-of-town tourists seeking directions to the homes of the "rich and famous."

When you arrive at the Mansion, you come to a magnificently designed iron gate. This is the house that Hef's girlfriend, Barbie Benton, had found for him. Just before the entrance, on the left side, is a large rock with a two-way radio system built into it so guests can identify themselves before being allowed entry onto the beautifully manicured grounds. Once past the gate, you pass the tennis court on the right and the wishing well Hef had built where he supposedly proposed to his beautiful wife, Kimberley. She lived next door in a fabulous house that Hef bought for her and their two sons because the marriage, like mine, didn't last. But, because of the boys, Hef still wanted them close.

Upon entering the Mansion, whom should I run into but none other than Mr. Lee Majors, who, according to Ms. Fawcett, was supposed to be meeting with her that very night to settle some business dealings. Although Lee and I had never met, we did make a movie together some years later (*Keaton's Cops* 1990). He graciously

HOLLYWOOD OR BUST!

introduced himself, and we started a conversation. He was charming, and I was at my charming best, but not a single word passed between us about Dan or Farrah. We chatted about everything except what we both wanted to sink our teeth into; our estranged spouses are sleeping together!

Ten minutes passed, and Lee and I were still chatting away when who should saunter in but famous NFL quarterback, philandering husband, Italian stud, and absentee father, Dante Pastorini.

Farrah had lied to Dan about her meeting with Majors for reasons only known to her and decided to pass on his company that evening. Farrah must have tired of Mr. NFL Greek God, and the affair eventually fizzled. She eventually took up with one of Lee Majors' dearest, closest friends, actor Ryan O'Neal, her longtime companion and father to their child Redmond. Although their relationship was stormy at best, Ryan remained by Farrah's side until her tragic death in 2009 at 62.

Anyway, back to the Playboy Mansion. Lee spotted Dan and was none too happy about it and must have decided this was the wrong place for a confrontation. He mumbled something to me and made a hasty retreat into the crowd. I smiled at Mr. NFL as he strode toward me, very much alone and without the beautiful Farrah with him.

I'll leave the details of the rest of the story of Dan and me for later. Stay tuned.

Chapter 2

So, where did this all begin? Well, I was born in Eastbourne, Sussex, England. It was March 27, 1940. World War II was in full swing as Germany dropped bombs on England like there was no tomorrow. After London, Eastbourne was bombed more than any other city. My Dad, Robert Pickett Wilkinson (everyone called him Robin), was born in Sunderland, England, on September 17, 1909. I don't know much about his childhood, but my birth certificate listed his profession as Master Window Cleaner.

Dad was a good-looking man who resembled the 1940s and 50's movie star Alan Ladd. When the war broke out, he was an English rowing champion set to represent England in the Olympics. He missed his one opportunity to compete in the Olympics. Growing up, I was fortunate to watch him practice and compete nationwide. I still have all his medals, and I treasure them.

My Mum, Lillian Rose Curryer (everyone called her Lily), a soft-spoken woman, was born in Eastbourne on April 15, 1915. Mum's father was a veterinarian from a well-to-do family in London. When he married my grandmother, his family disapproved of the union. They cut my grandfather from the family fortune from my great-grandfather's successful jewelry business. When I looked up the Curryer side of the family on Ancestry.com, they mentioned my grandfather was the only one left out of the will.

Before marrying Dad, Mum worked in a tailor shop. She could create anything on a sewing machine and was well-known around the area for her beautiful work at the local tailor shop before marrying Dad. Mum made just about every piece of clothing I wore. Being the macho man, Dad told her she should stop working because he believed only lower-class wives worked. He always insisted, with great pride, that we were middle-class.

My brother Robin was born in Eastbourne two years before me. Robin had big, beautiful blue eyes, a full head of thick, curly, blonde hair, and was the best-behaved baby ever... so I was told. On the other hand, I came into the world just after midnight, screaming my lungs out, totally bald, with a scrawny body, brown eyes, and a feisty personality that still gets me into trouble. As a young child, I always got into fights and sometimes came home with torn dresses. I did not own a pair of pants because my Mum thought they were un-ladylike.

JUNE WILKINSON

Many years later, long after I entered show business and my father had passed away, my Mum came to live with me in America. She still retained her old-world ways; for about ten years, she wore only dresses or skirts. Some habits are hard to break. Finally, she stopped wearing them except for essential affairs.

My brother Robin would remain picture-perfect once Mum got him dressed. I, on the other hand, *Little Miss Tomboy*, was a complete mess within minutes. If I heard it once, I must have heard it a hundred times—what a pity she is the girl. Women loved to run their fingers through Robin's hair, always making a big fuss over him or commenting on his good looks. Fortunately, all that meant little to Mum and Dad, who always treated us equally. It was outsiders that would go all goo-goo over Robin's looks. Although Robin was two years older than me, I looked out for him. Because he was so good-looking, with that blonde curly hair, other kids sometimes made fun of him. I, the tomboy, chased down those bullies and fought with them, which inevitably got me into trouble with Mum.

As the war raged, Mum feared Dad would get called up to join the fight. But, as it turned out, he was commissioned as a fireman in Eastbourne, which exempted him from the military. However, that job (with bombs constantly falling) was still hazardous and required him to live full-time at the fire station. While Dad was at the station, Mum, Robin, and I lived in a rented house at 85 Channel View Road in Eastbourne. It was the nicest house we occupied in England. Even though I was a child, I still have fond memories of the beautiful lilac tree that graced the front garden. I love

HOLLYWOOD OR BUST!

lilacs and, of course, *Lilly's* to this day.

I don't recall how many bedrooms there were, but I remember only one bathroom. Few people had two bathrooms; only those well-off lived in far bigger houses with more than one bathroom. Because everything was rationed, including water use, I was allowed to bathe once a week on Saturday nights. Sometimes two or three of us would share the water, but not simultaneously. A shower was unheard of! I never knew anyone who owned one and never experienced one until I came to America. Even when she came to live with me in America, Mum always wanted a bath. I could never talk her into taking a shower because she thought all that water pounding on her head would give her a headache.

Ah, yes, before I forget. One of my most vivid memories of living through the war as a child was a contraption made of steel that looked like a large kitchen table. The government issued them to civilians, and when the air raid warnings sounded, everyone with one of these devices was supposed to get under it until the all-clear sounded. If the house collapsed, the rescuers could come to dig you out. The warning sirens seemed to go off at least four or more times in the middle of the night, so my Mum put a mattress under this contraption, and that's where Robin, Mum, and I slept. If we happened to be out of the house when the alarm sounded, we ran like hell to the closest bomb shelter.

I was just too young to understand the severity of the War. Thankfully, my mother would turn it into a game. When the sirens went off, whoever got to the bomb shelter first—whether under or above ground— would win. I never realized the real danger we were in, but now that I think about it, if I were a German looking to bomb something, I would pick one of those above-ground shelters that weren't much more than corrugated tin over our heads. We were squashed in there like sardines. A direct hit would have annihilated the shelter and everything else in and around it. I'm sure my Mum was scared to death, but much to her credit, she never let her emotions show. She would cling to Robin and me until the all-clear signal sounded.

Because food was scarce, every family received a ration book that only allowed so much per person. We had powdered eggs; I never tasted a real egg until I was about four. A milkman delivered our milk, a profession held by my Uncle Tom that no longer exists. Most days, except in the summer, milk and butter were left outside on the window ledge to keep cool. The one thing Mum never let me forget (and, periodically, brought up over the next fifty years) was the time I ate a whole stick of butter that was supposed to last us for the month; so much for rationing. I was so young, about three or four, I don't remember it, but my mother never let me forget.

Rationing, as you can imagine, went on for years after the war had ended, and there were many times we would have to stand in line for hours to receive food, clothing, and most other essentials. Everything remained scarce for a long time because supplies were limited, and some items were available only on certain days. It was after the war—I probably was 7 or 8 years old—when my dad took me to a cafe in Eastbourne, sat me down, and said, *"I'm going to order a special treat for you."* It was my first taste of ice cream, and I remember that moment like it was yesterday.

HOLLYWOOD OR BUST!

While rationing continued, the stores' lines were so long that Mom would send Robin to hold a place for us. At some point, Mum would send me to replace him to give him a break because the wait could be two or three hours. To this day, I try to do everything I can to avoid standing in line because of the unpleasant memories of the war and those awful ration lines.

The war ended when I was five, and I remember Victory Day and all the celebrations. Dad returned to being a window cleaner, and life seemed to go on without much trauma until the owners of the house we were renting decided to sell it. My Dad, however, didn't want to buy it. My mother was upset because she had always hoped we would own a house one day. As usual, Dad made all the final decisions. He held the purse strings, so he got to call the shots.

We moved to a basement flat on Langley Road. It was a dark, filthy, and dreary place that my mother cleaned and scrubbed for over a week to make it livable. I don't remember how many rooms we had, but I recall the flat was in the basement.

Grandmother Rose, my mother's mom, would spend the day with us on Sundays. She lived in a cottage in Hastings's country area in a house that did not have indoor plumbing. The bathroom was in a shed out back, consisting of a plank with a hole in the middle and a bucket underneath. Yeah, kids, a plank, a hole, and a bucket. When we would visit her and stay over, I dreaded having to go in the middle of the night. There were no lights, and it scared me to death to sit on the plank in the tiny shed listening to all the strange noises out there in the pitch black. Trust me when I say I did my business as quickly as possible and scooted back to the safety of the house. If you wanted hot water, you had to heat it on the stove. During our stayovers, we had to take sponge baths next to the kitchen sink. I can laugh about it now, but it wasn't funny back then.

My grandfather died when my mother was only sixteen years old. Mum loved him so much; she was extremely close to him and never really overcame the loss. I'd never met anyone on his side of the family, but when I turned 12, I learned I had an aunt named Adelaide, my grandfather Curryer's sister. She lived in London, and one time she invited me to visit. So, off to Aunt Adelaide's house in London, I went. At that age, it was quite an adventure for me. I found out that eleven or so blocks away from Aunt Adelaide's home, which was in a not-so-grand area, my Mother's Aunt, Minn, and others from my Mum's mother's side of the family lived, but it might as well have been a world apart.

Aunty Adelaide lived in a vast, rundown mansion that must have been magnificent in its heyday. It was three stories and the most prominent house I could have ever imagined anyone living in alone. However, the place was a bit run-down, including the neglected gardens.

When I arrived, I knocked on the door, and a voice called for me to come in. The first thing that struck me was that the house was empty of furniture, but beautiful items like vases, bowls, and candle holders were scattered around. I remember thinking that my aunt looked very old. She had no household help, and the house was musty smelling. Adelaide was sitting in a chair; her hair was gray, pulled back in a bun, and her complexion was pasty with many wrinkles. She

HOLLYWOOD OR BUST!

welcomed me and told me I could sleep in any bedroom I wanted, there was food in the kitchen, and I could help myself at any time. There were no refrigerators back then; those who could afford them used ice boxes. Yes, kids, ice was used to keep food fresh before refrigerators came along. Can you believe it? Now we have fancy French door refrigerators with Internet connections. Who would have thought it possible?

England was cold most of the year and the rest of us who didn't have iceboxes put food on the ledge outside the windows to keep it cold and fresh. My, how things have changed over the years!

Upstairs in Adelaide's house were four large bedrooms, two completely empty. The other two had beds but little other furniture and no carpets or curtains. Another flight of stairs led up to the open attic room, which was empty except for cats' dried do-do all over the place that looked like it had been there for years.

Aunt Adelaide was a charming lady, but I had absolutely nothing in common with her, even though, looking back, she was kind and became very talkative once we got to know one another. But, each day, I waited until I could run off to Aunty Minn's house, where I could play with my cousin Janet, who was around my age. I also met Uncle Derek and Uncle Pip, two wonderful gentlemen who took Janet and me to my first fair. It was so exciting to experience the circus, carousels, and rides I had never seen before, let alone dreamed of. What a wonderful time I had. I still remember the taste of my first cotton candy; it was almost as good as that first ice cream cone.

After that visit, I never saw Aunt Adelaide again. It's

easy to second-guess yourself, but, looking back, I wish I had sat with her more and asked her all kinds of questions about my grandfather and that mysterious side of the family. I often wondered why I had never met them or why my mother was the only one who spoke about my grandfather. Mum loved him so much and talked of her memories of him often until she died, even though he had only been in her life for sixteen years. I think, being Daddy's only girl, he doted on her, and when he died, life changed dramatically for her.

Although Mum had six brothers, she was the one that was expected to take on the responsibility of helping in the household because, back in those days, taking care of the house was considered a woman's job. Remember, there were no washing machines, dishwashers, electric appliances, or vacuum cleaners. Everything was done by hand, which would take forever, especially looking after a family of eight.

One of the things that influenced me in later life was how Mum treated Robin and me equally. You see, growing up, she was never allowed to go out at night, like the boys were allowed, or do any of the things the boys were allowed to do. So, my mother vowed that if she ever had a girl, there would be nothing she was not allowed to do that the boys were allowed. Thank you, Mum!

Soon after that visit, Adelaide died. She left everything to my mother, which was very little. On top of that, English taxes were unbelievably high, the house was sitting on land with a 99-year government lease, and the lease had three months left before it ran out, so my mother received nothing from that source. She was entitled to the contents of the house, but when she returned to retrieve Adelaide's possessions, most of the personal contents were gone. Mum did find a full-length mink coat underneath one of the beds, but when she pulled it out, it was crawling with maggots. She took it outside and burned it.

Before returning home, Mum decided to visit Adelaide's next-door neighbor, where, much to her surprise, she saw many of Adelaide's belongings. The neighbor claimed Adelaide had given them to her as a gift. Mum knew that was a lie but could do nothing about it. When Adelaide's bills were settled, my Mum had just enough money to buy a second-hand car for my dad.

Around this time, my older brother Robin had been invited to a birthday party, and, boys being boys, they were climbing trees. One of the branches broke, and Robin fell. His arm was so severely broken that the bone protruded from his skin. Because the break was so severe, they decided to keep him overnight in the hospital. In the middle of that night, he stopped breathing but had just enough air to call for help before passing out. Fortunately, a nurse heard him, and they rushed a breathing machine to him, which most likely saved his life.

They discovered Robin had Tetanus poisoning, otherwise known as lockjaw. In those days, 90% of the people with Tetanus died. Robin became completely paralyzed. All he could move were his eyelids. He blinked once for yes and twice for no. My parents visited him daily, but I only went a few times as they did not want me to know what was happening until Robin was out of danger, which took months.

My distraught Mother was pregnant during this time, but I was not told. I don't understand why all the secrecy, but that's how they did things back then. I thought the stork brought me, and my brother Robin was found under a gooseberry bush. They thought I was too young to be told where babies came from.

One day I told Mum I thought she was getting fat, and she sloughed me off without an explanation. But, returning home from school some weeks later (Robin was still recovering in the hospital), I was walking down the hallway past my parent's bedroom when I heard a lot of commotion. Curiously, I entered the bedroom and saw a nurse slap a baby still connected to something (obviously the umbilical cord), and the baby started crying. The nurse held the baby up and said, "*Say hello to your new baby brother, John.*" I was in shock and couldn't believe what I saw. The baby was red and slimy. I ran to my bedroom and began crying. My mind was reeling, trying to sort out what in the world I had witnessed.

I think the baby's name, John, upset me more than anything. Why would they pick John, the most common name for a boy in English? I had always hated my name, the third most common for a girl behind Ann and Mary. What made it worse, at least in my mind, was that I wasn't even born in June! My mother cried when she realized how upset I was about my name. She said: *"I thought it was a beautiful name, and I always wanted a little girl named June."* Wilkinson was England's third most common after Smith and Brown. So, I felt I had two of the most common names around. As it turned out, Robin was responsible for naming the new baby because

HOLLYWOOD OR BUST!

my parents believed that would help keep his spirits up while he recuperated.

Thankfully, after many months of hospitalization, Robin came home completely cured. According to the doctors, one reason he survived was his calm demeanor, unlike his fantastic, marvelous, and incredible sister with the horrible name of June.

Chapter 3

Our next move was to 127A Terminus Road in Eastbourne in the downtown shopping area. However, my mother was unhappy with the move because Dad rented the flat without consulting her. Dad, as I said, had a habit of never discussing things with her before making decisions for the family. Mother was a bright lady, but the man was the boss and breadwinner in those days, and the little woman had no say. Mum, the only girl growing up in a household with six brothers, lived by one set of rules for the boys and another for girls. Luckily for me, Mum's attitude was that anything my brother Robin was allowed to do, I could do as well, so I never felt I was not equal.

Dad continued to run his own window cleaning company. Three other guys were working for him, and

HOLLYWOOD OR BUST!

Mum kept the books. Dad's big passion, outside of his work, was playing the alto sax. He formed a trio that performed on weekends at the Albion Hotel on the boardwalk. My Dad always told me that his band was rehearsing in the other room when I was born, so I came into the world to the sound of 1940s music!

The Albion Hotel was on the promenade across the street from the sea—the motion picture *Separate Tables* comes to mind as to the feel and look of the place. Dad played there for years, and to my good fortune, the owner's daughter and I became good friends. She invited me to stay over most weekends, which I loved. I felt like a princess eating in the dining room with the owner's daughter, and we got to sleep in one of the luxurious suites. Each New Year's Eve, the two of us girls would attend the New Year's Eve Ball, where my father played, and my mother was always invited.

And that brings up another fond memory. When I was 22 years old and living in America, I was in New York for something or other, and I remember seeing a beautiful dress in a department store window. I could just picture my mother in that dress. My Father's band was still playing at the Albion Hotel on New Year's Eve, and my mother was still attending each year. So, I bought the dress and sent it to her as a Christmas present. The gown was high-necked, with no sleeves, and flowed to the floor in a tight, sparkling fabric. She was thrilled because she would never have purchased it for herself, and my father certainly would never have bought it. Need I say, Mum looked stunning in that dress and never stopped talking about it!

JUNE WILKINSON

We moved to a flat between Marks & Spencer's department store and a dance studio called the Sussex School of Dancing. The dance studio and Marks & Spencer's had entrances from the street, but the only way to our apartment was from the back. To get to it, you had two choices: a dark, unlit, narrow, unpaved alley filled with potholes, which was about two blocks long and always scared the heck out of me at night because it was so dark. The second choice, not much better, was a bomb site, wholly flattened, with the usual debris from buildings having been annihilated after receiving a direct hit from bombs during the War. The bomb site was about two blocks long and two blocks wide; I usually chose to cross that way to get to the back alley that led to the steep, narrow, iron fire escape that led up to the front door.

These terrible things didn't bother Mum. What bothered her was the one thing that Dad had neglected to tell her—his mother and father were moving into the flat below us! Unbeknownst to me, there was bad blood of some kind between Mum and Dad's parents. I never did find out what had caused it. I just remember never being invited downstairs to my grandparents for breakfast, lunch, or dinner, and I don't remember them ever coming up to have a meal with us or even a simple cup of tea. They were always nice to me, but no one ever discussed what might have been behind the rift between them and Mum. I used to pop downstairs regularly to say hello. It wasn't until after I moved out that I thought the arrangement between them downstairs and us upstairs was strange.

I don't recall ever receiving any gifts from my

grandparents or, for that matter, us ever giving them gifts. I did get a gift once from my Auntie Marie, my father's only sister. Marie was always very sweet, and when she won a small amount of money in the lottery, she bought me a silver headband that made me feel like a princess. She married Philip, who would give us kids his loose change. Unfortunately, Marie and Philip ended up getting divorced. Later, Aunt Marie married Fred Payne, who was a lovely man. He died a few years ago, but Aunt Marie is still going strong at 90 plus as I write this.

Dad had a brother named Norman. Norman and their father were both in the insurance business. I don't remember visiting either family's home to share a meal. It seems odd to me now, although I never questioned it then. What was even stranger was that my grandmother occasionally would cook a meal just for my father and bring it upstairs to our flat. I never remember her bringing anything for the rest of us. Looking back on it, I find that very strange indeed. Families!

Thinking about strange things, my Mum told me that, one day, she visited her mother, and a man was there. She introduced him as Martini, whom she said she had married the day before—no explanation, and nothing was ever mentioned about it again! Martini was warm and friendly and always played with us kids. He was much friendlier than Granddad Wilkinson, whom I never remember playing with us.

Living in that flat between Marks & Spencer's and the Sussex School of Dancing would influence me and my future. I could climb up, sit on the wall separating the two buildings, and see into the Sussex School of Dancing window. Sylvia Fowley, one of the dance instructors, lived there with her mother and father. I thought Sylvia was the most glamorous woman I had ever seen. She had shoulder-length blonde hair, a petite, well-formed body, and always wore the highest-heeled shoes I had seen (that's when I began my love affair with high-heeled shoes). Dennis Byfield, another instructor, was Sylvia's boyfriend and reminded me of the dashing English actor David Niven. When they were not teaching students, they practiced ballroom dancing together for hours on end, and I would spend time sitting on the wall watching. Later I discovered that Sylvia and Dennis competed in dance competitions all over England. Eventually, I was lucky enough to accompany them to several of their dance competitions. Back then, that was a big treat for me.

    I begged my parents to let me attend dancing school, but my dad laughed it off. He thought it was a waste of time and money. I don't remember him ever encouraging any of my dreams. Thankfully, my mother promised me that, somehow, she would work it out so I could go to dancing school. She began taking sewing jobs, which didn't please dad, but she did it anyway. She was also an incredible knitter; after a few months, she saved enough for me to start dancing lessons.

    As I write this, I'm getting a little misty-eyed thinking of my mother's sacrifices for my brothers and me over the years. She never expressed her love verbally because my father disapproved of what he called "sloppy talk." One's emotions were not to be on display. I never heard my mother or father say, *"I love you."* Those words were

HOLLYWOOD OR BUST!

just not verbalized. But Mum showed us how much she loved us in a million little ways daily. I'm not suggesting Dad was not a good father. Heaven knows he did all he could for us. He was not the greatest husband, maybe because of his strict upbringing, the war, or perhaps just because he didn't know how to express his emotions. He never laid a hand on me in anger—never. We had a roof over our heads, food on the table, and clothes on our backs, and I enjoyed his great sense of humor. Looking back, I'm sure he tried to squash my dreams because he didn't want me to be hurt if I failed. In his awkward way, I guess he thought he was protecting me.

One specific time comes to my mind that I will never forget. We went to the movies. Sorry, I don't remember the film's title or the stars' names. The movie was about a circus, and the female lead played a high diver. She was very glamorous with blonde hair. She wore a silver sequined bathing suit, climbed a tall ladder, and stepped onto a platform. The camera cut to a shot looking straight down, which made the pool look as small as a teacup. She dove into the pool perfectly and quickly surfaced, still looking magnificent. The actress showed so much courage in what she was about to do. She was everything I dreamed of becoming.

When we returned home, I told my dad, with no uncertainty, I planned on becoming a movie star one day. He picked me up, took me to a wall mirror, and said, *"Now, does that look like the face of a movie star"*? His words, his tone, crushed me. I may not have been the prettiest girl on the face of the earth, but I was not ugly, and nothing would stop me from reaching my goals. If I wanted something badly enough, I did everything possible to get it all my life; fortunately, my mother was always in my corner. So, to this day, my motto is the word *"can't"* is spelled *"Try."* I may not always succeed, but I never want to be accused of not trying my best. So, there it was, my dream to become an actress, and I wasn't going to let anyone, let alone my father, deter me from finding a way into show business. Each day, I would come home and head next door to take dancing lessons, or if none were scheduled, I would sit on the wall and watch Sylvia and Dennis through their window do their thing.

Eventually, Sylvia and Dennis got married. Sylvia was the most beautiful bride I had ever seen, and Dennis was the most handsome groom. I remember thinking they were so glamorous, and, for those curious, Sylvia and Dennis are still happily married to this day, and their dance studio is still going strong.

Life seemed to go its merry way with nothing interesting happening, good or bad, until a stage producer came to the Sussex School of Dancing one day. I was taking a lesson with about twelve or thirteen other girls. I was not the best dancer in that class and certainly wasn't the prettiest. But after interviewing us, the producer chose me to appear in a pantomime version of *Cinderella* at the Devonshire Theatre. They picked me because they felt I wouldn't get inhibited, forget my lines, or become shy in front of an audience. I remember it like it was yesterday. It was a thrill to hear the orchestra warming up before the show. I was excited to put on makeup and exhilarated as I waited in the wings to go on. I adored everything about it. It was show

HOLLYWOOD OR BUST!

business, baby. That first experience remains one of the highlights of my young life. I was despondent when it came to an end, but, hey, what the heck, it was my beginning.

One of those little treasures that have stayed with me all these years came about because of actor Gary Webb, who played one of the ugly sisters in *Cinderella*. In England, pantomime female villains and comical old ladies are usually played by males. A female plays the leading man. It is considered part of the pantomime tradition. I asked all the actors to sign my program. Gary took my program and did the most incredible "J" I had ever seen when he signed, To June. I thought it was so fabulous that I practiced it for weeks so that June's boring, ordinary, horrible name would become memorable. To this day, I still sign the first letter of my name as Gary did all those years ago. I feel the name *June* is special, at least when written.

So there.

Chapter 4

Life moved on without too much drama, which was okay with me. The Sussex School of Dancing hired a new teacher, Joan Benson-Dare, who was terrific. I graduated from primary school, and my parents decided that I was too much of a tomboy and they would enroll me in a private school to turn me into a proper young lady, whatever that was supposed to be. They picked the Carlyle School for Young Ladies run by two old broads, Miss Carlyle and another lady, whose name I have conveniently forgotten. Whatever her name was, she was nothing more than Miss Carlyle's puppet. Both had gray hair pulled back in a bun and wore glasses, sensible shoes, and dark, dreary dresses. That tells you all you need to know.

From day one, they hated me, or, more correctly,

HOLLYWOOD OR BUST!

Miss Carlyle did, and I hated her. The school was in a two-story, private house with a large garden. I could tell she disliked me because, at her insistence, she made me sit at the front row desk right in front of hers so she could keep a close eye on me. I once overheard her make a rather rude remark about people in show business. Since I had not spoken more than six words to her, I figured she must have heard that I had been in one professional show and assumed that I had show business aspirations. Her assumptions were correct, of course.

There were backlashes against show business people in those days. When I first lived in London, I often saw signs in front of boarding houses and flats: ***"No Actors or Animals Allowed."*** Except for famous performers who had money, most people in show business were broke, and often they could not pay their bills. Miss Carlyle reasoned, "*No one with intelligence or class would be caught dead on stage.*" There are narrow-minded people everywhere who often make navigating our lives difficult. The way I overcame their bias toward actors was to ignore them.

While studying at Miss Carlyle's, I was lucky to get another professional show at the Royal Hippodrome Theater. Again, it was a Christmas pantomime called Babes in the Woods. Miss Carlyle, the curmudgeon, made several snide remarks about my being in that show. The few times our school put on a show, Miss Carlyle saw to it that I was never given a part, not even a walk-on. The only thing I can remember learning at her school was how babies were made, and it wasn't from Miss Carlyle. During a break in class one day, several girls huddled in a corner, and the conversation centered on how babies were made. God, I was so naïve. I found the details disgusting, and I was genuinely shocked. I could not believe what they were describing. Right then and there, I swore I would never get pregnant. I couldn't look my Mum and Dad in the face for weeks now that I knew how my brother John came into this world.

Chapter 5

When I woke up on my 14th birthday, there they were —*large breasts!* Unlike other teenage girls who were embarrassed by them, I loved them. I was the only girl in my class that had not been asked out on a date. But from that day on, guess what? Everything changed. I stood tall and suddenly received attention from almost every boy who had not given me a second glance. Not that I was interested in boys yet, you understand, but it helped my ego to know I would not be a wallflower.

This reminds me of the other reason my 14th birthday was the best ever: My first pair of high heel shoes was my gift. I wish I had tiny, delicate feet to go with them. Be that as it may, I went to bed feeling like the luckiest teenager on the planet. However, one day when I complained about not having tiny feet, my brother, John, said, *"Let's face it, June, you need big feet to balance your big breasts."* That's my baby brother, always with wisecracks.

I still had a year at the Carlyle School for Young Ladies, which took up much of my time. But my life was also filled with new wonders, exploring all kinds of things a typical teen would do. We played popular games at parties like *spin the bottle* and *postman's knock*. I don't remember how *Postman's Knock* was played, but it always ended up with a male and female kissing behind a door. I stopped playing when, one day, while I was postman, one of the boys stuck his tongue down my throat and started moving it back and forth. I thought I was going to vomit. I bit his tongue to make him stop. Today, kids that age would not even consider playing those innocent games. A fourteen-year-old would be under pressure to go all the way. Welcome to the new generation. After graduating high school, I began seriously considering what I wanted out of life. I discussed my future with Joan Benson-Dare, Dennis, and Sylvia. They thought ballet was out because I was too tall and not a great ballerina. I was much better at tap and modern; my bust would not be a problem in those dance categories. And then something happened that would change everything. My dance teachers suggested I audition for the Windmill Theatre in London.

The Windmill was famous for showcasing beautiful women. At this stage in my life, I wasn't ugly, but beautiful was a bit of a stretch. My dance teachers felt that my body would be an asset and that my dance abilities were more suited to musical review. I also had good comedic timing that would eventually place me in good standing with great English comedians like Peter Sellers, Tony Hancock, Harry Secombe, and others since it was a requirement to do skits with many of the great comedians who appeared at the Windmill.

The Windmill was renowned for being the only theatre that remained open during World War II. In fact, the Windmill became so famous that Hollywood made a movie called *Tonight and Every Night* starring the great American actress and beauty Rita Hayworth. It was a good film but couldn't match the excellent 2006 remake starring Judi Dench and Bob Hoskins, *Mrs. Henderson Presents*. I was teary-eyed watching it because it brought back so many wonderful memories. They must have filmed much of it on location at the actual Windmill Theater because it looked exactly like I remembered it, especially the scenes on the rooftop.

I remember my audition at the Windmill like it was yesterday. My dance instructors, Sylvia and Dennis, were kind enough to drive me to London. There was so much activity in the West End and so many theaters with big star names on the marquees. We drove around Trafalgar Square and then to the Windmill Theatre. My dream as a little girl was about to come true, and I recalled that movie with the beautiful blonde in her sequined swimsuit diving into that small tank of water.

I wore a black skirt and sweater, high-heeled shoes, a pink jacket, and a pillbox hat for the audition. Wow, after all these years, I still remember what I wore. I thought I was hot stuff, but looking back, I probably looked more like a fifteen-year-old trying to look like hot stuff. I quickly changed into my dancing clothes, gave the piano player my sheet music, and started my audition, a dance number I had been working on for weeks.

Sitting in judgment were Vivian Van Dam, who now owned the theatre (the original owner, Mrs. Henderson, had died many years before), Mr. Van Dam's daughter Sheila, and the dance mistress. Halfway through the audition, they stopped me. My heart sank! All kinds of evil thoughts were going through my head. They asked me to do some high kicks, followed by splits. I decided to show off and did some high kicks and then a cartwheel into a flying split! When I finished, Vivian Van Dam stood up and said, *"She's hired."* Needless to say, I was on cloud nine all the way home!

I was to be paid the enormous sum of twelve pounds a week, they would find me a roommate, and I would start rehearsals in two weeks. I was chosen as one of the dancers, but they said I might have a chance to become the lead fan dancer in the *Fan Dance*. Along with the *Can Can*, the *Fan Dance* was one of the two standard dances in every new production. I reveled in the idea that I was part of a group of women considered the most glamorous in London. I'm laughing while typing this, thinking, *"That's going just a little too far."* Performing at the Windmill was comparable to an American girl appearing in the famous Ziegfeld Follies; I was literally in seventh heaven. But, like everything in the theater, performing at the Windmill was hard work. Don't get me wrong; I'm not complaining; I loved every minute!

It wasn't until my ride home from the audition that Sylvia and Dennis mentioned that if I got the lead in the *Fan Dance*, I would have to dance naked! However,

HOLLYWOOD OR BUST!

throughout the dance, my body would never be exposed. Hmm. I knew wearing somewhat-see-through costumes would never bother me, but the *Fan Dance* routine was different: the lead fan dancer is nude and covered by two large fans, one in each hand. At no time during the dance can she expose her body. During the last part of the routine, the other six dancers had a single feather to cover the naked lead dancer. Then the lead dancer removes her two fans while assuming a statue-like pose, still covered by the other six plumes. The other dancers then remove the plume feathers from her body until she is naked. She must remain completely still for about another twenty seconds—hopefully, to roaring applause—then **Black Out!** I decided, right then and there, that I could handle that. It was a thing of beauty—not something rude, crude, or lewd—it was all part of the *Fan Dance* tradition.

The moral codes in England, set by the venerable Lord Chamberlin, stated that if you were naked on stage, you were not allowed to move and, in addition, not show the slightest hint of pubic hair—that was entirely out of the question. Every country seems to have different ideas about what is decent and what is not. Go figure. If I had been Lord Chamberlin, I would have made a rule that you had to cover whatever was the ugliest part of you! Problem solved.

There were two companies at the Windmill, *A* and *B*. I was in the A troop. When a new production began, the two groups would work every other day for two weeks. On the first day, *A* Company would perform at noon. The next day, *B* Company would do six shows. After the first two weeks of a new show, *A* Company, and *B*

JUNE WILKINSON

Company would begin rehearsals for the next production in four weeks.

I finished High School and began working at the Windmill Theatre full-time when I was just 15. I was now the youngest girl working there. While there, I created one of the worst habits that plagues me to this day. We had to grab food between numbers, and most of the time, we had less than a half hour to eat. There were no elevators in that building, so you had to run up six flights of stairs, grab whatever food you could, run back down, and don your costume for the following routine. You ask what this bad habit was; I eat too fast; I am always the first to finish. I also believe it is related to the War (food shortages). Then, my brother Robin would finish his plate and mine if I didn't eat fast enough (just kidding, Robin!). Truth be known, the Windmill is responsible for this bad habit of mine.

The Windmill retained a full-time press agent whose office was on the third floor. Part of his job was to gather the statistics on each girl: age, hair color, and bust size. The joke around the theater was I'd have to check in with him regularly as my breasts grew. Then they would send out a press release that Baby June's (they called me that because I was the youngest there) new bust measurements were such and such. In those days, any newspaper or magazine that featured a photo of a glamorous girl was sure to include her measurements: June Wilkinson 40-20-36, or whatever my measurements were. When I arrived in America, the press was more fanatical about my breast size. I would give a reporter an excessive number if I thought they were acting stupid.

Sabrina, an English lady with large breasts, became

HOLLYWOOD OR BUST!

famous on the Arthur Askey television show in England. She would appear in a very low-cut dress weekly and never say a word, while Arthur Askey would joke about her breasts. If someone from the press was a real jerk and questioned her measurement, Sabrina had a special tape; on one side, the inches were larger, and on the other, they were smaller. When a reporter requested a picture of the tape measure going around her chest, she would switch the tape to the more significant numbers and flip it to the smaller side for her waist measurement. Sabrina and I always laughed over that; the press never caught on.

Luckily, not all the press was breast crazy, and it stopped around 1968. That is when the sexist movement began, and pressure was put on newspapers to stop. However, that silliness never really bothered me. I just thought it was stupid and juvenile, and I think feminism is taken way too seriously, anyway. I always believed that what counted was the quality, not the quantity. I wonder how men would have reacted if their penis size had been posted along with their pictures. Now that I am thinking about it, what a great idea.

After several months, my roommate Linda Gray left the show to get married. By then, I had made friends with a Windmill girl who went under the stage name of Annie Donati (her real name was Ann Donahue). She lived in a flat on Great Newport Street. I moved in with Annie and paid four pounds a week in rent. The building had no elevator, and none of the flats had their own toilets. The toilet was in the hallway, and we had to share it with three other flats on the same floor. As I write, a thought comes back; who provided the toilet paper? I don't remember ever providing any, and I would bet my sweet ass the landlord didn't. The rest of the flat had one bedroom and a small living room. The flat was on the 6th floor, which helped keep me in shape. I was in seventh heaven because I was living my dream.

Meanwhile, back at the Windmill, my first day of rehearsal was a day of heightened excitement. I liked the girls; the dancing instructor and the choreographer were great to work with. Here we are all these years later, and I can still remember the first number we rehearsed: (Johnny's line, singing) *"Da Da Da Da Da DA —Da Da Da Da Da."* (My line) *"Hey, Johnny, what's that tune?* (Johnny) *I don't know; I just heard it in the rehearsal room."* Do I hear a yawn, dear reader? Well, imagine six girls from my age up to, I think, twenty-six, in cute, sexy costumes. Trust me when I tell you, nobody yawned!

In the third week of rehearsals, much to my surprise and delight, they gave me the lead in *Fan Dancer*. I was beside myself with excitement, but there was one little problem. I knew I had to perform naked and fretted over how I would do the routine while menstruating. Keep in mind that I was still a virgin, and although I had tried using a tampon, I couldn't do it. My Mother, bless her heart, came to my rescue by making an appointment with our family doctor back in Eastbourne. He fixed it without delving into the gory details so I could use tampons during my menstrual period. Now, aren't you glad I told you that story? Was it a big deal for me, then? You bet it was.

I began receiving a lot of press in the media, which

HOLLYWOOD OR BUST!

was great. Unfortunately for Mum, this generated a few nasty telephone calls from her so-called friends, complaining about my doing the fan dance in the nude. Our family doctor, Dr. Baron, had a young girl patient whose mother always accompanied her to the good Doctor's office. The girl's mother knew that I was also one of his patients, and she made some uncalled-for comments about my theatre performances. Dr. Baron, bless his heart, told the two of them, *"At least June is a virgin, which is more than I can say for many of the young girls I see in this office."* Dr. Baron called my mother and told her, (without revealing the woman's name), *"She had no right to bad-mouth June,"* The Doctor said, *"Her daughter has been sexually active for a year now."*

Mum felt much better about my chosen career after Dr. Baron's call. She was a pretty strait-laced lady, and I will forever be grateful for the loving support she showered on me. The fact that she trusted her 15-year-old daughter to go to London to pursue her dream. That is when I promised myself I would never do anything to disappoint her, and I never did. I never smoked, drank, or engaged in sex until I moved to America, but that's another story! I promise to get to it.

My roommate, Annie Donahue, was dating Harry Wolf, a nice Jewish boy who lived with his parents on the 3rd floor of our building. His mother, Dorothy, was a petite, slender lady with the sweetest smile, and his father went by the nickname Chubby due to his ample girth.

The Wolfs were very well off. Chubby owned a chain of drug stores and could afford to live wherever he wanted, but he loved living in this cheap flat because he could people-watch all day. One frigid winter day, my mother came into town to visit me and went downstairs to say hello to the Wolf's. Chubby told his wife, Dorothy, *"Go buy yourself a mink coat."* He handed her a wad of cash and asked Lily if she would accompany her. Dorothy, never one to flaunt their money, took my Mum by the hand, and they made a beeline to the department store. Dorothy picked out a mink and began to try it on when a sales lady came over and told her to *"Take that mink off immediately."* Dorothy explained that she wanted to buy it. The sales lady told her how expensive the coat was and suggested that neither Dorothy nor my mother looked like they could afford it. Dorothy returned the coat to the sales lady, turned to my mother, and said, *"Right, let's leave, Lily."* The two of them crossed the street to another department store, where Dorothy bought a magnificent full-length mink, put it on, and marched back to the other store across the street. Confronting the rude saleslady, she said, *"See this coat? I just paid cash for it. I just wanted to be sure you consider the big commission you just lost."* Until the day Dorothy died, my Mum loved telling that story.

Chapter 6

My Mum, Dad, and Grandma Martini visited London to see every new production I was in at the Windmill Theater. Robin never came, but now that I think back, one had to be 18 to get in. I don't understand now, nor did I back then, Lord Chamberlin's thinking on the subject. It was okay for a girl to dance naked at 15 and 16, but 18-year-olds were prohibited from seeing the show. Robin never saw me perform until forty years later when I performed in Calgary, Canada. My dear brother Robin never had an interest in show business. When one of my movies played in Eastbourne, Robin planned to see it, but the film ran and left before he got around to it. Bless his heart; Robin would much rather go fishing.

My roommate, Annie, stopped dating Harry Wolf and took up with a new boyfriend named Tommy Hicks.

Tommy was slim with blonde hair and flashed a great smile. He sang and played guitar in coffee houses around the West End. At that time, coffee houses became prominent for up-and-coming musicians and singers. Tommy was good enough that eventually, he landed a recording contract. The record company changed his name to Tommy Steele. *Rock and Roll* music had just started to come in, and there was talk of his becoming England's answer to Elvis Presley. When I didn't have a date, I hung out with Annie, Tommy, and his gay friend Lionel Bart. Lionel would become one of my best friends. It was, as I remember, an easy-going, fun-loving time in my life.

I don't remember much about my 16th birthday except that I was still a virgin. I just wasn't interested in physical relations back then. I had graduated to French kissing on occasion— "swapping spit," as it was referred to. With six shows daily, I ran on adrenaline and didn't have time for the opposite sex. I preferred winding down after performances by eating with my Windmill buddies. Call me *Miss Boring*.

We had our share of "stage door Johnnys"—guys who liked to hang outside the stage door hoping to get dates or autographs with one of the lady performers. I don't remember them ever treating us with anything but respect. As for the male stagehands, they were so used to seeing the girls working naked that they hardly took notice. However, they whistled and commented on how great we looked when dressed. How nice of them.

When I did date, the guys usually took me to dinner at some nightclub where there was dancing and a maybe

HOLLYWOOD OR BUST!

show at the more expensive clubs. I don't recall having a real problem with guys at the end of the evening. Perhaps it was because I was so young. Although, as we all know, some guys—perhaps more than just some—love the idea of "young girls." Or, maybe it was because I never played the teasing game or tried to be sexy. I have always been very good at handling men, even when their only interest was to get me into the sack.

One of these dates was with Charlie Chaplin Jr., son of the great silent screen star and director Charlie Chaplin. Charlie Sr. was no longer married to Charlie's mother, Lita Gray. He always insisted that his dad had married her because she became pregnant when she was 16 years old, and his dad was 36. If he hadn't married her, he would have gone to jail. The marriage only lasted a few years, and the divorce was ugly. Another interesting tidbit; Charlie Jr. told me his dad barely paid attention to him or his brother Sydney.

Most of the time, Charlie Jr. lived in America. I don't recall why he was in London at the time or who introduced us, but I remember how shy he was, and there seemed to be a deep sadness about him. He drank way too much when we were together, but it never bothered him that I didn't drink. Despite his troubles, Charlie was a sweet guy to hang with. He never made a play for me. Charlie loved talking about America and Hollywood, where he lived. Of course, the mere mention of Hollywood fascinated me, and the more he talked about it, the more I wanted to hear. When it came time for him to return to America, he gave me his address and phone number and promised to show me around if I visited Hollywood.

JUNE WILKINSON

If I didn't have a date after work, one of my favorite ways to relax and unwind was a disco club called *El Toro*, where I would dance the night away. Before disco music, depending on the club, they either had a piano player or a full orchestra. Using hit records instead of live music was a new concept and a cheap way for a disco to fill a club with music. At that time, the *Jive* was popular; if memory serves, the number one record was Louis Prima's *Just a Gigolo*. Louis and his wife, singer Keely Smith, were a major draw in Las Vegas during the '50s and '60s. I could have danced to *Just a Gigolo* all night. Little did I know then that one day I would be Louis Prima's leading lady in a dance film that highlighted one of the dance crazes of the 60s called *The Twist*."

After a year and a half of performing at the Windmill Theatre, I began getting interesting job offers. Comedian Bob Monkhouse, a prominent showman in England, asked me to perform a skit on his television show. When Vivian Van Dam, the owner of the Windmill Theater, got wind of it, he called me into his office and informed me in no uncertain terms that I was not allowed to work other shows as long as I was working at the Windmill. I told him there was no conflict because we had arranged to rehearse the TV skits on my off days. Van Dam was adamant and threatened to fire me if I accepted the Monkhouse offer. Even though the offer was just one show, I accepted. Defiantly, I marched into Van Dam's office, ready for an argument, but before I could say anything, he said he had changed his mind and I could keep my job as long as I agreed not to do outside shows in the future. Although I loved working at

HOLLYWOOD OR BUST!

the Windmill, the fact that they wouldn't allow us to better ourselves riled the hell out of me. I looked Van Dam into his eyes and said, *"Thank you, but I've decided it's time for me to move on."*

I had been with the Windmill from 1957 through 1958, and it was time to branch out. From my humble beginnings in Eastbourne, I had conquered the *Fan Dance* and the *Can Can* and was the lead performer of both numbers during my time there. I was almost 17, living in London, and about to be unemployed. I knew that I had to come up with something fast.

I had judged a few beauty contests in one of London's better nightclubs, so I called the Club owner and announced that I was no longer at the Windmill and would love to work for him. Off the top of my head, I told him I would do the dance of the seven veils, a dance I once saw Rita Hayworth do in a movie. Without hesitation, he said, *"You're hired. Can you start in two weeks?"* My answer was a quick *"Yes."* Thinking back to that phone call, I have no idea where I got the courage to do what I did. I'm not sure I'd have the courage to do that today.

The first thing that crossed my mind was the costume I would wear. Where would I get such a thing? Remembering my mother's extraordinary talent for creating clothes, I told her I was coming home for a few days. She could make costume veils that would look good when I moved but could also be removed easily as I danced. My musical-gifted Dad was tasked with coming up with the sheet music. I spent the entire week at my parent's house rehearsing the routine. But Dad being Dad, he tried his best to talk me into returning to the

Windmill Theatre. Thanks, Dad, but I was moving on.

For the younger people reading this—the MTV crowd—entertainment was very different in the 1950s. This is back before television was widely available in England. In fact, the first time I saw television was in the window of an electronics store when I was about fourteen. If I remember correctly, they showed an episode of the TV series *Dragnet*.

There were many movie theaters, and most films were in black and white. You could go to one of the nightclubs if you wanted live entertainment. At most clubs, the audience sat at tables facing a bandstand with a live orchestra. In front of the bandstand, there usually was an open area where each act performed. The space would become the dance floor when the show was over. Most clubs offered three-night performances, usually 10 PM, 12 AM, and 2 AM. The Master of Ceremonies presented each of the acts—singers, dancers, jugglers, comics, ballroom dancers, and magicians. The more successful live acts would travel from one club to another and often toured the world.

I don't recall much about that first veil dance on opening night; it must have been passable because I wasn't fired. The club manager offered me a steady job if I agreed to change the dance routine every few months. That made sense, especially since he had many return customers. I wracked my brain to develop unique ideas, and one day it just came to me. I don't know why it took me so long. Duh! Why not perform the *Fan Dance*? No club was doing it. After perfecting it at the Windmill, who could do it better than me? Where that cockiness came from, I don't know. Maybe it was from my mother,

HOLLYWOOD OR BUST!

who always told me I could do anything if I put my mind to it.

I bought some fans and worked out a routine to the tune *That Old Black Magic* since the fans I bought were black and white (makes sense, right?) Looking back, I think the fan routine was far better than my *Seven Veils* act. Then I came up with another brilliant idea: I asked the club manager to put me on as the first act at 10 PM. That allowed me to attend another club and perform the same act at midnight. Then I added another club and performed at the 2 AM show. I was raking in nice paychecks from three clubs: one outside the West End and the other two in the West End.

In the 1950s, the two top nightclubs in London were the Embassy and Stork Clubs. The booking agents were Lew and Lesley Grade, better known as Sir Lew and Sir Lesley Grade. Both became wonderfully talented stage and film producers and all-around entrepreneurs. But, at that time, they were just promoters and agents. Mr. Black, who I think may have been related to the Grades', worked for the agency. Black was in charge of booking the acts for the Embassy. He called, offered to have me perform exclusively for them, and asked what the other clubs paid me. The Embassy would pay me the equivalent of what I earned at all three clubs if I signed an exclusive contract. I couldn't wrap my fingers around that pen fast enough!

Settling into my new life at the Embassy Club was easy. The girls in the chorus were friendly as well as good dancers. I still lived in the flat with Annie, within walking distance of the Embassy, which was a big plus. I walked to and from the club alone every night unless I had a date. I took the same route each night; it was always the same prostitutes in the same doorways. They greeted me with *"Hello, Dear,"* once they knew I was not looking to take away any of their customers. Tuesdays through Sundays, I walked home alone around 3 AM, never considering possible dangers until I recalled the story of *Jack the Ripper!* Perish the thought.

There were two Masters of Ceremonies at the Embassy. One was Davy Kaye, who performed at the Embassy from 1954 to 1968. He did take breaks to do other things, like starring opposite Raquel Welch and Robert Wagner in *Biggest Bundle of Them All*. The other comedian, Richard Dawson, filled in when Davy performed elsewhere. As many of you will recall, Richard Dawson became famous in America as a regular cast member in *Hogan's Heroes*, starring Bob Crane. Later, Richard became the host of the hugely popular ABC television game show *Family Feud*. In England, Richard was known as Dickie Dawson and married the famous English sex symbol, Diana Dors. Unfortunately, the marriage didn't last (an unfortunate end in many show business marriages).

After performing the fan dance routine to death, club management decided I needed to do something new. Davy Kaye came up with the idea for the new act. It started with an introduction by Davy: *"Ladies and Gentleman, please give a warm welcome to Miss June Wilkinson."* I would step into the spotlight in a gold evening gown and slowly walk around the perimeter of the audience, trying to look as magnificent as possible. At the same time, Davy was ad-libbing jokes with the audience. A seven feet tall sheet of glass was mounted in the center of the stage. I stepped onto the stage and stood behind the glass.

Let me back up. Before my entry, three members of the audience were chosen to participate. Three chorus girls would give each participant a toy gun and arrows with rubber suction cups that stuck to the glass. Wherever the arrows stuck, I would remove a piece of clothing while Davy continued with funny lines keeping the audience (most nights) in stitches. My dress was in sections that allowed me to strip down to nipple cups and G-string. The winner is the shot that hits the G-string. The lights go out, and, in the dark, a stagehand quickly covers me with a cape. Then the lights come up, and I present the winner with a bottle of champagne to thunderous applause. I never understood why this act became such a huge success, but we packed them in every night, so who am I to have questioned it?

Though the press coverage was incredible, one London paper ran a negative article with a tasteless headline that read, *"Dad, Come and Clean Up Your Daughter's Act."* The critic claimed I was naked when I handed the bottle of champagne to the winner. That, of course, was a bald-faced lie. My Dad, bless his heart, came to London with a ladder, water bucket, and chamois and invited the press to watch as he "cleaned up" his daughter's act. He washed the glass in front of where I stood and then announced to the press, *"Now it's nice and clean, and you can see my daughter's beautiful body."* Dad's statement made all the papers with a photo of him cleaning the seven-foot glass window. That little stunt had customers lining up around the block to see Daddy's little daughter Baby June Wilkinson. Put that in your hat and smoke it (whatever that means).

The Embassy Club's owners were thrilled with all the business and were very protective of me. They only asked me to join anyone for a drink after a performance if Lew or Lesley Grade were in the house entertaining some of their clients. I was lucky enough to meet many interesting and famous people because of that.

One was the American singer Johnnie Ray, a major worldwide celebrity at that time. While appearing at the Palladium, he and his entourage would come to watch my late show. When the news got out that he was there frequently, hundreds of adolescent girls would show up each night, hoping Johnnie would be there. After one of my performances, he and his business manager, Saul Lazarow, came backstage to say hello. That night began a beautiful friendship that lasted almost forty years until Johnnie's death in February 1990.

American actress and pin-up Jayne Mansfield, who was at the height of her popularity, also came to see me perform. She was in town promoting her first big movie, *The Girl Can't Help It.*" After my act, she graciously invited me to join her at her table. Jane was charming but a little shy despite her public sex symbol persona.

American bandleader Ray Anthony came to see my act. He was married to movie star Mamie Van Doren. After the show, I was invited to his table for a drink (I always drank soft drinks, never alcohol). I'm mentioning my meeting with Ray because, years later, Mamie and I were in a movie together (*The Candidate* - 1964), and she recalled that night at the Embassy. She told me Ray claimed to have made a play for me, but I had turned him down. That was not true. He did not make a play

HOLLYWOOD OR BUST!

for me; he remained a perfect gentleman. Ray has always been a good friend of Hugh Hefner's, and we met again at the Playboy Mansion years later. We joked about Mamie's story; he thought she was just trying to catch him in a lie. Spoiler alert; it didn't work, Mamie.

One of my favorite people was the dashing English movie star, Michael Wilding. Michael came to my show regularly and, after the show, would take me out for dinner. As you can tell, there have been many dinners in my life. My relationship with Michael was purely platonic, and we became very close friends even though he drank too much. After a few too many, Michael would reminisce about the good old days. One night, when talking about his former wife, Liz Taylor, he said, *"I should have married Marlene Dietrich instead of Liz. Marlene and I were much more suited to each other. But Liz was stunningly beautiful with a strong personality and pushed the marriage, so I finally gave in."*

I detected a deep sadness about Michael. As I said, he loved to talk about the old days and would go on and on about it once he started. I didn't mind because I loved hearing tales of famous movie stars and the early days of Hollywood. Often, we would meet up with some of Michael's buddies. The English actor Stewart Granger, who enjoyed great success in Hollywood, was a close friend of Michael's, and we spent time with him. I loved listening to them reminisce and joke because Stewart had great humor. He and Michael talked about all the girls they had affairs with or those they didn't manage to take to bed. The three of us went to a movie one night, and on the screen was this gorgeous Lady. Michael said, *"I suppose you've had her too."* Stewart Granger responded,

"Be quiet; I'm having her now."

Another star that comes to mind is Cliff Richard, an English singer who enjoyed great success. My friend Lionel Bart, a famous songwriter back then, invited me to join him to hear the newcomer Cliff Richard sing. Lionel wanted to see if the young man had talent. We drove out into the suburbs where 16-year-old Cliff lived with his parents. Cliff, his mom, and his dad were waiting for us, and Cliff sang in their small family living room. My heart went out to Cliff that day because it was not the best or easiest environment for a performer to show off his talent. However, Cliff did a great job under the circumstances. If Cliff could shine in that environment, he could make it anywhere. Lionel thought so, too because they teamed up and worked together in the following years.

HOLLYWOOD OR BUST!

Chapter 7

Lew and Lesley Grade booked all the big stars from America. Most were young Rock & Rollers like Buddy Holly and the Crickets, Charlie Gracie, and Jerry Lee Lewis, with an occasional Mario Lanza, tossed in for good measure. Since I grew up during the rock and roll era, the Grade's arranged for me to see many of the shows and visit performers backstage, and they also brought some of them to see my shows.

One night, I was in Buddy Holly's dressing room, and he and his band members were joking and fooling around. One of the Crickets accidentally hit Buddy in the face with his guitar and broke Buddy's two front caps five minutes before they were to go on. Buddy came up with the idea of using chewing gum to cover the missing caps and trying not to smile when he went on stage. His sense of "the show must go on."

In five minutes, Buddy was on stage singing with gum that looked like teeth. He looked up, down, and sideways the entire show, but not out front. I respected him for not canceling the show, which he could have quickly done. When I saw the movie about Buddy's life, they showed the scene with his band members fooling around and breaking Buddy's front teeth. They placed the location not in England but a theater in America. I have no idea why they did that, especially when portraying someone's life. The truth would've been much better because the movie—at least for me—lost its credibility over that one scene.

Another American rock star the Grades booked in England was Charlie Gracie. I did not go to see his show, but a couple of days after his opening, someone from the agency brought him to the Embassy Club and invited me to join them. Charlie was from Philadelphia and had written and recorded the song *Butterfly*, which sold over a million copies. Charlie was shy but very charming, and before I knew it, I had developed my first big crush. I'm sure everyone remembers the excitement of their first crush. For me, it was like the clouds parted and the sun shined.

Each night after Charlie finished his show, he would come to the Embassy, and we would talk until the wee hours of the morning. There were passionate kissing sessions that lasted for hours, but I was still a virgin, and the kissing was as far as it went. Now that I think back, he was 21 and maybe a virgin too. Maybe not.

The press got wind that we were dating, and the rumors flew. I didn't care because I was happy to be

HOLLYWOOD OR BUST!

with Charlie, and the nosy media be damned. I couldn't wait to see him every night after the show, and I was sure he felt the same. When his father came into town for the last two weeks of Charlie's tour, Charlie took him to the Embassy Club to meet me. His father was polite, but I could sense he didn't approve of me or what I did for a living.

It was a sad time for Charlie and me when it was time for him to return to America. His appearances had been so successful the Grade Agency planned to bring him back a few months later. That gave me something to look forward to. I couldn't wait; I filled my time with work and friends as I marked the months until Charlie would return to England.

I had no phone in my flat when I was dating Charlie. Very few people had phones in their homes, and cell phones were yet to be invented. I don't remember asking Charlie for his address or even giving him mine, but about a week before Charlie returned, I got a call from Mrs. Hicks, Tommy Steele's mother, who said she would like to meet me. I thought that was strange, but I went to her house anyway. She sat me down and said, *"June, I have some bad news for you. Charlie got married and is bringing his wife on his trip here."*

I was crushed, devastated! I couldn't believe it—my heart was broken as only a teenager's heart can be. It took me the longest time to get over Charlie. Thankfully, Annie, Tommy, and Lionel stood by me and were great company as I worked my way beyond any further thoughts of Charlie Gracie, my first big crush. Easy come, not so easy to let go.

I don't recall how we met, but I did go out with the

American movie star Steve Cochran. When Steve was in town, he would take me to dinner and drop me at the Embassy Club just in time for my first show. He never tried getting romantic, even though he had a reputation for being a notorious womanizer.

Steve began his career in the theater and later was signed to a contract with Samuel Goldwyn Studios. His first movie was *Boston Blackie Booked on Suspicion - 1945*, starring Virginia Mayo and Danny Kaye. Eventually, Steve did several films for Warner Brothers playing gangsters. Backstage at the Embassy, the chorus girls would fill me in on all of Steve's Hollywood affairs with the likes of Merle Oberon, Joan Crawford, Mamie Van Doren, Mae West, Kay Kendall, and the list went on and on; we girls always had a great time gossiping. Steve's 1951 movie *Inside the Walls of Folsom Prison* impressed me the most. The title inspired Johnny Cash to write and record *Folsom Prison Blues*. We said goodbye on Steve's last night in town; I thanked him for his company and all the dinners and wished him a good trip back home. And that was that.

How does that Sinatra song go: *"When I was 17, it was a very good year."* I would have been the envy of every teenage girl in England if they had known the many opportunities I had to meet all the hot, young rock stars like the young Canadian singer Paul Anka. Paul was smart, talented, very cocky, and just 17 years old, like me. I thought he was a much better showman onstage than most young singers.

Paul and I quickly became friends, but we disagreed on sex. He was sexually active and thought I was immature because I wasn't. We had hot and heavy petting sessions, but I would never go all the way even though I liked him a lot. He was the first one I had shown any interest in since Charlie Gracie, but, damn it, I was not ready for sex, and that was that. I don't know if it was because my mother trusted in me or if I was just not ready—so, no sex at that time. Paul and I kept seeing each other until his gig ended, and he returned to Canada.

At the end of 1957, a night at the Embassy Club changed my life forever. At one of my late shows, a bunch of middle-aged, boisterous men and their wives were in the audience. They were drinking heavily and having a great deal of fun. After my act, the Club Manager knocked on my dressing-room door and said this group had invited me to join them at their table, and, out of courtesy to management, I did. The group was from American Plastics, a company owned by Joe Sholkin. The Company had such a profitable year that he took all the executives and their wives on a European trip. They'd been to France and Germany—England was their last stop. Though they had too much to drink and were loud, I thoroughly enjoyed them and their wives.

The next day, I got a phone call from a newspaper reporter who said he had received a call from a gentleman representing American Plastics. The caller said he had seen my show, was impressed, and wanted to bring me to America to promote his products. He asked the newspaper reporter for my telephone number, and the reporter said he would prefer to contact me and, if I were interested, he would bring me to their hotel as long as they would allow him to take a photo of us together. I don't know why they didn't contact me instead of the reporter. Anyway, when the reporter called, I agreed to the meeting, and yes, I would pose for pictures for the reporter's newspaper. The reporter/photographer picked me up, and off we went.

Mr. Sholkin answered the door. When he saw who I was, he got this funny look. He pulled me aside and said he was pretty surprised to see me. Then he chuckled and said that, throughout their trip, he and his executives played practical jokes on one another and thought this was one of them. *"This has got to be one of my guys playing one of their practical jokes on me, and a good one at that, so I'm going to go along with it, and I hope you will too."* But then, as if a light bulb went off in his head, Joe said, *"Hey, wait a minute. My company will be on display at the Chicago Home Convention. How would you like to come to America and be the hostess at that convention?"*

So, ladies and gentlemen, boys and girls, what began as a practical joke became a reality for Little Baby June. I quickly accepted Joe's offer, but on the condition that my mother could accompany me, and he agreed. It's nice to meet with influence and money.

Mr. Sholkin introduced me to Jimmy McCullough and Tony Charkha, who were friends of the Sholkin's and were traveling with the group. McCullough said he had some connections in show business and would use those connections to try and get my career off the ground in America. As it turns out, he was responsible for bringing sex-goddess Anita Ekberg to America. I was definitely in the right company.

In the 1950s, the only way to become an

international star was to make it in America. When I returned to my flat, I called my Mum and shared the news. Imagine her surprise! The only traveling she had done until then was a short plane trip to the Isle of Wight, a trip she repeatedly recounted over the years. I was thrilled that this was a way to repay my Mum for all she had done for me. We were going to America; Merry Christmas and a Happy New Year, Mum!

Chapter 8

On January 15, 1958, my Mum and I boarded a Trans World Airlines propeller-driven plane in London because there was no jet service for public travel back then. We were accompanied by Joe Sholkin's English friend Tony Charkham. We were decked out in our finest clothes because, back then, unlike today, flying was considered very chic. The trip took 15 hours, with one stop for refueling. In those days, airline food was like dining in a fine restaurant with China and linen napkins —they treated passengers like Kings and Queens. What a difference a few years make. We can now fly to the moon, but it's impossible to get a decent meal on today's airlines; you're lucky to get pretzels and a soft drink.

When I arrived in New York, the press awaited me. Good old Jimmy McCullough had arranged everything;

HOLLYWOOD OR BUST!

a fancy hotel in midtown Manhattan and an interview on the *Today Show* with host Dave Garraway. Jimmy wanted me to look perfect for my first TV appearance in America, so he visited designer Oleg Cassini's salon to select a dress for the *Today Show*. Oleg was already well known in the fashion world but hit it big when he became a designer for President John Kennedy's wife, Jacqueline.

As soon as we arrived, Cassini showed us a new line of clothing he had designed that featured the bust, waist, and hips. Perfect, I thought, because the "in fashion" at the time was the sack dress, which was not a good look for me. His new style sounded suitable for my body type. I would wear it on the *Today Show* and again that evening to a party where Oleg would show off his creation. For agreeing to accompany him to the party, he gifted me four dresses to keep on the condition I wore them while I was in America. I couldn't make that deal fast enough.

On the way to the party, we stopped at a hotel to pick up Oleg's friend, Zsa Zsa Gabor. Zsa Zsa was very charming and friendly. She told me if I was ever in Hollywood to look her up, she would show me around and introduce me to all the right people. Hey, you can't beat an offer like that.

I didn't know it then, but attending that party would change my immediate future. The party was at an elegant estate somewhere on the water. Two of the people I met that night were Ray Stark and Elliot Hyman. "What do you do, Ms. Wilkinson?" Stark asked. I told them that I was in show business. Ray told me he and Elliott were filmmakers. What they said next floored me. Elliot said, *"What would you say if we offered to place you under contract?"*

Huh? They just met me. Did I hear him right? Was I dreaming? Pinch me!

"If you're interested, June, our attorney will contact you as soon as tomorrow to discuss details. What do you say?"

Yes, yes, and yes, again, gentlemen. I'm all yours. However, thankfully, my answer was a bit calmer than my thoughts. *"Yes, I would love to consider it."*

After Oleg dropped me off at the hotel that night, I told Jimmy and my mother what happened—neither couldn't believe it. *"Ray Stark and Elliot Hyman own Seven Arts—they're big-time! Sign, June. Sign. You have nothing to lose."* Jimmy said.

So, here I am, four days in the United States, and the following day I'm off to the Hampshire House to meet with Greg Bautzer, attorney for Seven Arts, to sign a movie contract! Lady Luck was perched on my shoulder. When I arrived, I called Bautzer's room, and he invited me to come up. Nervous as hell, I knocked on his door; he let me in, sat me in a chair opposite his desk, and placed a contract in front of me, which I read carefully. The agreement called for a weekly salary of $250, a place to live, and acting lessons, all paid for by Seven Arts.

The next part didn't go so well.

After I signed the contract, Bautzer crawled over the desk and landed on top of me, and my chair fell backward to the floor. What the hell was happening? He crawled on top of me, talking a mile a minute, nothing of which I understood. His hands were all over me, and the damn fool was trying to kiss me. He told me that all

HOLLYWOOD OR BUST!

men in Hollywood were wolves and not to trust them. What? What was he doing? Then—are you ready for this? —he promised to look after me, all the while groping me.

I pushed at his chest and told him I was still a virgin, worsening matters. He kept babbling about how he would take care of me, set me up in my own apartment, pay all my bills, and see that no one took advantage of me while he frantically tried to unhook my bra. All I could think of was what a jerk this guy was. I had just signed a contract for $250 a week (a lot back then), providing me housing and acting classes—what did I need him for? Did he think his clumsy groping would make me want him?

Mr. Bautzer was married to movie star Dana Wynter. While he's groping me, he tells me how his wife didn't understand him, that she was cold, and all the other BS. I suppose he thought I would get into bed. It sounded like a bad screenplay.

I wiggled out from under him, grabbed the contract, and headed for the door. I thanked him for his *"kind offer to take care of me,"* but I would prefer to work in Hollywood for a while first. Now that I think of it, that dumb line made it sound like I might be available in the future. Hmm, choose your words carefully, June.

On the way back to my hotel, I couldn't stop thinking about what had almost happened and what a jerk Bautzer turned out to be. Are all men in Hollywood like that? I never said anything to my Mum or Jimmy; I just showed them the contract.

Thankfully, I never crossed paths with Bautzer again until 1982. Susan Stafford and I went out together one night with our dates. Before Vanna White, Susan was the original hostess on Wheel of Fortune. Who do you think was Susan's date that night? None other than Greg Bautzer. I wanted to take Susan aside and put the fear of God in her about Bautzer, but I didn't—maybe I should have. When Susan introduced us, Bautzer, *the non-stop talking groper,* acted like we had never met. Who knows, perhaps he didn't remember me? This I know; he was and remained a first-class jerk to me.

The day after signing the Seven Arts contract, Jimmy McCullough, Mum, and I drove to Atlantic City to attend the premier of a movie. That evening, I was introduced to actor Jackie Coogan, who first became famous for playing the kid in *The Kid*, a favorite Charlie Chaplin movie. Jackie became famous again thanks to a new generation of kids growing up with TV watching the series *The Addams Family*. I was delighted when Jackie and his wife invited me to lunch on the boardwalk. I liked the Coogans; they were a lot of fun. They shared their telephone number and told me to look them up when I moved to Los Angeles.

Jimmy invited Mum and me to dinner at the 500 Club that night. He suggested I wear one of the Oleg Cassini dresses because my mother and I would be the guest of Paul "Skinny" D'Amato and his wife, a very beautiful lady. It was a wonderful evening with good food, dancing, and a great show. The D'Amato's proved to be very charming and friendly. I had no idea who Paul D'Amato was until I read Kitty Kelley's 1986 biography of Frank Sinatra; she revealed that Skinny D'Amato was one of the biggest mobsters in America. I was blown over that we had dinner at the 500 Club with a gangster and his wife; for those too young to remember Mr. D'Amato, Google him.

After a few days in Atlantic City, we returned to New York. Jimmy was going to be busy, so he thought it would be nice if he arranged for a friend of his to take Mum and me to dinner. Hey, why not? The gentleman was the great New York Yankee hero Joe DiMaggio. Neither my Mum nor I knew much about Joe other than he'd been married to Marilyn Monroe, which in itself was exciting. But why would Joe DiMaggio want to have dinner with us?

Joe picked us up at our hotel and took us to a nice Italian restaurant. He was polite but had almost nothing to say, which we found odd. I remember thinking, *"I don't think he wants to be here."* Looking back, maybe Jimmy and Skinny D'Amato told him to take us to dinner as a favor to them. It probably was the last thing Joe wanted to do, and I felt he couldn't wait to drop us back at the hotel. Joe never once mentioned his marriage to Marylyn. In fact, he never had much of anything to say.

Joe and I had one more dinner date about six months later. I was in New York before moving to Los Angeles to officially begin my contract with Seven Arts. Not knowing my way around New York very well, when Jimmy McCullough called to check on me, I asked him if he knew any good but inexpensive restaurants. He promised to call me right back. When he called, he said he had talked with Joe DiMaggio, and Joe was looking forward to seeing me again and would happily take me to dinner. Really? All I could think of was, *"Oh, no, not again"*!

JUNE WILKINSON

Joe took me to another Italian restaurant. He knew everyone there, and they all fussed over him talking about baseball, which meant nothing to me. I had never seen the game or knew anything about it. It's not an English sport; it never was played there. I tried my best to converse with Joe, but he made little attempt to respond beyond sentences with less than half-dozen words. It was a relief when someone would stop at our table to speak with Joe. It helped to fill the uncomfortable and long silences between us. If you've ever experienced being with someone like that, you know how painful it can be. I never did understand Joe.

I've been in the company of celebrities all my life (I don't mean to brag), but I don't remember any of them that received as much attention as Joe DiMaggio. Because of my lack of baseball knowledge, I probably didn't appreciate him as much as I should have. I wanted to talk about Marilyn Monroe, but I'm sure it would have made him uncomfortable, so I never brought it up, and neither did he.

It wasn't until I read Joe's biography that I learned of his connections to the mob. That may have explained why he took me to dinner twice. He was doing someone a favor. If that were the case, think of the hold the mob must have had on him that he had to do them favors like taking me to dinner. I'll never know.

Chapter 9

After my stay in New York and the brief interlude in Atlantic City, we were off to Chicago to fulfill my job as a hostess for Joe Sholkin at the convention. The hotel was excellent. My Mother had never stayed in such a fancy place and was having the time of her life.

Tony Charkham invited my Mum and me to join him for lunch at the hotel restaurant, where he ran into his friend, the singer Jane Morgan. Readers of a certain age will remember Jane's huge hit, *It Was Fascination.* Jane's husband, Jerry Weintraub, a film producer, was a legend in the entertainment business. In his autobiography, he revealed the arrangement he and Jane had. Although he adored and loved Jane, he also loved and adored his mistress. Oddly, neither lady objected to this arrangement. Jerry had a reputation as one of the best negotiators in show business. But his arrangement with Jane and his mistress must have been among his most successful and rewarding. Talk about *Fascination*! The pun was intentional.

After lunch, we went to the convention floor to see Joe's booth. Then it was on to the hospitality suite, where I played hostess and became reacquainted with many of the company executives I had met in England.

I loved Chicago; there were so many little clubs with great jazz combos and talented piano players and singers. I wished I had time to visit, but my time in Chicago was short. Mum and I had a lovely dinner with the group at the famous Pump Room. Someone had a copy of Playboy magazine, and the conversation centered around that issue. Someone passed it to me. After glancing through it, I told the group, *"My body is as good as anyone in the magazine."* When you're 18, like I was, you think you're God's gift to the world. Then, Jimmy said, *"You know, June, I agree; let's try and get you into the magazine."* I thought he was just joking! *"You know someone at Playboy, Jimmy?"* Jimmy smiled. *"Yeah, June, I do."*

It was around midnight when we returned to the hotel. What happens next only happens in the movies, or so I thought. Well, not this time; this time, it was real. Despite the hour, Jimmy called the Playboy office. Believe it or not, the man himself, Hugh Hefner, was alone in his office and answered the phone. After exchanging a few pleasantries, Jimmy pitched me and said I was interested in appearing in the magazine. Then there was a long silence while Jimmy listened. Finally, Jimmy said, *"Great, Hef. If you're that interested, you have to*

HOLLYWOOD OR BUST!

act fast as June's scheduled to leave town tomorrow.

To my utter surprise, Hef told Jimmy he'd seen my *Today Show* interview and said we should come right over, and he would try to round up a photographer. This was crazy; things like this don't happen this fast, except this one was. This had to be a dream I would awaken from at any moment.

Wrong!

I looked at Mum; she looked at me with a puzzled look, and reality set in. Mum said, *"Go for it, June."* I gathered my swimsuit, a nightgown, and a few other things I thought would photograph well, and Jimmy, Mum, and I were off to the Chicago Playboy offices. When Hugh Hefner greeted us, my first thought was how handsome he was, tall and slender, and to boot, he was very polite.

Hefner had found a photographer despite the hour. I slipped into my blue swimsuit with its bullet-bust line, which was in vogue then, and we started shooting under the watchful eye of Hefner. Back then, bras had a harsh, pointed look that was later brought back by Madonna. We did a few shots in my brassiere, which also had that harsh, pointed look, and a few shots in a petticoat my mother had made for me. Eventually, we got around to taking some nude photos on a bed. The bed was actually Hefner's that he used when working late in the office. He gave me one of his shirts to cover parts of me. I admit to being a bit uncomfortable about the nude shots with Mum there, but she seemed to enjoy it.

I don't recall how long the session lasted. When it was over, I began to get dressed when Hefner decided to take a few more shots with my dress unbuttoned and wearing no bra. It all happened that quickly. Today, they spend hours and hours doing test shots, hair, and makeup, choice of clothes, or the lack thereof. The difference between then and now is that, back then, the girls looked more like the girl next door. Today it's more of a glamorous fantasy image. And remember, when I posed, it was before boob jobs and pubic hair was ever shown.

The following day I was booked for an early appearance on a local morning TV show before I headed off to Los Angeles. Hefner sent a photographer to the studio to cover my appearance, and then it was off to Hollywood alone while Jimmy and Mum headed back to New York City. Jimmy was friends with singer Patti Page and her husband, Charlie O'Curran. He arranged for them to look after me in Los Angeles. Patti was the number one singer in America at the time with two huge hits, *The Tennessee Waltz* and *How Much Is That Doggie in the Window."* Her husband, Charlie, was a well-known choreographer. So, off I went to Tinsel Town to fulfill a dream I'd had since I was a little girl, and, to top it off, Patti Page would look after me. Pinch me once, pinch me twice. They put me up for three days at the Sheraton Hotel in downtown Los Angeles. One evening I had dinner at Patti and Charlie's house and watched TV with them.

The next day Charlie took me to Paramount Studios. When you approach Paramount Studios, you approach those most magnificent gates. I had only seen them on the screen when I watched the opening of one of Paramount's films and fantasized about walking through those gates one day, which I was about to do. Some fantasies do come true.

Charlie was there to stage the musical numbers for the 1958 Elvis Presley movie *King Creole*. As we entered the soundstage, Elvis was in the middle of an argument with one of the dancers. When Elvis spotted Charlie, he strolled over to us. Charlie introduced me, and we stood around talking until it was time for Elvis to shoot a scene. I couldn't believe I had just had a conversation with Elvis Presley. Between takes, Elvis would come over and talk with me. At the end of the day, he asked if I would have dinner with him that night. Are you kidding? This is Elvis Presley, June, so open your mouth and graciously accept the man's offer, girl.

Elvis sent a car to pick me up, and we were off to the Beverly Wilshire Hotel in Beverly Hills, where he was staying. When I arrived at Elvis's suite, about five guys with thick Southern accents around Elvis's age were there. Dinner was brought in. It would not be an intimate dinner with Elvis but with him, me, and his *Boys*. They talked about the women they knew, the ones they thought were the most beautiful; actress Natalie Wood's name came up the most. Elvis insisted that Deborah Paget, who starred with him in the 1959 film *Love Me Tender*, was the most beautiful woman he had ever seen.

After dinner, Elvis took my hand and said, *"Let me show you around."* In no time flat, we ended up in his bedroom. Here we go again, I thought. He wasted no time and kissed me and said he wanted to go to bed with me. I responded with, *"I'm a virgin,"* a line that was starting to sound monotonous, even to me. To my surprise, it didn't bother him at all. He sat me on the edge of his bed, got his guitar, and started singing. All I could think of was, *"If my friends could see me now."* I could hardly wait to tell Paul Anka to make him jealous. Boy, how stupid youth is sometimes.

Elvis sat there and sang most of his repertoire, stopping between songs to kiss me, and yes, girls, his lips were soft and tender, and he remained a perfect gentleman. When it was time to leave, he called for the car to take me to my hotel. At the elevator, he planted a goodnight kiss on me, and I thought that was the end of my encounter with Elvis Presley. It wasn't.

Elvis called the next day to invite me to dinner again. I was surprised because I thought our first meeting would be the only one. This was Elvis Presley, the man who could have any woman he wanted, and since I hadn't come across in the bedroom, I assumed that was the end of that. I told him I had to pass on dinner because I was flying back to New York at midnight. He said, "Pack your bags, and I promise to get you to the airport on time."

A car picked me up and whisked me off to the Beverly Wilshire Hotel. It was the same scenario, same guys, conversation, and little of it directed my way. When it came time to leave, Elvis and some others piled into the car with me, and off we went. At the airport, Elvis got out of the car, hugged and kissed me goodbye; no one in the surrounding area even noticed that it was Elvis Presley. I waved goodbye to Elvis and the gang as the car left.

Several years later, Max Baer Jr., who starred in *The Beverly Hillbillies*, called to invite me to a party at Elvis's

HOLLYWOOD OR BUST!

rented home in the swanky neighborhood of Bel Air off Sunset Boulevard. We spent about an hour driving through the maze of streets that can be confusing to non-residents. We never found the house, and Max had never thought to get Elvis's phone number, so we gave up and went home. I never crossed paths with Elvis again.

    A couple of years go by, and I'm working in Las Vegas, and Elvis was married to Priscilla by then. I was strolling through the casino at 3 in the morning when three guys—some of Elvis's Memphis boys whom I'd never met—approached and asked if I wanted to meet Elvis Presley. Without hesitation, I said, *"Been there, done that,"* and kept walking. These guys had no earthly idea what I was talking about. To this day, I believe they were trying to round up girls for themselves, using Elvis as bait, and were not told by Elvis to "troll" for him.

Chapter 10

I returned to England to organize and prepare for what would be my permanent move back to America. Before my first trip to the United States, I had committed to a variety show for producer Paul Raymond that was to travel throughout England. Unfortunately, I had to tell him I could not proceed because of my contract with Seven Arts. He was not happy, of course, but as they say, that's show business. My focus now was my return to the United States for what I hoped would be a successful acting career.

Leaving England was difficult; I had to leave my family behind in Eastbourne, and that was hard. Looking back, I realize how brave and selfless my mother was to let her only daughter, now 18, go to a foreign country to live alone. But there she was, hugging me, giving me her full support, and not knowing if or when she would see me again.

Remember, this was before jets, e-mails, or cell phones, and we were a lower-middle-class family, and we could not afford expensive long-distance calls to another country. Calls in those days were much more costly than they are now. Today, I pay an extra $25 a month, and I can call and talk all day long to Europe, Canada, and Mexico. I was 18, and if I did call home, a three-minute call cost over $10, a lot of money in those days. That was out of the question for my family, and I could only afford it occasionally.

As a mother, I'm not sure I would have been as unselfish as my mother. I would give anything to spend just one more day with her to tell her how much I love her and thank her for all the gifts of life she bestowed on me. If I face similar decisions, I hope to be as great a mother as she was. There are tears in my eyes as I write this. I admit I was negligent at the one thing I could have done but seldom did; I never wrote a letter—how Mum would have treasured them.

Chapter 11

When it came time to leave England and return to America, my friend Lionel Bart drove me to the airport. As nervous and excited as I was, Lionel was equally excited about his new project: he was about to write what would become the musical version of Charles Dickens's *Oliver Twist*. When I asked him why he chose *Oliver Twist*, he explained it was in the public domain, and he wouldn't have to pay royalties. I didn't give it much thought then, but when it opened on June 30, 1960, it became the most successful musical hit ever. I read there was a time when Lionel was making over 16 pounds a minute from his royalties from *Oliver, his* pop hits, and the James Bond theme song *From Russia with Love*. Unfortunately, Lionel lived a high life and threw huge parties and invited anybody and everybody: the rich and

HOLLYWOOD OR BUST!

the poor, the famous, and even royalty like Princess Margaret and the Beatles. Speaking of the Beatles, there are pictures of the late George Harrison and me floating around, and I'm always asked if we ever had a romance. To set the record straight, no, he was never a romantic boyfriend of mine, just a friend.

Back to Lionel Bart; initially, he would keep in touch by phone or write letters. He was much better about keeping in touch than I was. When his show opened on Broadway, I was busy touring, and we never got to see each other, nor did I know how bad his drug consumption was. When we talked or wrote a letter, he sounded fine. Unfortunately, I found out too late. As I said, Lionel lived high, and many people took advantage of him. When he died of cancer in 1999, he was flat broke. I will always be grateful for the significant role Lionel played in my early life. I wish he had confided in me; maybe I could have helped.

I don't remember much about the flight to America, but I remember the press making a big fuss and taking pictures at my departure from England and arrival in New York. As I said, flying was considered glamorous back then, and the newspapers always took photos of movie stars and famous people whenever they traveled. Now, the paparazzi follow celebrities everywhere, looking to get that one embarrassing shot.

Seven Arts put me up at the Lexington Hotel in New York, where I stayed for six weeks before transitioning to Hollywood. The only people I knew in New York were singer Johnny Ray and his business manager, Saul

Lazarow. Saul was also Paul Anka's business manager and regularly teased me about my crush on Paul.

In New York, I had time to do whatever I wanted. The only negative was the heat and humidity; I had never experienced that weather in England. Luckily, almost every place had air-conditioning, another luxury that was still hard to find in England at the time.

Ray Stark called from Los Angeles to be sure I was okay. I assured him I was. He said he'd been speaking with Prince Aly Khan, known as Aly Khan. He was a Pakistani diplomat of Iranian-Pakistani descent and Prince Aga Khan's son. He was a well-known socialite, racehorse owner, and jockey. Ray mentioned to Khan that he had signed a new actress and told Khan a little bit about me. *"June, would it be all right to give Aly your telephone number?* Ray asked. *"The prince would like to take you to lunch."* Okay, since it was Aly Khan, I agreed. I was well aware of who Aly Khan was. I knew from the tabloids he was a notorious playboy and rumored to be quite the lover, dating the most beautiful single and married woman in the world. That included the beautiful movie star Rita Hayworth—he became her third husband.

Prince Khan called me the next day. We made arrangements to meet at an upscale Manhattan restaurant for lunch. I admit to spending a long time preparing, trying to look as perfect as possible. One of my good qualities, or at least I think of it as one, is that I'm always punctual. I arrived on time, and there was a reservation in Khan's name. Khan had not arrived yet, so I ordered a cup of tea and waited and waited and waited. After too many cups of tea and too long a wait to

HOLLYWOOD OR BUST!

suit me, I left. To add insult to injury, Mr. Khan (notice I'm not calling him Prince anymore) never called to apologize. I had begun to think of myself as the cat's meow, but being stood up by Kahn certainly put me back in my place, so much for Aly Khan. He was out of my life before he entered my life. It was his loss.

I had been in New York for about four weeks when I got a call from Paul Anka. He was flying into New York to work with his musical arranger, Don Costa, and would be staying at the St. Moritz Hotel, within walking distance of the Lexington Hotel where I was staying. Saul Lazarow gave Paul a heads-up that I was in town and had given him my phone number. When Paul called, we decided to meet on his first night in the city.

Charlie Gracie and Paul Anka were the only two real crushes I'd had until then. They were totally different personality types, both singers and teen idols. Even though we spent hours kissing, Charlie never laid an inappropriate hand on me. On the other hand, Paul was the opposite, always trying to get me to go all the way. Although to give him credit, he never got angry when I didn't. Why he even bothered with me was a mystery. He could have had any number of his groupies who have jumped at the opportunity. I seem to recall he lost his virginity when he was around fifteen—but don't hold me to that—you'd have to check with him!

Even though Paul was young, he was brighter than most recording artists I had met. One example: Paul noticed that Johnny Carson did not have a theme song, so he wrote one and submitted it to Carson. Paul offered to split the residuals of his creation with Johnny 50/50. That clinched the deal, and Paul received thousands a night in residuals for years.

I saw a lot of Paul while he was in town, and yes, the inevitable happened; we finally went all the way, and I lost my virginity. I admit it, bells rang, the heavens opened, and I was in utopia. Okay, I'm just kidding. As I sit here writing about it, I'm trying to recall what it felt like, and for the life of me, I can't. I have been racking my brain, trying to remember, but I honestly don't recall. I remember Elvis's lips and how they felt when he kissed me. Maybe that's because I knew my girlfriends would ask what Elvis's kiss was like, and I would have to describe it in detail. Sorry, Paul. However, I must have liked it because I kept seeing him.

Saul and Johnnie Ray always asked if I had lost my "cherry." When they finally wrangled the truth out of me, they placed a big bag of cherries at the front hotel desk for me with a note. *"We found these cherries at the St. Moritz Hotel. Do you recognize yours?"*

After eight weeks of being wined and dined at swanky places like the Copacabana, with its excellent chorus line, and the Waldorf-Astoria featuring great bands like Guy Lombardo and his Royal Canadians, I was beginning to feel like a princess again. And, I might add, without the company of Prince Aly Khan.

When the call came from Seven Arts to fly to Los Angeles, I bid goodbye to my New York friends who had shown me such a fabulous time. Now it was goodbye New York; hello Hollywood, here I come.

In Los Angeles, a private car took to the Beverly Comstock Hotel. A note was waiting, reminding me that Ray Stark would pick me up for lunch at noon. At lunch,

HOLLYWOOD OR BUST!

Mr. Stark told me he had arranged for me to stay at the Hollywood Studio Club, a special place for young girls only. Seven Arts was producing the 1959 film *Thunder in the Sun* with Susan Haywood and Jeff Chandler and cast me in a small part. Wow! Susan Haywood and Jeff Chandler! Again, I hit the jackpot. My dreams were coming true faster than I would have ever believed.

I was excited about moving to the Hollywood Studio Club for Young Ladies. That was overshadowed by my first big dumb mistake. Ray Stark and Seven Arts offered to buy me a car, to which I stupidly replied, *"Oh, but I don't drive."* It would be another year and a half before I owned a car, and then I had to buy it myself. *DUH!*

I packed my belongings the next day and moved to the Hollywood Studio Club. The Club was the donation of some very generous ladies connected to show business in the mid-1920s, spearheaded by the wife of the great film director Cecil B. DeMille. The idea was to provide a safe environment for young girls trying to break into show business. The club had strict rules and regulations and was known for its respectability, virtue, and a safe haven in a profession where one could easily get into trouble. The house was a big, old mansion with a beautiful garden and courtyard and, of course, the dreaded reception desk, where rule number one was enforced—no men allowed in your room. There were many stories about men trying to get in through the coveted rooms with balconies. When the famous actress Kim Novak lived there, she lived in a room with a balcony, and the rumor is that one night Frank Sinatra serenaded her from the street until the authorities came and told him to leave. Another Hollywood rumor or fact?

One of the enforced rules at the residence was the nightly curfew. The door was locked by 10 PM. If you tried to enter after that, your name was entered into the dreaded *Late Book*. If your name found its way into that book once too often, you were out on your ass. Management put it more delicately, but the result was the same. As you can imagine, there was a long waiting list of young aspiring lady actresses hoping to move there, not just because of the impressive facilities or the fact that it was affordable. I think it was because management showed genuine concern for the well-being of the girls and not so much about making a profit.

The club had a large dining hall, a rehearsal room with a stage and piano, and a reception room; the only room men could visit. Over its lifetime, the Hollywood Studio Club was home to Kim Novak, Marilyn Monroe, Donna Reed, Zazu Pitts, Sharon Tate, Marie Windsor, Evelyn Keyes, Janet Blair, Rita Moreno, Shirly Knight, and many others.

My favorite person was a girl no one thought would become a star. She had the wackiest sense of humor and was always pleasant to everyone. And, good for her, she did make it. Miss JoAnn Worley hit the big-time in the television comedy *Laugh-In*, with the wildly popular comedy team of Rowan and Martin. JoAnn also performed in dinner theaters, so our paths crossed many times over the years. As for me, I had that Seven Arts movie contract while living at the Club, so that gave me a bit of importance in the eyes of all the other "wannabes."

Chapter 12

When I walked onto the *Thunder in The Sun* set, I was surprised at how many people there were: stand-ins for the stars, makeup artists, prop men, and sound and camera technicians. When I first set eyes on Susan Hayward, I thought she was stunning. She was petite with a trim figure and thick red hair. Unfortunately, I didn't have any scenes with her, so we never got to speak beyond passing hellos. I never saw her standing around chatting with anyone. As soon as her scene was over, she went straight to her dressing room. And although my part was small, I was excited and grateful to be in the movie.

The male star, Jeff Chandler, was a frustrated baseball player. When he wasn't shooting a scene, he spent his time tossing a baseball back and forth with his stand-in. I don't think he ever noticed me; he was too busy throwing that bloody ball. The other male lead in the movie was Jacques Bergerac, a French actor who married actress/dancer Ginger Rogers. At the end of each day, everyone gathered to watch the dailies of previously shot sequences. Jacques, a pleasant enough fellow, would take a seat next to me. Once, when the lights went out, he dropped to the floor, took off my shoe, and tried to suck my toe. Jeez, here we go again. I jerked my foot away and put my shoe on like what happened didn't. When the lights came on, he got up and left without saying one word leaving me to wonder why he would do such a thing. I never let him sit next to me again. Yet another Hollywood jerk.

I took Charlie Chaplin, Jr. up on his previous offer to contact him when I was in California. Charlie took me to dinner when I was free, and his friend Marty Barth often joined us. Marty was such a lovely man, and we became good friends. By now, you must know I am a people person and make friends easily. Marty never had much money and drove around in an old clunker of a car. But clunker or no clunker, when I had somewhere to go and needed a lift, Marty was always there for me.

One day, one of the girls at the Hollywood Studio Club ran into my room waving a magazine. *"June, June, you're in Playboy!"* Playboy had released its September 1959 issue featuring my photos and had dubbed me "The Bosom." I thought the pictures presented me well, and I was happy with the corresponding article, so everything was just fine. Little did I realize what a stir I had caused. Seven Arts, who had no idea I had posed for those pictures, was not so pleased. They huddled with the Roger & Cowan PR Agency, who handled all Seven Arts press. They were concerned it would blemish my image. Nudity was a big deal in America, and censorship was far stricter than in Europe. There was no nudity in American films. On TV, married couples slept in twin beds. Since my Playboy photos were out and the damage was done, Roger and Cowan's answer to the problem was to take advantage of the situation and hire a photographer to take even more pictures and make me the most photographed-pin-up in the world. Lady Luck was still perched comfortably on my shoulder.

On the flip side, Hugh Hefner was ecstatic because the issue I was in was flying off the newsstands like crazy. Remember, this was way before bust jobs, and a bosom my size was definitely not the norm! Ever the sharp businessman, Hefner was keenly aware I had become established in show business, so next he published a six-page feature story on me.

Rogers and Cowan hired Russ Meyer, the number one pin-up photographer in the business, and asked him if he'd be interested in being the exclusive photographer for June Wilkinson. Russ thought he had died and gone to heaven. Russ was a big bust man (excuse the pun), and they'd handed him a female whose breasts Hugh Hefner thought were good enough to call The Bosom. They asked Russ to get me into as many magazines as possible. Of all the photographers they could have hired, Russ was the right man to do it. In Russ's 2008 biography, he wrote that he had never made that much money in his entire life before working with me. But I'm jumping ahead.

Russ picked me up at the Hollywood Studio Club on the first day because, damn it, I still didn't have a car! Russ was a large man. He wasn't fat but stocky, with big hands and a kind of blue-collar look about him, and he always sported a big grin. The conversation came easy between us, with Russ doing most of the talking. For our first session, I wore red Capri pants that were very popular at the time. I had packed about six different selections of clothing that I thought would photograph well, and I thought the Capri pants would look good with no top.

Our destination was a house in the Hollywood Hills that had once belonged to the great silent film star Rudolph Valentino. While he was shooting photos, Russ never stopped talking. He kept shooting roll after roll of film while instructing me to keep changing poses. He kept telling me how fabulous I looked. One of those first photos later appeared in Playboy. We were off and running.

Russ talked a lot about his wife, Eve, and told me how madly in love he was with her. While shooting away, he would go on forever about how he and Eve had met and how beautiful she was. All this while he continually barked out commands, "Change position, June, move, chin up, head up, don't slouch, your breasts will look better if you do this." It was continuous shooting, nonstop talking, and, eventually, a break for a quick breakfast or lunch, which was always a hamburger or hot dog at some fast-food joint. Russ never took me to fancy places. At the end of the day, Russ couldn't wait to get home to be with Eve. Years later, I was shocked when I heard they had divorced; what would have happened if he had been so in love with her? Russ never shared the details with me. Russ and Eve remained friends and business partners until she tragically died in a plane crash. Russ raved about Eve's business savvy and credited her for making him wealthy. Sorry, Russ, I may have had something to do with that too.

After several months of photo sessions, Russ told me he was thinking of producing and directing a movie titled *The Immoral Mr. Teas* and asked me to appear in it. I was still under contract with Seven Arts, and my agreement would not allow me to appear in Russ's film. So, after some deliberation, we decided he would not use my name in the credits or on any advertising, and he would not show my face, but he could show my breasts. Let's face it; my breasts were all he was interested in. When *The Immoral Mr. Teas* was released in late 1959, everyone knew it was me, even though you never saw my face. I guess breasts are like fingerprints; there are no two alike. *The Immoral Mr. Teas* became a massive hit for Russ.

In return for my appearance in his film, Russ agreed I could access any of his photographs. I never took advantage of the deal, except once when I used one of his photos of me lying in the sand in an ad for a film I was in that year. (*The Private Lives of Adam and Eve, (1960)*, starring and directed by Mickey Rooney.) Years later, I asked Russ for some photos, but he told me there had been a fire and all the negatives were lost. I don't know if that was true or if he didn't want to give them to me. Russ went on to churn out hit after hit. All his films were visually explicit and X-rated, all made on minimal budgets.

JUNE WILKINSON

In 1968, Richard Zanuck and David Brown, hot producers at 20th Century Fox, had trouble with Jacqueline Susann's script for the sequel to *Valley of the Dolls*. This successful team had a distinguished reputation for producing quality movies like *Jaws* and *Driving Miss Daisy*. After seeing how much money Russ's movies made, they hired him as the film's director.

I had not heard from Russ in ten years. I had moved on to several stage shows and a stint on Broadway. Russ called and said he wanted to meet for dinner. By then, I knew he would be directing *Beyond the Valley of the Dolls*, and I was very excited for him. We went to a chic, ultra-expensive restaurant, unlike the dives where we'd had lunch or breakfast in the old days. He dove right into the reason he'd wanted to see me. Much to my disappointment, the conversation did not go as I expected. Russ told me he was directing *Valley of the Dolls* and felt he owed me a role because of my tits—his words, not mine. He went into a long monologue about why he could *not* offer me a role. He was stuck with actress Edie Williams, the mistress of one of the big shots at 20th Century Fox. To say it ruined my lunch was an understatement. Russ, however, could not have been upset for long because, to everyone's shock, he and Edie married on June 27, 1970. Marital bliss did not last very long; neither party seemed to like the other very much, and they soon divorced. There's no business-like show business, like no business I know, folks.

I did not see Russ again for some 25 years until an excellent writer, Steve Sullivan, interviewed me. Steve, who had written several books on glamor girls, was now writing one titled Glamour Girls Then and Now. He

HOLLYWOOD OR BUST!

mentioned he would be interviewing Russ Meyer the next day, so I asked if he would tell Russ that I said hello and hoped he was doing well. The next day Steve called and said Russ would love to take me to dinner. Could he give Russ my phone number? Of course, I said yes.

The following day, Russ called and said he wanted me to see his house, and then we'd go to dinner. So, two days later, I'm off to his home under the Hollywood sign, which I thought was appropriate for him. I could not believe what I was seeing: every room, and every inch of the doors, walls, and ceilings, was covered with photos and posters of nudes or semi-nudes. At first, I thought, "Oh, my God, what poor taste," but I took a long, hard look and thought, *"No, I'm wrong; it's perfect, Russ Meyer."* Everywhere I looked, there was a photo of a woman's body in some form of dress and undressed with breasts so large it made me feel inferior, and that's saying a lot. He had pictures of ladies with breasts so large they defied gravity or, to put it another way, they'd be uncomfortable sleeping on their stomachs!

We had dinner on Hollywood Blvd., at Musso and Frank's famous Hollywood restaurant. Russ suggested we sit at the bar, which was his favorite spot. After, we returned to his place, and he gave me DVDs of every one of his movies, including the one we made together, which I did not have. He hugged me goodbye and sent me on my way.

We'd have dinner together from time to time after that. One evening, Russ had this sad look and told me he was suffering from the early stages of Alzheimer's disease. At times he was fine, but sometimes he would not remember things, and other times he would.

Fortunately, Russ had help at the house, so I assumed he was adequately cared for. I took him out whenever I could to places like the Playboy Mansion or a stage play I thought he would enjoy. I did this because I feared it would get to the point where he could no longer get out on his own. Russ would talk endlessly about making another movie with me, but I knew he could not make more films mentally. I always led him to believe it would be wonderful to work together again.

It was time for me to leave town to do a stage show. Several months later, when I returned to Los Angeles, I visited Russ at home. All the walls and ceilings were bare —not one photo was in sight. For fear that I might embarrass him, I didn't say anything. I left with a terrible, sad, empty feeling, knowing I could do nothing about it.

Russ Meyer died in September 2004. His funeral was the saddest I have ever attended. Not in the sense that people were sad because of the death of a loved one, but this was one of the worst, coldest send-offs I had ever witnessed. The viewing and the service were private, and no one was allowed in unless they were on the guest list.

As sure as I'm sitting here typing this, Russ would have loved every woman he had known or lusted after to show up naked or, at least, in something sexy. He would have wanted a big, happy, boisterous party to celebrate his life. Instead, the service was pathetic. It was held at the Old North Church in Forest Lawn Memorial Park. The minister mispronounced Russ's last name as Mayer, instead of Meyer, throughout the entire service. The only time during the service anyone felt connected to Russ was when film critic Roger Ebert got up and gave the eulogy. There was no gathering after the service to share moments of Russ's life. There was no effort to make him look like himself; he looked strange. We just shuffled quickly past his coffin. Everyone, including me, got into our cars and left when it was over.

Chapter 13

I was sitting around having coffee and chatting with some of the girls at the Hollywood Studio Club, and the talk was all about Spike Jones auditioning for a singer. His wife, Helen Greco, the lead singer who usually sang in the band, was pregnant and would be out of commission for about six months. The gig would be at Harrah's Casino in Tahoe, Nevada.

Spike Jones, for those of you who don't remember him, was a bandleader who specialized in wild, insane, crazy music and employed all kinds of strange instruments: washboards, bicycle horns, pie pans, garbage can lids, car horns, cowbells, frying pans—anything he could find that made noise. Although my contract with Seven Arts was still intact, I wasn't doing any acting for them other than the acting class I

HOLLYWOOD OR BUST!

attended one day a week. The lack of activity drove me crazy, so when I heard about Spike Jones's casting call for a singer, I thought, why not audition?

There was, however, one little problem; I couldn't sing. But, what the hell, why should I let a little thing like that get in the way? I had good comedy timing; my body would suit many gags and comedy skits. I thought I would be an asset to his show—no modesty here.

In addition to the lack of vocal skills, I had another problem. I had to get permission from Seven Arts before taking any job. I knew they had nothing immediately coming up for me. They were in preproduction on a film titled The World of Suzy Wong, with William Holden and newcomer Nancy Kwan. There was certainly nothing in that film that I would have been right for. So, I decided to go to the Spike Jones audition.

Spike recognized me as soon as I walked in. We talked for about an hour. He gave me a few lines to read and a couple of jokes. He asked me to sing, but surprisingly he didn't seem concerned that I couldn't carry a tune and offered me the job. I explained I was under contract with Seven Arts and was required to get their permission first and would call him as soon as I spoke with them.

I returned to the Studio Club, put a call into Seven Arts, and asked to speak to Ray Stark. They didn't know who I was or why I needed to speak with Ray. Although my ego was a little crushed, I put that aside since they sent me a nice weekly paycheck. Although I didn't talk to Ray Stark, they promised to get back to me. The next day, I got a call from someone at the Seven Arts office, giving me the okay to accept Spike's offer. Since I was getting more money from Spike than Seven Arts was paying me, I figured they were happy to be off the hook for the money while I was working elsewhere. I have always believed that things turn out for the best. Lady Luck was still perched comfortably on my shoulder.

Spike's contract listed me as a singer (that was a real stretch!). I promptly sent the contract to my father with the word singer underlined. He returned a note saying, "Now I know all Americans are absolutely crazy."

Rehearsals were great fun, and the guys in Spike's band were terrific. But it was Billy Barty that I fell in love with. He was known as one of the little people because he was only three feet eleven inches tall. But Billy had the biggest heart and considerable talent. Billy was an old hand who had been in show business since the 1920s when he starred with Mickey Rooney in the Mickey McGuire silent shorts.

Billy's act was to come on stage dressed as Liberace, wearing a glitzy costume and large rings on his fingers. He would sit at a tiny miniature grand piano with a candelabra and do an incredible Liberace imitation. He received standing ovations almost every night. Billy loved the showgirls, and they loved him back. He was always sitting on one of the showgirls' laps when I visited his dressing room.

In the following years, Billy was the only person from Spike's band with whom I crossed paths. He lived in Los Angeles and was active in movies and TV productions. He did a great deal for the little people, and in 1957, he started the Billy Barty Foundation. As much as he seemed to love tall, statuesque showgirls, when he finally married, it was to a beautiful lady who was his size.

HOLLYWOOD OR BUST!

Unlike Spike, who I never heard crack a joke off stage, Billy always seemed to be having a good time. Spike didn't seem happy. I never heard him laugh or have fun around others.

I was working the show for about two weeks when I found a long, black dress that was tight fitting with a high neckline. I thought the dress was beautiful and an improvement over the gold dress Spike had chosen. I bought the dress and put it on the next night. I walked up to Spike and stood next to him, waiting in the wings to go on. Spike turned to me and said, *"Good evening, June,"* and then he turned back. It took a second or two before Spike realized what I was wearing. He did a double take, saying, *"Change that dress really fast; you don't sing that good."* The band and I laughed at that one.

One of the cleverest publicity stunts that Harrah's Casino came up with was perfect for a Spike Jones show, and Spike loved it. They photographed me standing at the border between Nevada and California, with my feet on the Nevada line while my breasts stuck out into the California side. As they say today, that picture went viral, and we played to packed houses after that.

I loved working at Harrah's Casino but could not gamble or linger at the gaming tables because I was underage. The rules were, and still are, if you are under 21, you can walk through the casino, but you can't stop until you get to the other side. I walked as slow as I dared, but the security guys were on to me and would move me along.

I usually had dinner after the show because I needed a little time to come down from the highs of a performance. I went to bed around four and usually fell asleep immediately. Spike, on the other hand, suffered from insomnia. Often, I would arrange for no calls because people think nothing of calling at about 9 A.M; that's far too early when you are working in nightclubs.

One particular morning, after I had been asleep for a couple of hours, the phone rang, and it was Spike. *"Spike,"* I said, *"I arranged for no calls. How did you get through"*? Without skipping a beat, he said, *"I told them I was Spike Jones; this was an emergency, and they put me through."* I asked what was wrong, and he said, *"I can't sleep, and now you're awake, so come on down and have coffee with me."* All he wanted was someone to talk to because he couldn't sleep. That became a habit that I was none too happy about. But he was my boss, so I always got up and met him in the coffee shop whenever he called. Most of the time, Spike would talk about his family and his wife, Helen Greco, pregnant with their child. Helen eventually gave birth to a baby boy and named him Spike Junior.

One time Spike asked me if I was interested in anybody in the band, and if I were, he would arrange it. I thanked him profusely and said the only thing I wanted was sleep, a hint that he never seemed to take.

I enjoyed my time immensely with Spike and all the boys in the band and was sad when the Tahoe gig ended. Spike had two weeks off, and then the show would continue for two weeks in a theater in Phoenix, Arizona. I wasn't contracted to do the show there, but Spike invited me to join them, and I accepted. I don't remember much about the Phoenix show, but it was in a theater, not a casino, and not as much fun. Thankfully, Spike found another early morning talking buddy.

HOLLYWOOD OR BUST!

Finally, I was able to sleep!

I don't recall why, but someone loaned Spike a brand-new Rolls Royce to run around in while he was in Phoenix. When I woke up one morning, I turned on the radio and heard that Spike and his talking buddy had run into a brick wall in the wee hours of the morning. They weren't hurt, but it was bye-bye to the completely ruined Rolls.

After the Phoenix show, I returned to Los Angeles and learned my contract with Seven Arts was up; they were not renewing it. Bummer! If I hadn't gotten in touch with them to do Spike's show, I could have paid my expenses and collected my $250 weekly paycheck for another nine or ten months. Oh well, easy come, easy go. That chapter of my life was now over. I have no regrets because working with Spike and his Merry Men was a blast that I will always treasure.

Chapter 14

Soon after my gig with Spike, Ernie Kovacs, who had a top-rated TV comedy show, chose me to be in a cigar commercial that featured him. It was just the two of us. He wanted me to play an American Indian in a black wig. We shot it in one day. Unlike most comics or comedians I was used to being around off-camera; Ernie never cracked a joke or did any shtick. He was very polite and pleasant but didn't talk a lot. I had never appeared in a commercial before, and I had no idea that when you did a commercial, you were paid a residual every time it played. Fortunately, the commercial ran for several years during Ernie's live show. He always mentioned, *"In case you didn't recognize her, June Wilkinson plays the Indian girl."* That was terrific publicity for me.

We were all saddened when Ernie died in a car

accident on January 23, 1962, in the wee hours of the morning. My commercial with him was taken off the air, and they shot a new one with Ernie's beautiful wife, Edie Adams. So, that very lucrative payday was over. But more importantly, the world lost an extraordinary talent in Ernie Kovacs.

I did commercials for Carnation Milk, Frederick's of Hollywood, and others in the following years. The most lucrative by far was The Mark Eden Bust Developer. The device worked on an isometric system: You squeezed the Bust Developer between your palms. The device made your pectoral muscles move and, consequently, firm and increased the size of your breasts. Yes, I was well compensated on that one.

A momentary step back to the Hollywood Studio Club. One of the rules stated that if you had a date, the date was required to wait in the foyer. The person staffing the front desk would announce the date's arrival, and you then met and greeted them in the lobby. That was how I became cast in my first independent movie.

As I said, Seven Arts had enrolled me in an acting class, and even though I was no longer with them, I was still attending Joe Graham's acting class. One of my fellow students was Bill Wellman Jr., son of famous director William Wellman, known in Hollywood as "Wild Bill Wellman." Bill Jr. was a good-looking young man, and although there was never anything romantic between us, we became good friends and have remained so to this day. Since I still had no car, Bill would drive me to class, then back to the Studio Club.

JUNE WILKINSON

One day, Bill was waiting for me in the lobby when a man named Doug Fowley was waiting for his date. Doug introduced himself to Bill, and they were in deep conversation when I arrived at the foyer. By the time we left to go to our acting class, Doug had decided that Bill and I looked really good together and suggested we be cast as the newlyweds in his new movie, but he needed to get the approval of the Executive Producer, Mike Ripps. Doug was on hiatus from Hugh O'Brien's hugely popular Western television series, "Wyatt Earp." In the series, Doug played the infamous Doc Holliday. The movie he was about to do would be his first as a Director/Producer titled "Macumba Love," a 1969 horror film about Voodoo to be shot in Brazil.

About four days later, my agent received a call from Mike Ripps. He was a stout man who owned a couple of drive-in movie theaters in Mobile, Alabama. This man had never produced a movie before but felt that Hollywood was sending him such crap that he was sure he could produce something better than what he was getting. Ripps gave his approval to Bill Wellman and me as the newlyweds. The part was mine. Brazil, here I come!

Around this time, several girls decided to move out of The Hollywood Studio Club and asked if I would like to share an apartment. As much as I loved the Club, I felt it was time to move on, so I joined them. We found two small studio apartments a few blocks from the Studio Club and rented them for $90 a month each (Oh, for the good old days!). Shirley Gardner and I would be roommates; Lillian (I forget her last name, sorry, Lillian) and Evy Norlund, a pretty girl who was Miss Denmark

HOLLYWOOD OR BUST!

in 1958, would share the apartment above us.

Evy was madly in love with the handsome actor James Darren. Darren was getting the star build-up at Columbia Studios when someone at the studio discovered he could sing, which led to two huge hits, *Good*bye Cruel World and Gidget. James and Evy were married on February 6, 1960. I boarded a flight a few years ago, and who should I run into but James Darren, whom I had not seen in years. We chatted and caught up, and I was so pleased to learn that he was still married to Evy. Some Hollywood marriages *do* work out.

While I was getting ready to go to Brazil to film Macumba Love, I received a message from my agent that actor Steve Cochran, whom I had not seen or heard from since my dinner dates with him in London, was trying to get in touch with me. He saw my name in *Variety* and asked my agent if I would call him, which I did. Steve told me that Yvonne De Carlo and her husband—a top Hollywood stuntman—were having a Western theme party, and he asked me to go with him. Many will remember Yvonne De Carlo from the endless reruns of the hit TV series The Addams Family. But not everyone remembers that Yvonne was a famous movie star long before she joined the cast of *The Addams Family*.

I wore blue jeans, my only Western attire for the Western-themed party. Yvonne's house was packed with many interesting people, but within thirty minutes, Steve seemed anxious to leave and insisted he show me his house. I would have preferred to stay at the party, but I was Steve's guest, so I agreed.

Halfway through the house tour, a young girl, who could not have been more than fourteen (I was still 18 at the time), ran into the house. She told me she was Steve's girlfriend and begged me not to go to bed with him, which I had no intention of doing anyway. Steve was furious with her, rushed me out of there as fast as he could, and took me home. When we arrived, he parked the car a block away on a dark street. Suddenly, his hands were all over me, and he was literally tearing at my clothes. Fortunately, I had those tight jeans on—not easy clothing to get off. After what turned out to be a nasty struggle, I exited the car and ran as fast as my feet would take me to my apartment.

Shirley and Lillian were there and had been drinking, and they were a little out of it. I tried telling them what had happened in the car, but they weren't listening. I got so angry that I picked up their bottle of scotch and started drinking it like soda. Dumb move! I threw up and then passed out. The next day, I woke up on the floor amid all my puke. It had been my first and only hangover. To this day, I have never touched scotch or been drunk again. It would be years before I even tried alcohol since I didn't have much desire for it. I like champagne, wine, and an occasional beer, but I never want more than two glasses.

Needless to say, I never went out with Steve Cochran again. Unfortunately, he met a very ugly end. In 1965, while sailing his yacht, supposedly looking for suitable filming locations, he died of a lung infection. Several underage girls sailing with him had no idea how to manage the boat. They drifted with Steve's dead body for ten days before being rescued.

It was a tragic end to another Hollywood story.

HOLLYWOOD OR BUST!

Chapter 15

It was time to leave for Brazil to film *Macumba Love* and my first significant movie role. Walter Reed, an outstanding actor who was never out of work, was cast as my father. Walter was in the very first Superman film in 1951. In 1970, he appeared in Tora, Tora, Tora and hundreds of other movies. One of his most memorable performances was as the Western as the husband of actress Gail Russell in Seven Men from Now. He and his wife remained my friends until they both passed away.

The role of the Voodoo Queen went to Ziva Rodam, an Israeli living in America. Ziva was Miss Israel and had also served in the Israeli Army. She was exotic looking and had an amazing body. Unfortunately, I don't think she liked me. I can't remember her ever talking with me other than when we were shooting, unlike the rest of the cast and crew, who went out of their way to befriend everyone.

Getting to Sao Paulo, Brazil, would take three days (remember, no jets yet, travel was still on prop-driven planes). The first stop after leaving Los Angeles was an overnight stay in Miami. The weather was balmy and warm, like a blanket wrapped around me. I would love to have spent a few more days there. The second stop was Caracas, Venezuela, where I had difficulty sleeping because the natives insisted on playing their bongos all night. They sounded great, but by three or four in the morning, they were driving me crazy. The following day, tired but excited, we made the last leg of the journey and arrived in Sao Paulo, Brazil. We were tired, but I put on my best smile for the press. We settled into the Continental hotel in the center of town. I would have slept for three days if they had let me.

The cast reading of the script was set for the following day. It was nothing like the old Windmill Theater rehearsals where the piano player, dance instructor, song instructor, and line instructor fought for a space in the rehearsal hall to work in. We gathered around a long table in a conference room. I was not impressed when I'd first read the screenplay, so I was pleased to hear Doug Fowley announce there would be changes to the script. On a scale of *A* to *Z*, I had given *Macumba Love* a giant *Z*. Hopefully, Doug would improve it.

Doug told me not to be concerned about my English accent. The script would refer to my being born in England, which was a great relief because I was worried about my accent. Unfortunately, the script changes did little to improve the film, but we had fun making it, so that made up for it. Turning a sow's ear into a delicate purse isn't easy.

The day we shot the swimming scene, we had to stage it two ways because of the no-nudity rule in American films. So, in the American version, I was shown swimming in the ocean in a one-piece, high-neck swimsuit that revealed little cleavage. In the European version, I was in the same swimsuit and hit by a giant wave that pulled my top down and exposed my breasts. Playing my protective husband, Bill Wellman, quickly covers me. I remember thinking, *"Why are they bothering with the nude scene? It added nothing to the movie."* I would rather they worked on what I thought was some pretty bad dialogue.

Brian Donlevy, the American movie star, was shooting a movie in the area and was staying at our hotel. He finished each day before us and then could be found sitting at the table in the bar next to the piano with his ever-present drink. I once introduced myself, and he was polite, but it was evident that he preferred sitting by himself.

The producer of Donlevy's film, Marc Frederic, introduced himself and invited me to join him and his wife at their table. They seemed interested in knowing a bit about my life and career. About a week later, again over dinner—there's always a dinner involved—Marc told me he had an idea for a movie about a girl who goes to Hollywood and becomes a huge success. She joins a nudist camp to escape the constant stress of her rising career, where she finds peace and tranquility.

Knowing nudity wasn't allowed in American films, I

didn't see how they could shoot an entire movie in a nudist camp. I expressed my reservations but indicated an interest if they thought they could pull it off, and we spent a few dinners discussing the project. His wife gave me their phone number, I gave her my contact information, and she asked me to let them know of my further interest in the film when I returned to Los Angeles.

After a month of shooting, we moved to another location that was so beautiful I thought I had gone to heaven. We had a two-hour drive through a jungle area before reaching the ocean. Off the coast, we could see an island known as a top vacation destination for wealthy Brazilians. It was our next film destination, where we would spend several days. From my hotel window, I could feel the warm balmy air and hear the sounds of a live band playing Brazilian music. The lighting was soft and beautiful, there was romance in the air, people were dancing, and dinner was served by the swimming pool. I showered, dressed, and joined the others.

About an hour into the evening, a rather shy, handsome young man approached me and asked me to dance. His name was Carlos Eduardo Estefano. His English was impeccable, which was fortunate because I only knew about five words in Portuguese. At the end of the evening, he walked me to my door, kissed my hand, and asked if I would dine with him the following evening. That began a routine; working on the movie all day, then dinner and dancing every night with Carlos by the pool. I put away all thoughts of Paul Anka out of my mind and began a hot romance with Carlos.

Vacationing on the island was seasonal. When the

HOLLYWOOD OR BUST!

season ended, there was no more music, dancing, or socializing by the pool. Carlos returned to his home in San Paulo, but we arranged to meet in three weeks when I was back.

Carlos lived with his family in a big house in the middle of town. When he took me there, I noticed two men in military-style uniforms. They had rifles over their shoulders and walked the perimeter of the house in opposite directions. Carlos told me there was so much poverty and that if they did not protect themselves and their property, mobs would force their way in and rob or possibly kill them. Pretty scary way to live!

Mike Ripps, the Executive Producer of our film, showed up halfway through filming. This loud American with a Southern drawl sat around the hotel swimming pool every day, but for whatever reason, it took him two days before he introduced himself. I never remember seeing him on the set—probably just as well.

On March 27, we were still in Brazil, and I celebrated my 19th birthday. With a heavy heart, I thought it was time to leave Brazil because I loved every moment there. Carlos, who I knew was crazy about me, promised to visit me in America. I boarded the plane to Los Angeles with a heavy heart, leaving Carlos behind.

Chapter 16

When I entered the apartment back home, my roommate broke the news that Buddy Holly, Richie Valens, and Big Bopper had just died in a plane crash. I hadn't had contact with Buddy Holly since London and never met Richie Valens or the Big Bopper. Buddy once told me that he dreamed that one day he could take care of his family financially; then, his life was over in a flash. It seemed so unfair that their families had lost them all. I recall waking up the following morning thinking how short life is and that we should never waste the time we are given. How sad that it is late in our lives when we realize that tragic fact.

It was time to concentrate on making a living since I no longer had those weekly checks from Seven Arts. I

HOLLYWOOD OR BUST!

thought about all the money Russ Meyer had made from the photos he had taken, including his pictures of me that were currently in Playboy. So why not capitalize on that? I would make myself available to the photographers. They could sell the images, split the money with me, and we'd all benefit nicely.

That's when photographer Earl Leaf entered my life. He was a skinny, hippy type with a full beard. He never liked posed pictures; candid shots were his style. He loved to catch models when he thought they weren't looking. Earl and I enjoyed great success together professionally, and as a bonus, we became close friends. He found out I didn't have a car, and in LA, a car was a must-have. So off we went, and with his help, I found a second-hand, blue and white Mercury. I now had a car —*that I had to pay for*! With much trepidation, Earl, bless his heart, taught me how to drive. Thanks to Earl's patience, I'm happy to report I passed my driver's test.

The next two photographers I worked with were incredible, but I never developed a close relationship with either of them. Cavalier magazine hired George Hurrell to photograph me for an issue. I was excited because I had seen several of George's photographs and his outstanding work. However, it was a bit painful working with him. During shoots, he hardly said anything other than *"don't move."* He spent an eternity on each shot—changing the lighting, rearranging my costumes, and fixing my hair. By the end of the day, my muscles hurt so much from trying *not* to move that I couldn't wait to get into a hot tub and go to bed. But it was worth it because George was one of the best.

The other photographer, Andre De Dienes, had a

working style that was much easier for me. Andre was born in 1913 in Transylvania (I thought Dracula was the only one born there). Sadly, his mother committed suicide when he was fifteen, so he had little choice but to venture into the world to seek fame and fortune. After working throughout Europe, he came to America and became a successful and in-demand photographer. But unlike Hurrell, whose specialty was glamor shots, Andre's specialty was nudes. He took his time with each shot and was very particular about the lighting, which is extremely important. He made me feel beautiful and encouraged me while clicking away, saying things like *"You're incredible, you're so beautiful,"* which helped the pain of sitting stationary for long periods. If he didn't like a pose, he'd say, *"Try another."* After each session, he thanked me profusely, showered me with compliments, and bid me goodbye until the next time. I have fond memories of working with Andre, a true artist.

Chapter 17

Marc Frederic was about to start production on his nudist camp movie he had talked to me about in Brazil. The title of his screenplay was *Career Girl*. After reading the script, I thought it was one of the most impossible and weirdest movies anyone would want to make. The entire movie was to be shot in a nudist camp. Good luck with that. Male torsos couldn't be shown below the stomach, female breasts could only be displayed above the nipple, both men and women could only show legs halfway up their thighs, and no private parts were to be shown ever.

Trust me when I say the script was truly bizarre! I thought it was the dumbest script I had ever read, but since I had told Marc I would do it, true to my word, I did. We shot the movie in a real nudist camp with men, women, and children who were regular customers. I talked at length with some of the families, trying to understand why they went there, but I never did get it. If I chose to be nude, I would prefer to be naked in the privacy of my backyard.

As the saying goes—"*To each his own.*"

The only exploitation nudity that director Harold David thought he could get away with in order not to be censored was at the end of the film. He had me running naked onto a diving board in a long shot. I dive head-first into the pool and disappear under the water. The camera pans the length of the pool. When the shot reaches the pool's edge, my head, shoulders, and breasts are exposed in a close-up for one brief second. The camera pans to my face, then **blackout**—*The End.*

As I suspected, the nudist movie did not get good reviews, but none were as bad as I would have given it. Oh well, so much for nudist camps; I have never wanted to return to one!

Around this time, Albert Zugsmith contacted my agent and offered me a small part in a movie titled *The Private Lives of Adam and Eve (1960)*. He produced *Written on the Wind* starring Rock Hudson, Robert Stack, Dorothy Malone, and Lauren Bacall. *Adam and Eve* had a cast list as long as the phone book: Mamie Van Doren, Martin Milner, Mickey Rooney, Mel Torme, Tuesday Weld, Faye Spain, and—wait for it—*Paul Anka*! I had no idea Paul was even in the movie until I saw his name on the cast roster. Then I found out he had shot his scenes before I was even offered the job, and he'd already left town. Now, let's back up. I did see Paul a couple of times after I returned from Brazil, but the romantic feelings

HOLLYWOOD OR BUST!

between us were no longer what they once had been. My heart was still with Carlos. However, the good news is that Paul and I remained good friends.

My next project was the lead female role in the Tennessee Williams play *Baby Doll*. I was thrilled to get the part. The play was staged at the Theaterama, close to Sunset Blvd., in Hollywood. Henry Beckman, an outstanding Canadian actor, was also in the cast. Henry frequently appeared on Broadway and won two Genie awards, the Canadian equivalent of the American Oscar. Later, he became a regular on two popular television series, *Here Come the Brides* and *McHale's Navy*.

I will never forget an incident that occurred four days into rehearsals. Henry became so frustrated with me that he yelled, *"You know what? You're giving a mediocre performance. I beg you to be brilliant or lousy, but don't give me in-between."* After that scolding, I vowed to work harder. Looking back, I think part of the problem was the director, who gave me minimal direction nor did he correct me if I was playing a scene wrong. The producers must have agreed because they brought in a new director who was better.

I received terrific reviews thanks to the support of cast members Henry Beckman and Terry Beck. One reviewer wrote, "*June Wilkinson presented a top-notch characterization of the virginal child bride despite her incredible assets.*" We had a good laugh over that one.

We were blessed with full houses every night. Unfortunately, it was a small theater, or we could have sold more seats. I did the usual TV and newspaper interviews to promote the show. One of my TV appearances was on the Max Baer Sr. show. The name Max Baer meant nothing to me. It wasn't until later that I discovered he had been the world heavyweight boxing champion. I had never been to a boxing match, and to this day, I'm still not interested in boxing.

Years later, a World Championship title match was held while I performed in Las Vegas. People flew in worldwide to see the fight, and tickets sold for a small fortune. I was given a gift of two seats, which I eventually gave back because it was a crime to waste them on me. But if those tickets had been for the final marathon tennis match at Wimbledon with Roger Federer and Nadal or the Djokovic/Nadal 2012 Australian Open final—which lasted nearly six hours—they couldn't have wrestled the tickets away from me.

Anyway, back to 1959 and Max Baer. After appearing on his TV show, he and his friend, Slapsy Maxi Rosenbloom, a boxer turned actor who appeared in movies and on TV, asked if I wanted to join them for dinner. Since I hadn't eaten, I accepted, and off we went to *Panza's Lazy Sue*. It was not exactly a hole in the wall, but it was not fancy either. What made up for it was listening to these two characters trade stories like it was a well-tuned routine between them.

Max loved my company but always waited until the last minute to set up a visit. He would call, *"June, do you need to be fed?"* If I said yes, he would have me meet him wherever he planned dinner. Invariably, he would have other boxers tagging along with him. Most of what I had read or been told about Max made him sound loud, crude, a bully, and a vicious fighter in the ring. I only knew Max outside of the ring. He was a quiet gentleman

HOLLYWOOD OR BUST!

and never made a move on me—we were just friends. Let's face it, I was only 19, although that didn't and wouldn't stop many other men from taking a run at me. It was a sad time for all his friends when Max died. He was a dear friend who was kind to this 19-year-old and remains in my memory.

Another memory comes to mind, so here it is before I forget. One Sunday night at the Playboy mansion, I sat with my regulars, comedian Chuck McCann, his wife, and Gale and Vincent Bugliosi. Vincent was the lead prosecutor in the Charles Manson trial for the murder of Sharon Tate and others. We first met in Canada on a TV show where Vincent was on a book tour to promote his book *Helter Skelter*, and I was promoting my aerobic studios. The conversation got around to boxers and boxing. I mentioned I knew the boxer Max Baer and some of his boxing buddies. My stories of Max and his friend Slapsy Maxi Rosenbloom mesmerized everyone.

Speaking of *Helter Skelter*, I once dated Jay Sebring, a famous hairdresser to the stars. Jay was one of those tragically killed by Charles Manson, along with Sharon Tate. Jay and I met at a club called *The Factory*. He introduced himself, and we made a date for dinner by the end of the evening. Jay had just broken up with Sharon Tate, and I think Jay asked me out because, at our dinner at *The Factory*, he mentioned I reminded him of her. He was charming and fun to be with, but unfortunately, he was into drugs. Drugs have never been my scene. When we went out, he would think nothing about lighting up a joint, even in restaurants, which made me nervous. Back in the sixties, if you were caught with illegal drugs and were not a citizen, the offender would be put on a plane and sent to whatever country they were from. I wasn't a citizen. If Jay was ever busted, I feared I would be found guilty by association and sent back to England.

But I digress.

Thanks to good reviews for my performance in Tennessee Williams's *Baby Doll*, my new agent, Sam Armstrong, received calls from three producers offering to make firm commitments for my services. The first was from Stan Seiden, who was going to stage *Pajama Tops* at the Le Grand Theatre in Hollywood. Mr. Seiden had produced the show twice before; one time with Mary Beth Hughes, best known for her 'B' movies, and then with Barbara Eden, the star of the hit TV show *I Dream of Jeannie*. A bit of nostalgia was also connected to the Le Grand Theater. During World War II, it became famous as the *Hollywood Canteen*, where movie stars gathered to dance and entertain soldiers to help keep morale high.

The second offer was from the Jolly Playhouse in La Jolla, California, close to the famous Del Mar horse racing track. The show they offered me was *Marriage-Go-Round*. It ran for several years on Broadway and starred Charles Boyer, Claudette Colbert, and an old friend, the stunningly beautiful Julie Newmar.

The third offer was from the Circle Arts Theater in San Diego. They were planning to stage the Broadway musical *Fanny* starring Walter Slezak, who starred in the role on Broadway. The part they offered me was the belly dancer. All of the offers were for next year's season, and the timing for me was perfect. Usually, if you received offers for three things in show business, they invariably fell on identical or close dates, leaving the performer with the difficult decision of which show to accept.

Pajama Tops was set to start rehearsals in January and run for six months, depending on business. I could give two weeks' notice any time after the second week, and they, in turn, could give me two weeks' notice. The other two shows called for one week's rehearsal schedule and two weeks of performance. I would have a small break between the end of the *Marriage Go Round* (set to open in July) and rehearsals for *Fanny*.

Then, Mike Ripps, the Mobile, Alabama, producer of *Macumba Love*, called and said they were premiering the film at a drive-in theater in Phoenix, Arizona. The director, Doug Fowley, would be there, and they would pay me and cover my expenses if I promoted the movie before and after the opening. I had never been to a drive-in theater. With all the rain in England, I'm sure no one has ever been foolish enough to open one.

Phoenix was in desert country, with cacti everywhere, a very different terrain than in jolly old England, and I found it fascinating. The first night I had dinner with Mike Ripps, Doug Fowley, and Bob Steuer, who had agreed to help. Finding a distributor for the movie had been a hard sell. Finally, United Artists decided to give it a try. They had three drive-in movie theaters in Phoenix, and the Acre's Drive-In, where the film would premier, was the least successful. Determined to do everything possible to make it successful, Ripps, Bob Steuer, Doug Fowley, and I got to work. I don't think there was a university, newspaper, radio, television show, or a gathering where I didn't appear. Newspaper ads also said opening night tickets would include love potion, shrunken heads, and all kinds of free stuff; Bob Steuer didn't miss a trick. When Doug and I arrived at the drive-in, there was a line about a mile long waiting to get in. We arrived on a motorcycle—Doug was driving, and I held on tight behind him. The crowd went crazy when we approached. The police had a hard time keeping the public under control. I had never seen anything like it, and I loved every minute.

People were lining up to get the advertised love potion. They didn't know it was candy tablets you placed in liquid, which would make a fizzy like soda. Bob Steuer had everyone believing it was a real love potion. We would run out of tablets daily, and Bob would rush out and buy more for the next day. For months afterward, I kept getting letters asking me where they could buy more love potions, insisting it worked. Needless to say, our film out-grossed every theater in town.

United Artists hired me to appear at important openings. With the power of the pen, I would stay in first-class hotels and order room service or eat in any restaurant I chose. To this English-born war baby, that sounded like heaven on earth. Bob Steuer, representing the producers, traveled with me and John L. John, field representative for United Artists. And to think little Baby June had something to do with the film's success—well, maybe a bit more than a little.

Chapter 18

My roommate Shirley and I were tired of sleeping on the two couches that opened up to beds, so we decided to move to a bigger apartment on Laurel Avenue between Santa Monica and Sunset Boulevard in Hollywood. We also added a new roommate, a Greek girl named Helena Kallianoites.

The three of us were quite different, but regardless of our diversified looks and personalities, we got along very well. Shirley was a redhead and very intellectual. Helena was an incredible belly dancer with long, wild, black hair. I was the natural blonde—yeah, I wish!

We had been in the apartment for about a month when I received a call from Doug Fowley. He was back working on the *Wyatt Earp* TV series as Doc Holliday. Hugh O'Brien, the star of *Wyatt Earp*, heard that I was in the movie Doug directed, and Hugh was bugging him to arrange a date with me. Doug said bluntly, *"He's a jerk, June, but go on a date with him to get him off my back."* I was hesitant at first but agreed as a favor to Doug. Twenty-four hours later, Hugh called, and we made a date for that Saturday. His secretary called me three times to be sure I hadn't forgotten.

Helena and Shirley teased me about my *big* date. *"June, you better buy a new dress because he must be taking you to some special place,"* Shirley said.

On date night, an hour before Hugh was due to pick me up, he called and apologized; he was running late and asked if I would mind meeting him at his house. My dear roommates teased me again, saying, *"Well, I guess I should take off this dress; it's much too fancy for a casual dinner at his house."* Little did I know.

When I arrived, Hugh was shoeless, shirtless, and wearing just a pair of shorts. I found it odd that the house was sparsely furnished, nor do I recall much about the dinner Hugh prepared. He remained in minimal attire all evening. Thank goodness I'd changed out of my Christian Dior—just kidding. But even if I had bought a dress at K-Mart, it would have been too fancy for this date. We dined at a small round table in the kitchen, and I tried to make small talk, *"Did you just move in?"* His answer was a simple, *"Nope."* Most of my questions were answered with a simple *"Nope."* The conversation was strained and limited throughout the dinner—shades of Joe DiMaggio. I did all I could think of to keep the conversation going.

After dinner, Hugh gave me a guided tour of the house. I wondered why there was so little furniture. I

HOLLYWOOD OR BUST!

asked him if he was redecorating, and his answer was *'Nope.'* If you haven't already guessed, the last room was his bedroom. At least the room had a bed, if nothing else. He asked me straight out if I wanted to make love; I don't remember his exact words, but my answer was short and sweet, *"Nope."*

I have to say, unlike actor Steve Cochran, Hugh didn't hassle me about leaving. In fact, he was very polite, which surprised me. I bid him goodnight and made a beeline for home, where my roommates eagerly awaited the *big* date. When I told them about the dialogue—or the lack of it— they wouldn't stop laughing. I told them about Hugh's one-word answer; *"Nope."* That became a standard answer in our vocabulary from then on.

I thought that—no, I wished—that would be the last I would hear from Hugh O'Brien, but he called me every few weeks to see if I wanted to go out. I was always polite and thanked him and said, *"Nope."* You'd think that was the end, but it wasn't.

One day, Hugh called, and I was about to say, *"Nope,"* when my brain kicked in. Helena had a job belly dancing at a Greek Club on Hollywood Blvd. It was opening night, and Shirley and I planned to attend. If I showed up with Hugh O'Brien, it would be great publicity for Helena and the Club. So, I told Hugh where I was going, that I didn't have a date, and if he wanted to take me there, that would be great. He agreed.

Everyone made a big fuss over him when we entered the club. However, as soon as Helena's performance ended, he wanted to leave. He took me home, and I invited him in for coffee. I know what you are thinking, but I was trying to be polite. As soon as we entered the apartment, he walked through the living room straight to my bedroom, removed his clothes, climbed into my bed, and yelled, *"Come and join me."* I yelled back: *"Nope."*

I watched TV in the living room while Hugh stayed in the bedroom. Then, Shirley and Helena arrived home. *"Oh, you got rid of Hugh,"* Shirley said. *"No, he's in the bedroom with all his clothes off, waiting for me to join him."* When Hugh heard other voices, he asked who was there. I told him my two roommates were home. He yelled, *"Well, tell one of them come in and take care of me?"* In unison, we all shouted, *"Nope!"* Poor Hugh put on his clothes and left without even a goodbye. Welcome to Tinsel Town; never a dull moment.

I ran into Hugh a few times while I was married to Dan Pastorini, and he was always very polite. Some years later, comedian Buddy Hackett would attend the Hugh O'Brien Youth Leadership charity function in Beverly Hills. My best friend, Sherry Hackett, Buddy's wife, couldn't go, so she asked if I would accompany Buddy. The work Hugh was doing with his charity organization was impressive. I was far more impressed with the mature Hugh than the youthful Hugh. We all have to grow up sometime.

Hugh remained a bachelor until 2006. As I write this, he's in his eighties and married to Virginia Barber. I met her at the Playboy Mansion when she and Hugh attended one of Hef's Sunday movie nights. She was lovely and pleasant to speak with, and I wished them the best of luck. The word *"Nope"* will forever remind me of

HOLLYWOOD OR BUST!

Hugh O'Brien.

Chapter 19

My roommates Helena, Shirley, and I got along quite well, making living conditions very comfortable. Shirley became engaged to a lovely man, who unfortunately died before they could tie the knot. Helena began dating Billy Gray, who played the son on the popular TV show *Father Knows Best*. Eventually, they married, but, like so many show business marriages, it didn't last.

Meanwhile, I snagged a job on the Garry Moore Show, doing a comedy skit with Carol Burnett and comedian Ed Wynn. It was a one-time shot, but I got a kick working with two accomplished actors like Burnett and Wynn, a sweet man who sent me a beautiful bouquet on my final day. Later, I did a show with Carol Burnett's ex-husband Don Saroyan titled *Will Success Spoil Rock Hunter*. We performed at many Army and

HOLLYWOOD OR BUST!

Navy bases—Camp Pendleton was one I remember fondly. The enlisted men and women were great audiences, and I loved performing for them.

My agent Sam Armstrong had arranged for me to meet producer Irv Levin. Levin had learned I was no longer under contract to Seven Arts. His company was planning on producing several movies over the next couple of years, and he thought maybe there was something that I might be suitable for. Irv was involved with Eugene Klein of National General Theaters, one of America's larger theater chains. The interview went on until about six that evening. He asked me if I was available to join him for dinner. I had no choice, really, so I accepted. I honestly don't remember much about the dinner, but it was pleasant enough, and he didn't hit on me. He invited me to join him for dinner for two more nights. Oops, here we go again.

Enter Maurice Duke. I will spend a few moments here on Duke because he was about to become a critical component of my future.

Following my third dinner date with Irv, I received a phone call from this gentleman Maurice Duke (*I'm using the word 'gentleman' loosely here—you'll see*). Irv and Duke were friends. It turns out that Irv called Duke every night after he had dropped me off, providing Maurice with a blow-by-blow description of everything that happened during our dinners. Duke warned me that Irv only wanted to get me into the sack, which I had already anticipated. Duke said Irv might cast me in one of his movies, but his genuine interest in me was sex. Isn't it always with men who wear their penises on their sleeves?

Remember, I had no idea who Duke was before he called, so let's give the man a round of applause for his concern for a lady he had never met.

Here is where it gets strange. On the third and final night, Irv called Duke and said he was no longer interested in me sexually (might my attitude have sent a message?). It was more important, Irv said, that he and I were friends. I didn't believe what Duke said next. *"I'm calling you because I had to meet the "cunt" that out-maneuvered Irv."*

Now, I've heard my share of foul talk—not from my parents—but certainly from others while living and working in London. But not to the extent that a man would have the audacity to use that word when speaking to a woman. If that wasn't enough, every other word out of Duke's mouth began with *"F"* or *"C."* Duke insisted we meet, so, grateful for his giving me a heads up on Irv, I accepted his offer for breakfast at Nate n' Al's deli, one of his regular hangouts. To be honest, I had to meet this character in person.

Maurice Duke (real name Duschinsky) was born in New York on October 30, 1910, to a poor Jewish family that had managed to emigrate from Hungary. When he was very young, Duke contracted polio. Of his three brothers and four sisters, he was the only one with the dreaded disease. In those days, doctors didn't know how to cure or treat it. In Duke's case, they put casts on his legs and left them on way too long, which stunted the growth of his legs. When they finally removed the casts, his legs had withered. Duke wore braces and walked with a cane for the rest of his life. He grew to only five feet and had difficulty getting attention from adults or other kids. Duke's answer was to be the loudest kid on Coney Island. I can attest that as an adult, he was still the loudest and crudest. But even with all the profanity coming out of his mouth, you couldn't help but like this guy.

While still young, Maurice changed his last name to Duke. He began his show business career playing the harmonica with the *Cappy Barra Boys*. He began managing the group and decided he liked that better than performing. Eventually, he went to Hollywood, where he became a manager and producer and made many 'B' horror movies. *Bela Lugosi Meets a Brooklyn Gorilla* comes to mind. When I first met Duke, he was still managing actor Mickey Rooney, actor/comedian Zero Mostel, newscaster Tom Snyder, and Lassie, the dog, to name a few. Not a lousy roster of clients to be representing, especially the dog.

Duke was dating a beautiful lady named Evelyn (he called her Evie), who was 20 years younger than him. Evie became pregnant. Duke had no desire to have children or, for that matter, get married, so he arranged for Evie to have an abortion. Evie was on the operating table, ready to seal the baby's fate, when Duke yelled, *"Stop, get off that table; we are getting married!"*

For years, Duke would tell me how he had nightmares over the moment he almost lost his son. Alan was a wonderful son and grew into a wonderful young man. He was a lead attorney for the Walt Disney Company for many years. Duke and Evie had a daughter and named her Fredricka. She worshipped the ground her dad walked on, and Duke adored her. Fredericka went on to become a successful child actress and produce and write. In fact, we have worked on several film productions together.

Yes, Duke was a loudmouth and trash-talker, but I didn't care because he always had a twinkle in his eye and a way about him that made everyone love him. He was one of my closest friends and mentors. Occasionally, I would join Duke and his cronies on a Sunday at the famed Matteo's Restaurant in Westwood. Duke, along with songwriters Sid Robins and Foy Willings and Doris Day's husband, producer Marty Melcher. Although I had met Doris a few times at Duke's apartment—always with at least three of her dogs—she never joined the guys for dinner. Doris used me on her TV show, and producer Stanley Shapiro hired me to pose for the movie poster used for a Doris Day movie. But, for those dinners, she never joined us; I was always the only lady.

HOLLYWOOD OR BUST!

Chapter 20

One of my favorite places to spend an evening was a country-western club called the *Palomino Club* on Lankershim Boulevard in North Hollywood. Singer, songwriter, guitarist, and actor Billy Strange and songwriter and singer Homer Escamil took me there first and introduced me to their friends. You could go to the Palomino alone and feel comfortable; it was that kind of place. Everyone—and I mean everyone—was friendly. There was always someone to dance with or sit around and listen to music. The owners were Bill and Tommy Thomas, and the place was a hole in the wall. But the most prominent country-western artists hung out or performed there: Johnny Cash, Buck Owens, Merle Haggard, Jerry Lee Lewis, Willie Nelson, and many more.

Billy and Homer became lifelong friends. Unfortunately, Homer's life was cut short. He was in a terrible car accident and later died from brain cancer. The doctors thought the head trauma from the accident caused a tumor that killed him. Homer would have left a great legacy if he had been with us longer. He wrote *The Battle of Chavez Ravine* and *Are you Satisfied*, which singer Sheb Wooley recorded.

Billy Strange died on February 22, 2012, in Nashville at 81. During his career, he teamed up with songwriter/singer Mac Davis to write several hits for Elvis Presley, including *A Little Less Conversation*, the theme from *Charro!*, and *Memories*. Strange also composed the musical soundtrack for two of Presley's films, *Live a Little, Love a Little*, and *The Trouble with Girls*. He wrote *Limbo Rock* which The Champs and Chubby Checker recorded; Nancy Sinatra's *These Boots Are Made For Walking;* and *Somethin' Stupid,* which she sang with her dad Frank Sinatra. Billy also conducted for Dean Martin, composed and arranged music for the Ventures, and worked with producer Phil Spector, singer Ricky Nelson, and the Everly Brothers. I could go on and on and fill thirty pages about the prolific Billy. Billy, you are missed, but your work lives on forever. Wherever you are now, Billy, I know Homer is there with you. Hug him for me.

HOLLYWOOD OR BUST!

Chapter 21

The Playboy office asked if I would come to Chicago and help with the first Playboy Club TV show, and I accepted. They even made a custom-made bunny outfit for me. I thought it looked adorable on me—again, no modesty here.

The kickoff of the show was on February 29, 1960. They asked me to be the greeter at the front door. The lines waiting to come in were unbelievable. Having never done a job like that before, I pretended it was show time and I was on stage; it was a real happening. There were three-floor levels, and members were given a club key with a bunny rabbit stamped on it. The beautiful girls in their bunny costumes had to perfect the bunny dip when serving. The food was incredible, and so was the entertainment. When I finally climbed into bed in the wee hours of the morning, I knew the Playboy Club TV would be a real winner.

While in Chicago, Hef wanted me to appear on his other television show Playboy Penthouse. Those of you too young to have seen the show, let me tell you, it was great fun. The set was made to look like Hef was at home having a party with an incredible collection of spectacular-looking ladies dressed in sexy cocktail wear. The music featured a lot of jazz, which I suspect was Hef's favorite. There were always big-name singers on the show, like Sammy Davis Jr, Nat King Cole, Ella Fitzgerald, or Mel Torme, and great comics like Lenny Bruce, Bob Newhart, and Joe E Lewis. The talent was always first class.

That night, I was wearing a strapless blue cocktail dress. We gathered on the set about an hour before the show started. Drinks and finger food were served, so you felt like you were at a real party. I had a cocktail glass in one hand filled with champagne when the floor manager yelled, *"We're on in three minutes."* Before I knew what was happening, someone put another champagne glass in my other hand. There was no place to put them down. All the waiters had left the stage area with filled trays. The director yelled, *"Action,"* and we were on the air. Knowing the jokester, I am, I took the two glasses and balanced them on my breasts. My masterful feat was captured numerous times by the photographers there.

Then a waiter with an open bottle of champagne poured more into the half-empty glasses while I still balanced them on my breasts. There was a round of applause. I laughed, and that was the end of it. The November 1960 issue of Playboy hit the newsstands, and

HOLLYWOOD OR BUST!

there I was in all my glory, balancing the champagne glasses on my breasts. Hef said it was one of the most talked about photos in the magazine. He even put more pictures of that moment in two later issues.

If you glossed over it, look at this book's cover.

Chapter 22

When I returned to Los Angeles, I only wanted to spend a few days relaxing at home. My trip to Chicago had been fun, but there were too many late nights for me. But then Duke called and asked if I would drive him to Las Vegas. I was tired and tried begging off, but Duke is a hard person to say no to. He was going to Vegas to meet with Marlene Dietrich and didn't want to make the drive alone. I recall how Michael Wilding spent many hours talking and raving about Marlene when I was seventeen, working at the Embassy Club in London. This was a woman I would love to meet in person. So, Duke and I were off to Vegas.

Duke had meetings all day but told me to be ready to go to Marlene's dinner show that evening. Wow, what a show. Marlene was a fabulous performer. She didn't

HOLLYWOOD OR BUST!

have the most remarkable voice, but it was distinctively hers. She oozed glamour and sex appeal, and showmanship. That Lady knew how to work a room. Her conductor, Burt Bacharach, was one of the most flamboyant conductors I had ever seen. Many will remember that he and Hal David became a successful songwriting team. Later Burt married the beautiful and talented actress Angie Dickerson.

After Marlene's show, Duke and I visited her in her dressing room. She was charming and talkative, and I'm glad I had this once-in-a-lifetime opportunity to spend a short time with a legend. When we left, I walked through the backstage area when Burt Bacharach stopped me and asked for my phone number. Hmm, here we go again. I didn't know Burt, and I thought it was pretty bold of him to ask a stranger for their phone number, but Duke said, *"Give him your number; he's better than most of the jerks you're dating."*

I took Duke's advice, which began my romance with Burt Bacharach. We dated over the next year, but keeping the romance going with both of us traveling so much was hard. What made it worse was that I lived in Los Angeles and Burt in New York. I would visit him in New York and sometimes on the road, but it was challenging, to say the least. Between his work and mine, our visits dwindled to nothing. Here comes the fun part. About thirty years later, I was reading Marlene's bio. She talked about Burt Bacharach being her last lover. Last Lover? I couldn't believe it! I had no idea he was having an affair with Marlene and me simultaneously. My friends have never let me forget that one.

One night my girlfriends and I were at the Palomino

Club. We sat at a table next to a group we didn't recognize. We struck up a conversation, and they told us they were actors. One, Seymour Cassel, was from New York and seemed a little out of place at a country joint. Seymour told us he had recently acted in an offbeat movie called *Shadows* for actor/director John Cassavetes and was also John's Associate Producer. Cassavetes and his actress wife, Gena Rowlands, had rented a house in Brentwood on Sunset Blvd., which included a guesthouse. Seymour stayed there while he was in Los Angeles.

At the end of the evening, Seymour invited me out for dinner. Ah, yes, another dinner; here we go again. The truth is I found Seymour to be interesting, so I accepted. We met at the *Rain Check* restaurant on Santa Monica Blvd the following day. Now that I had a car when meeting someone I didn't know well, I took my own wheels. That way, I wasn't trapped if I wanted to leave. Seymour was with John Cassavetes and some other guys when I showed up at the Rain Check; so much for a private dinner with Seymour. The group hung on to every word that came out of Cassavetes's mouth because he was considered the actor's director and an innovator who consistently turned-out films of great interest.

I readily admit that I was attracted to Seymour and, after that first night, began going out with him. One night, when Seymour, Cassavetes, and I were having dinner, they had planned to stop by actor Nick Adam's house to see his new baby and invited me to come along. When we arrived at Nick's house, he told me we had met a few years back, but I didn't recall meeting him. *"June,*

HOLLYWOOD OR BUST!

don't you remember that night in Elvis Presley's suite at the Beverly Wilshire Hotel when we all had dinner and took you to the airport?" Oh, my, he was one of the guys there, and, shame on me, I had zero memory of him. I assured him my full attention had been on Elvis, and Nick laughed.

As many will recall, Nick was the star of *The Rebels* television series. He must have been a tortured soul because, in 1968, he committed suicide. Years later, I was watching a telethon on Suicide Prevention. Elvis called in and donated $10,000 in Nick's name. Nick, my friend, I hope you are in a better place wherever you are.

My friendship with Seymour meant I could spend time with John and his wife, Gena Rolands. Gena was and is an incredibly talented and successful actress. When I first met her, I thought she could have been Grace Kelly's sister; that was her kind of look. She also made what I thought was one of the best westerns ever; *Lonely Are the Brave (1962),* in which she starred opposite Kirk Douglas. I'm bringing this up because the film failed to receive much exposure when it was first released. Seymour, John, and Gena had to go to a small theater out of town to see it. If you ever have the opportunity, don't miss this film; it's one of the great ones. You'll be in for a treat.

Seymour and John took their work seriously, and being with them made me think long and hard about my career. They got on my case about how I relied on my obvious assets and not more on my acting. It's true; I have relied on my body all my life. I argued there was nothing wrong with using your assets: Durante's nose, Gene Simmon's tongue, Kim Kardashian's ass—and I don't mean Kanye West. From that day on, I began taking my work more seriously, relying less on my *World's Greatest, Magnificent, Fabulous, Incredible, One-of-a-Kind Breasts*. All kidding aside, it wasn't because I didn't take acting seriously, because I did. But I could be a better actor; that became my goal, and I worked diligently. Nothing is wrong with my assets, and if it's right for the part, absolutely use them. But from then on, I wasn't going to rely on *them*.

HOLLYWOOD OR BUST!

Chapter 23

My next gig was a rather strange project. I was cast in a film that was already in production in Germany. It was being shot in black-and-white and directed by Fritz Umgelter, who had many television and movie credits to his name in Europe. In 1967, he won the prestigious TV Film Teleplay award at the Baden-Bade Film Festival.

The production company hired a twenty-something-year-old film UCLA graduate to add a new section to the movie. You may have heard of him; he was this Italian kid, Francis Ford Coppola. Francis decided to produce this segment in English, color, and 3D. The German title was *Mit Eve Fing Die Sunde*. The English title was *The Bellboy and the Playgirls*, and starring in Francis's segment was none other than yours truly. Sorry, I don't remember anything about the storyline or who else was in the cast. I have, however, found in my scrapbook a synopsis of the movie used to promote the film.

George, a bellboy at the hotel, takes a correspondence course in detective work because he hopes to become the house detective. When June Wilkinson checks into his hotel with a bevy of beautiful lingerie models, George decides they are not what they seem. Wearing various disguises, he joins the girls at work and play, trying to get proof that the male lingerie buyers go to the girl's rooms for purposes other than to buy lingerie; George is not able to get the proof he needs; the reason being that the girls are models and nothing more.

When the movie opened in Los Angeles, thank goodness I saw it alone because I hated it. The script had called for minor nudity, mostly when the models changed clothes. I kept my clothes on by taking Seymour's and John's advice. There was no reason to be naked since I played the company owner, so my clothes stayed on. Otherwise, the film was a total, absolute bomb. I left the theater quickly, praying that no one recognized me.

Thankfully for Coppola, his talent shone through. He is one of the most celebrated directors America has ever produced with films such as *The Godfather*, *Apocalypse Now*, and *Patton*.

I read an article in the Los Angeles Times years later about the video release of Coppola's first movie starring June Wilkinson. I honestly had no idea what they were talking about. When I realized they were referring to *Bellboy and the Playgirls*, you could have knocked me over with a feather! Had I known then that this awful movie

HOLLYWOOD OR BUST!

was partially directed by a director who would someday become one of the most renowned directors in film history, I would have stayed in touch with him. Oh well, I screwed up again. My apologies, Mr. Coppola; feel free to call me anytime.

To my dismay, Hefner ran the film at the Mansion one night. When the movie ended, Hef told me he thought it was sweet and enjoyed it. Hmm, there's no accounting for taste! Although it has been years since I have seen it, I might take another look—maybe—no promises.

JUNE WILKINSON

Chapter 24

John Cassavetes made a deal with Paramount Studios to write and direct a movie titled *Too Late Blues (1961)*, starring Bobby Darren and Stella Stevens. John's choice for the male lead had been Cliff Robertson, but Paramount insisted on Bobby Darren. John cast his buddies Seymour Cassel and Everett Chambers and told me: *"June, there is only one small part that you would be right for, and it can be shot in one day. I know Paramount will not go for a big salary because it's such a small part, so trust me and tell your agent to go for a daily salary."*

Wait until you hear the end of this story.

On the first day of filming, Stella and I were in the makeup room getting makeup. I was on the call sheet daily, but they never got to my scene. This went on for days, but I didn't care; I was having a great time and

HOLLYWOOD OR BUST!

being paid for every day I was called to the set. Bobby Darren had just finished making a movie in Italy with Sandra Dee titled *Come September*. Rumors were flying about whether they were married or just engaged, and neither was shedding any light on the subject. Sandra wore a beautiful ring, which she referred to as her *engagement ring*. I remember when she visited the set, she was always looking at the ring like maybe it might disappear.

My scene was the final shot on the last day of filming. It was a nothing scene involving me, Stella, Bobby, and others. John's assistant said, *"John, we kept June here all these weeks for that one scene?"* John smiled, *"Yes, and wasn't she great."* John turned to me and winked. That was the most significant paycheck I ever got for doing nothing, and I would gladly do it again.

In 1959 I received a call from J. C. Agajanian, who looked and dressed like a cowboy. He always wore a Stetson hat and cowboy boots and was the first generation of his family to be born in America. His mother was about three months pregnant with J.C. when his Armenian parents survived the devastating war there and escaped to America. They settled in California and, through tenacity and hard work, had two successful businesses, a pig farm, and a trash collecting company. J.C. had always dreamed of becoming a racecar driver. By the time he was nineteen, he had enough money and bought his first racecar. His parents went ballistic, justifiably so, because the fatality rate for racecar drivers was very high in those days. They reached a compromise, and, lucky for me, J.C. became one the most prominent promoters and racecar owners. Racecar enthusiasts will remember J. C. owned the car that won the Indianapolis 500 twice and held the track record four times.

J.C. asked if I would like to present the trophy to the race winner in Riverside, California, the following weekend. We agreed on a price, beginning a new career and one of my most enjoyable jobs. So much so that I almost felt guilty about accepting the money. I met many racecar drivers who were diverse in class and personality; drivers like Lance Reventlow, Augie Pabst Jr (yes, the beer company), and Pedro and Carlos Rodrigues, Mexico's youngest and most successful racers. Big sponsors backed drivers like Sterling Moss. Those without sponsors put their cars together with spit, chewing gum, and big dreams.

Sterling Moss reminds me of something I hadn't thought about in years. In 1957 after I had left the Windmill Theatre, I was performing the *Fan Dance* at a couple of nightclubs, and I got a call asking me if I would perform the *Fan Dance* at Sterling Moss's bachelor party before his upcoming wedding. I had never done anything like that before, but Sterling Moss was a big celebrity at the time (later knighted by the Queen and is now *Sir Sterling*), so I figured, why not.

The night of the party, a gentleman greeted me in the hotel lobby, took me to the suite, and snuck me into a back room to prepare. I gave him the LP with my music, and as soon as I was ready, he turned on the music and turned out the lights except for the area where I was going to dance. I couldn't see well because the light was shining directly on me. What little I could see didn't look or feel like a party. There were only five or six men there who were very quiet and somber. It felt more like a wake than a pre-wedding party. Unlike the Windmill Theatre, I did the fan dance in pasties and G-string, where it was just a G-string. After I finished, I returned to the dressing room and dressed. The gentleman who greeted me in the lobby escorted me downstairs, paid me, and thanked me profusely. That was it. I never did another bachelor party, not that the guys weren't well-behaved because they were, but I wasn't comfortable doing it.

Sterling and I only crossed paths one other time. In 1960 he was racing in the Riverside Grand Prix, and I was presenting the trophy. We had several photographs taken together. He was very polite and never mentioned having met me before, and neither did I. And who knows, he may not have even remembered. To gossip here a little, Sterling has been married three times. Number three was Suzy. He met Suzy in the 1950s when she was just five years old. They wed in 1980 and have remained happily married. It was meant to be.

So, if your first two marriages fail, do not despair; the third time will probably work unless you're Dan Pastorini.

Back to the dangerous sport of racecar driving: I continued to present racing trophies throughout California and occasionally in other parts of the country. I did this from 1959 to around 1962. It was great fun getting to know all the drivers and seeing the action in the pits. I was closest to the Rodriguez brothers because we were around the same age. Pedro had a bit of a crush on me because he would take me to dinner often when he was in town, but that was as far as that went.

Pedro's brother Ricardo drove most of the time for Ferrari. However, in 1960, Ferrari dropped out of the Mexican Grand Prix, held at the Magdalena Mixhuca Circuit in Peraltada, Mexico City. But Ricardo managed to secure a spot as a driver for the Johnnie Walker Lotus. But on the practice run, his rear right suspension failed at the dangerous Peraltada corner. His car hit the barrier, killing him instantly.

Ricardo was only 20 years old. In his memory, Mexico declared a National Day of Mourning. After Ricardo's death, Pedro considered retiring, but his love of racing was too great. In 1963 he won the race at the Daytona International Speedway, and by 1967 had won his 9th Grand Prix in South Africa. He was the two-time world champion driving the Porsche 917 with his co-driver Leo Kinnunen.

Pedro died in a crash while racing in a Ferrari 512M4 for Herbert Muller at Norisring, Nuremberg, Germany. On July 2006, 35 years later, a plaque was placed on the site of his death.

HOLLYWOOD OR BUST!

Chapter 25

On March 3, 1961, I opened in *Pajama Tops* at the Le Grand Theatre, Cienega Blvd., in Hollywood. As I wrote earlier, the theater was famous in World War II as the place the soldiers visited when on leave and where they would meet the movie stars of their dreams. Members of the industry guilds and unions paid the expenses. The Board of Directors named the building *The Hollywood Canteen*. Actress Betty Davis was president, and actor John Garfield was vice president. Crooner Rudy Vallee, who served in the Coast Guard, led the band on opening night in a grand march to the front door, and The Hollywood Canteen was officially opened. My opening night was not quite that spectacular.

Audie Murphy, the most decorated American soldier in World War II who became a major movie star, and singer Guy Mitchell were riding their horses in the area of the Hollywood Canteen. They were both friends of mine, but as usual, both had been drinking. I was performing there that night, and these two wise guys decided to ride their horses into the theater to say hello. They got as far as the lobby and, still on their horses, managed to open the door to the theater. The audience was stunned; management was not amused.

The incident happened in less than a few minutes but seemed like an eternity. I kept quiet, never mentioning I knew either of these crazy cowboys. Murphy and Mitchell showed up on my doorstep the following day, still very drunk, laughing and joking about what had happened the night before. I threatened them both with their lives if they ever did that to me again.

I don't recall how I first met either of them, but periodically they would show up at my place, usually in the early morning after they had spent the night boozing it up. Both men were married, although I never did meet their wives. I can only imagine their wives' thoughts about boyish behavior and heavy drinking. I admit they were sweet guys; neither one ever got fresh or out of hand with me. Although Audie and Guy were alcoholics, they had friendly dispositions, and I really liked them both a lot.

But I digress again, back to *Pajama Tops*.

It was a typical farce written by Jean de Letraz and was initially performed in France as *Moumou*, the lead character's name. The cast consisted of a wife, her cheating husband, his mistress, the mistress' husband, the maid who wants to become the mistress of the house, and the husband's gay friend Moumou. This flimsy plot

HOLLYWOOD OR BUST!

was and remains quite stupid and is not worth discussing in any detail. The gags, sexy costumes, and all the outrageous fun things we did in the show made it an audience-pleaser, and that was enough. Since it was a farce, we could get away with almost anything. And although the audience loved it, the critics hated it. I didn't realize it then, but this silly, stupid little play would become the most important show I would do for the next forty years.

When *Pajama Tops* closed, I had a week off before rehearsals began for *Marriage-Go-Round* in La Jolla, California. We were the season's first show and only had a week to get the show up and running. Opening night was June 26, and closing was scheduled for July 8. Everyone was friendly, but I didn't get close to anyone in the cast or crew. Sandor Szabo and Jeannie Cagney were delightful onstage and off, but we never hung out together. The other cast member, Reid Hammond, always disappeared when the curtain came down, so I was pretty much left alone. I hoped that Jeannie's brother, film star James Cagney, would come to see the show. I was a big fan and knew it would impress my dad if I met him. *Yankee Doodle Dandy* (1942), one of James Cagney's biggest hits, was one of Dad's all-time favorite movies. Unfortunately, Cagney then lived in New York and never saw the show.

Several weeks later, I began rehearsals for the musical *Fanny* in San Diego. What a difference between *Marriage Go Round* and *Fanny*. The boys and girls in the chorus line were excellent dancers and singers and fun to be with onstage and off. I was still worried about my big number, even though the producer and director knew I could not sing well. I had lunch with the director, who reassured me the chorus would sing with me and the only thing I had to worry about was dancing. Boy, was that a big relief. From then on, I had a wonderful time and no longer agonized over my lack of singing skills.

Around this time, my romance with Seymour Cassel had begun to wane. And although we were still seeing one another, we had agreed it would no longer be exclusive. One night while out with some friends, Seymour had a eureka moment and decided he missed me. Bidding his friends goodbye, he hopped in his car and sped to San Diego to catch my show. On the way, he was stopped by the police and given a speeding ticket. By then, it was too late to catch my show. He had to work the following day, so he turned around and sped home, only to receive another speeding ticket. Thirty years later, my ex-roommate Helena and I were having dinner in Malibu when in walked Seymour. The first thing out of his mouth was, *"You owe me for two speeding tickets."*

Some things are forever amusing and never to be forgotten.

Chapter 26

I almost forgot another moment in my life that I didn't mention when talking about racecar driving. It was the last race trophy I would ever present for Curtis Turner for the grand opening of Charlotte Motor Speedway. He was born on April 12, 1924, in a small town on Bent Mountain in Virginia. He learned to drive before he was of legal age during prohibition. Even though Curtis was underage, his job was to drive the moonshine to buyers. Sometimes he would have several cop cars chasing him, but he never got caught. Curtis could turn a vehicle on a dime, knowing exactly how much space he needed to squeeze into the smallest spaces. The man was a legend in the moonshine business long before he became one in the racing game.

When I arrived, Curtis picked me up at the airport

and insisted I accompany him on his private plane to Roanoke, Virginia, to meet and have dinner with his family. I don't recall much about the aircraft, but it was small. But I will never forget the ride back. He flew low over acres of trees to show off his timber business. Then, much to my chagrin, he decided I needed a thrill, so he began doing stunts in that little plane that scared me to death. He found my screaming amusing. How I managed not to throw up, I will never know. I swore I would never get on any plane if Curtis was the pilot!

When I arrived back at the hotel (my stomach was still in my throat), there was a message from Maurice Duke to call him immediately. He was in New York City and had just gone to a Club called the Peppermint Lounge. He told me to fly there immediately to see how people were going crazy over a new dance called *The Twist*. If he was that excited, I thought, I better go. So, after I presented the winning trophy the next day, I caught a flight to New York.

On the way to the airport, Curtis asked if it would be okay if he mailed me my appearance fee. I said that would be fine. I didn't know then, but they went over budget on the track opening, and he was financially unstable. He and his partner, O. Burton Smith, would eventually lose the track. Curtis tried to raise money from the Teamsters Union, but that failed. Sadly, he was barred from racing for several years.

Curtis may have been down, but counting him out would be a mistake. Eventually, he was reinstated into racing and became a multimillionaire via his timber business. Sadly, Curtis tempted fate once too often. On October 4, 1970, my friend Curtis Turner was flying his

HOLLYWOOD OR BUST!

Aero commander with passenger and professional golfer Clarence King when the plane crashed into a mountainside shortly after takeoff near Punxsutawney, PA. Neither survived.

Curtis was inducted into the International Motorsports Hall of Fame in 1992. There will never be anyone who lived as much and as fast as he did. Curtis Turner was definitely one-of-a-kind.

When I arrived at my hotel in New York, a message awaited me from Duke. After checking in, I was to get to his room ASAP. As I approached his room, I could hear Duke (always loud) on the phone conversing with Sid Robins, one of the all-time great songwriters. Sid wrote the lyrics for many big standards. *Undecided Now* was a hit when released in 1938 and then again when revived by the Ames Brothers. It is still a big jazz staple today. And many big-name singers have recorded his *I Miss You So* over the years. Duke told Sid about the new dance craze called *The Twist* and told him to get his f***ing ass down to The Peppermint Lounge on 128th Street.

I had never been to the Peppermint Lounge. There were a lot of mirrors and a dance floor swarming with celebrities. The place had an extensive gay clientele, and notables like Marilyn Monroe and Frank Sinatra visited. Even Greta Garbo had shown up one night to dance to the house band *Joey Dee and the Starlights*. I had a great time dancing the night away and was exhausted when I got to bed. And I must say, Duke was pretty savvy to latch onto that dance craze, as you will see.

I was awakened at the crack of dawn. It was Duke calling. *"Get your f***ing ass up."* (The man could never complete a full sentence without several *F* words). *"I've rented a limousine, and I'm going to show you Coney Island, where I was born; then we're flying back to Los Angeles tonight. I spoke with Louis Prima* (the singer). *Louie's performing in Las Vegas and thinks he can put enough money together to make a movie featuring this damn new twist craze."*

That was Duke, he may have been operating with two short, withered legs, but he had more get-up-and-go and connections than any man I ever met. I never heard him complain about his legs. He never wanted to be pushed around in a wheelchair unless there was no other way. Every day he got up, put his braces on, clicked them into position, and, with a cane and his overactive computer brain, was ready to conquer the world.

Not everything goes well in this life. Eventually, Duke and Evie divorced. He gave her the house in Beverly Hills and rented an apartment for himself. He lived fast and often recklessly; one moment, he was rolling in big bucks; the next, he would ask if I could cover his rent. No matter that he was loud and that every sentence that slipped out of his mouth was filled with obscenities. To me, Maurice Duke will forever be my hero.

In three weeks, Duke's buddy, Bernie Gould, wrote a script for a film about the dance craze sweeping the country. Louie Prima managed to get the Las Vegas mob to come up with the money, or at least that's what Duke told me; I never really knew. The film would star Louie Prima, Sam Butera, the Witnesses (Louie's band), and little old me. Louie's company, Keelou Productions, would produce the movie. William J. Hole would direct, and they would use my favorite designer at that time, James Ottobre, to design my costumes. The project was

HOLLYWOOD OR BUST!

moving along like a speeding train.

The first day of shooting was great fun, but there are downtimes when shooting a movie. So, during those breaks, the band and I would sit around and exchange jokes. One day, Louie walked in when one of his guys was in the middle of telling a rather raunchy joke. Louie gave him a lecture in front of everyone. *"You don't talk that way in front of a fine lady like June."* Thank you, Louie, but I'm a grown girl who tells raunchy jokes too. Duke walked in a few minutes later and began talking in his usual potty mouth. For a moment, there was silence. Then everyone looked at Louie and started laughing. So much for Louie's tongue-lashing, thanks to Duke.

All fun aside, I knew Louie might have a problem in the romance area. I always liked him, but I wasn't interested in him romantically. But here we go again; I could tell he was interested in me. Lucky for me, my girlfriend, Quinn O'Hara, was a big fan of Louie's. I invited her to the studio cafeteria the next day to meet Louie, knowing he would go crazy over Quinn. She had long, gorgeous red hair, a beautiful face, and a great body. Sure enough, he thought she was fabulous; she thought he was fabulous, and I was off the hook for the rest of the shoot. Thank you, Quinn.

When we completed filming, Louie presented me with a gold watch with the inscription, *"To the finest lady from Louis Prima."* I was sad when the production ended; I would miss Louie and the boys dearly.

The movie was released as soon as it was ready because there was competition with two other twist movies, Chubby Checker's *Twist Around-the-Clock* and *Hey Let's Twist,* starring Joey Dee and the Starliters.

JUNE WILKINSON

Ours, titled *The Continental Twist* (1961), was released first. They flew me all over the country to promote the film. The extensive PR included TV, radio, and newspaper. Everywhere I went, I was asked to demonstrate *The Twist*. By the end of that tour, my hips hurt, and I was sick and tired of that dance. To this day, although I love to dance, the only dance I *won't* do (unless they pay me) is—you guessed it—*The Twist*.

Photo Gallery

Lily & June

Eastbourn

Father & Robin

JUNE WILKINSON AGE 14
Helping Her Dad With His Window Cleaning Company

June Wilkinson

girl watcher

JUNE 1959   PRICE 50¢

A GUIDE TO GIRL WATCHING

Bonnie Logan and June Wilkinson

Love Goddess Issue

Duke, June & Duke's kids

Duke, June & Duke's kids

June Wilkinson Spike Jones

GEORGE HARRISON
"The Beatles"

JUNE WILKINSON
Playboy's "The Bosom"

Playboy after Dark 1970

June & Dan's Wedding 1973

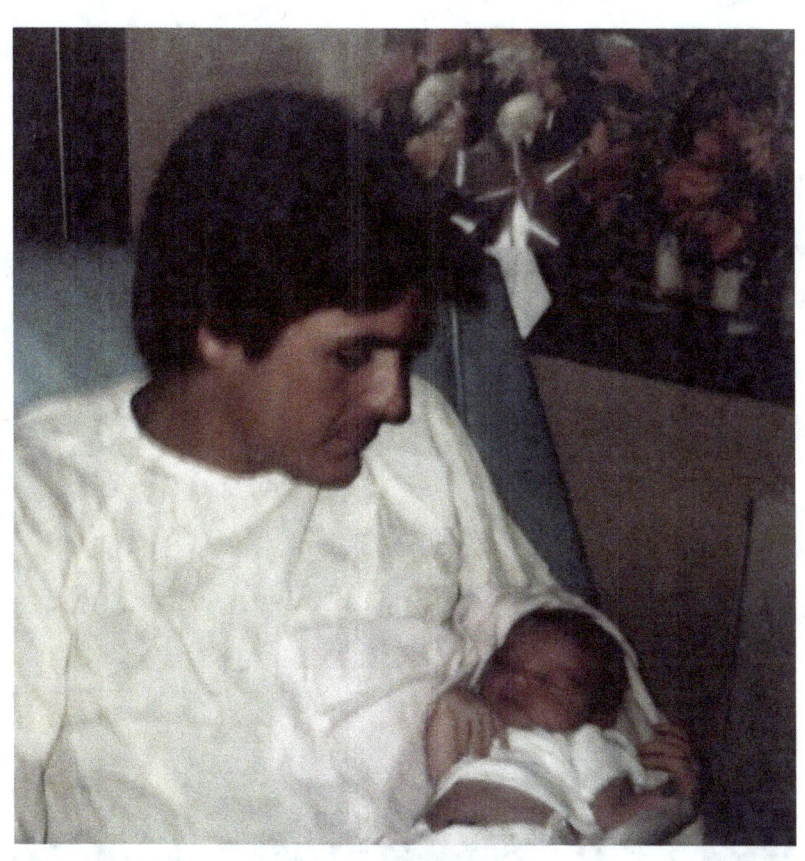

Dan & Brahna

Dan & Brahna

Dan, June & Brahna

June, Brahna, Dan, and Dan's father Dante

Lily & Brahna

June & Brahna

June, Brahna & Sheshe

June & Brahna

Brahna & June

Dan & Brahna

June, Brahna, and comedian Avery Schreiber

June & Brahna

June & Brahna

June, Brahna & Lily

Brahna & June

June, Todd Pastorini, Jennifer Pastorini, Stefani Pastorini and Brahna

Brahna & June

June & her dance teacher, Sylvia Byfield

Helen Wilkinson, Megan Thomas , Steven Wilkinson & Brahna in England

June & boyfriend Peter Hughes

Chapter 27

I had saved enough money and was considering buying a house. The Lazarow office was looking after my money now, and Saul Lazarow, like most New Yorkers, thought it was best to rent unless you were a multi-millionaire and owned skyscrapers like Donald Trump. Donald who?

Seymour Cassel had moved out of Cassavetes's guesthouse and rented a small place in Laurel Canyon. Although we weren't dating anymore, we were still good friends, and I had gone to see his new place. In the early '60s, many hippies made their homes in Laurel Canyon. You remember hippies, right? Laurel Canyon takes you over the hill from Sunset Boulevard to North Hollywood's valley.

When I left Seymour's house, I decided to look

around the area. I turned onto a street called Weepah Way and saw a sign for a home for sale there. The house was small, tucked away on top of a hill. I arranged to see it. It consisted of one bedroom, a bath, a small kitchen, and a tiny living room, but it was on two lots. Even though Saul disapproved, I went ahead and bought my first house. I was very proud and wished my Mum could see it. Owning a home was a dream she and my father never fulfilled.

One morning I was sitting on my patio in my new house having coffee, and my phone rang. A writer named Leo Guild from Holloway Publishing was on the line. He explained that he specialized in female biographies and received a call from a Chicago publishing company interested in publishing my life story. Of course, I was thrilled and knew my Mum and Dad would be impressed.

I arranged to meet Mr. Guild a few days later at his office at Holloway Publishing. When I arrived, I was greeted and ushered to the third floor. The room was sectioned off into a number of small cubicles, each with a desk and a couple of chairs. Mr. Guild introduced himself, and we made ourselves comfortable in his cubicle. We exchanged pleasantries, and he asked me to tell him about myself. That told me he had not done his homework, but I began anyway.

I started with where I was born and my life there. He wanted to know about my performing the *Fan Dance* at the famous Windmill Theater. I told him it was like a ballet with six girls in tutus. He wanted to know how I felt about being nude in front of so many men. Was it a sexual turn-on for me? I told him I found no difference

HOLLYWOOD OR BUST!

if I was dancing dressed from head to toe or naked behind feathers.

This cat-and-mouse performance went on for about four weeks. Guild kept trying to get me to talk about the sexual thrills I got from turning men on with my photos in Playboy. I tried to explain as best I could that it was part of my job, but he kept pushing it, and I began to get suspicious. Guild handed me two books he had written and asked me to read them. He said they contained the kind of stuff that sold books. That was that, and I left.

That day, when I reached the elevator, a young man caught up with me and introduced himself as Ray Locke, and he wanted to shake my hand. He was a writer and editor for Holloway Publishing House and occupied the cubical next to Leo Guild. He rode the elevator down with me, told me he'd never had as much fun eavesdropping, congratulated me on how I handled Leo, and offered to take me to lunch. At lunch, I asked a question about Mr. Guild, but Ray remained the loyal employee and said little other than, *"They want a book that will sell, June."* That began a lifelong friendship with Ray Locke until he died in 2002. I'm happy to report that Ray became a very successful writer. His book on the Navajo Indians is now in its sixth edition and is considered the most successful book written about the Navajo Tribe. More about Ray is coming up.

The two books Leo Guild gave me to read were two of the most disgusting, revolting, nauseating books I have ever read. The first was a biography titled *I Am Not Ashamed* by Barbara Payton, an actress who supposedly wrote it with the help of none other than Leo Guild. Barbara married actor Franchot Tone after his marriage to Joan Crawford ended. Franchot starred in movies with the likes of Gregory Peck and Jimmy Cagney. But poor Barbara didn't fare so well in her career. Franchot divorced her after he found out she had been sleeping with some guy named Tom Neal and others in Hollywood. According to her book, she became a drunk and a prostitute within five years. Sadly, Barbara died at 37, fat and unrecognizable as the beautiful starlet she once was. The tragic stories from Hollywood never end.

The second book was Jayne Mansfield's biography. It was such salacious garbage; I didn't believe a word I read. If Jayne's book had been true, it would have made headline news in the mainstream media, but reviewers mostly ignored it. That was it for my relationship with Leo Guild. He called several times and left messages, but I never returned the calls.

Six months later, I received a bouquet of beautiful red roses and a bottle of champagne from Guild and the Chicago publishing company with a note saying, *"This is to help you have a wonderful day. Now you could help us have a wonderful day by sending us the manuscript of your life story."* I called Ray Locke, told him about the champagne and roses, and invited him for lunch. He read the note, shook his head, and suggested I tear up all of Leo Guild's notes on the so-called story of my life that I had made. We flushed all the pieces down the toilet laughing and toasting Leo with champagne with every flush! I never heard from Leo or the publishing company again.

There are hucksters everywhere just looking to exploit people for a quick buck, especially in Tinsel Town. Not this time, Leo Guild, not this time, thanks to the support of Ray Locke. Oh, and yes, thanks to those

HOLLYWOOD OR BUST!

two books you gave me, Leo. They convinced me to flush you and your publishing company from my life.

Chapter 28

Louie Prima called to let me know that he, Sam Butera, and the boys were booked to play a lounge in Las Vegas and wanted me to join them. I would have loved to any other time, but I had signed up to do *Pajama Tops* at the Moore Theatre in Seattle, Washington. The opening coincided with the beginning of the Seattle World's Fair.

This time Stanley Seiden was going to coproduce *Pajama Tops* with Zev Bufman, a young Israeli producer. If that name sounds familiar, it's because Zev hit the big time with Elizabeth Taylor and Richard Burton years later. Although they were divorced by then, they continued to appear in stage plays together—never let business get in the way of a failed marriage. Zev was their producer, which led to his becoming one of the top producers in show business.

HOLLYWOOD OR BUST!

For the current run of *Pajama Tops*, my agent Sam Armstrong wrote a contract that gave me a piece of the action not from the profits but the box office gross. Either the producers had not noticed or thought I would not check the numbers. Wrong, Kimo Sabe; June always checks the numbers!

Stan and Zev rented the Moore Theater, a wonderful place with all the accouterments of a grand old theater: a live-in cat, bats, rats, and excellent acoustics. You could whisper and be heard clearly on the balcony. John Agar, who Sam Armstrong also represented, was cast as my leading man. In 1945 John was serving as a training instructor in the military when a friend arranged for him to escort America's sweetheart Shirley Temple to a Hollywood party given by her boss, film kingpin David O Selznick. The rest, of course, is history. John married Shirley, which opened all the right doors for his entry into show business. But like so many Hollywood marriages, John and Shirley went their separate ways after five years. As many of a certain age will remember, John went on to star in many films and TV episodes. If you check John's credits on IMDB.COM, you'll see he had a long career through 2005, mostly in forgettable science fiction films.

John was a lovely man, but he was a reformed alcoholic and very nervous about this being his first stage play. Unfortunately, we got off on the wrong foot because Lee Hewitt, the road manager—in my eyes, a nasty piece of work—told us he was at one time the right-hand man to gangster Mickey Cohen. I guess he told us that to be sure we knew he was *our* tough guy boss. He also shared the details of my contract with John

Agar, including that I was getting a percentage of the show's gross. Ordinarily, that sort of thing is never discussed, nor is it anyone's business. Well, as expected, that upset John Agar. Angrily, he called Sam Armstrong. Sam did his best to explain the situation and told John, *"What I was able to get for you, John was the most money, not the most money of anyone in the show."* From then on, John had a bit of a vendetta against me. He'd pick on almost everything I did, and I did my best to hold my tongue and ignore him.

One particular incident comes to mind. I appeared as a guest on a local radio show to promote the play, and they asked me if I had a boyfriend. *"No,"* I joked, *"but I'm looking."* John started in on me when I arrived at the theater that night. *"How dare you go on the radio and tell the world that you are looking for men?"* His outrageous behavior floored me; I didn't know how to react. He's lucky I didn't smack him. It took his current wife, Loretta, a lovely lady, to calm him down and mind his business. What a jerk.

Another incident involved Lee Hewitt. When I returned from cutting the ribbon on the restaurant's opening day at the top of the Seattle Space Needle and later a TV interview, Lee Hewitt asked me to come into his office. This jerk pulled out a gun, placed it on his desk, and mentioned that he was unhappy about something I said that day during my TV interview. That day, he threatened me and warned me never to do that again. But before he could finish his tirade, I did something I'd never done in my career—I completely lost it. I stood there looking at this small-time wannabe gangster with his little gun, stared him right in the eye,

HOLLYWOOD OR BUST!

and said: *"Fine, go ahead and cancel all of the press. I'm the only shmuck who gets up early or stays up late and does ninety percent of all the TV, radio, and press interviews. So, Lee, you can forget all of that now!"*

I spun around and walked out. Lee ran after me but remembered that he had left his gun on the desk, so he ran back, swooped it up, and continued yelling at the top of his lungs: *"You will do all of the publicity that we decide you will do!"* I turned around, marched to him again, got in his face, and told him to read my contract carefully. It called for six shows a week and two on Saturday and Sunday but said nothing about my having to do publicity. Then I walked out.

What planet are these jerks born on?

The next day Stanley Seiden flew in from Los Angeles and took me to dinner. He had heard of the dust-up between Lee and I and was there for no other reason than to sweet-talk me into doing the publicity again. Now, in truth, it was an easy show to do. However, the press promotions can be killers; interviews on the radio can take place early morning or after midnight and go on into the wee hours of the morning. It's the same deal with TV interviews. It becomes a real drag, along with all the other things they ask you to do to promote shows. I agreed to do the publicity again for two reasons: I don't enjoy doing shows for a small audience when I was getting ten percent of the gross. The truth is, I did PR diligently no matter what I was paid because I considered it part of the job whether in my contract or not.

To everyone's delight, the show was so successful Stan and Zev received offers to send us on a national tour starting in Miami for the Caplan family, who owned a chain of movie theaters. However, believing *Pajama Tops* was ending in Seattle, Duke had made a deal with his friend, Henry Ehrlich, for me to appear in a motion picture *The Rage* (1962). Ehrlich was now living in Mexico City and producing Spanish-speaking films. It was a good screenplay. Most of the films offered weren't even *B*-quality, but one has to make a living. Fortunately, *The Rage* rated an *A* as far as I was concerned.

The story centered around a bank robbery. I would play an American working as a stripper in Mexico in love with a local gang leader. He talks my character into seducing one of the bank clerks they plan to rob. That would give the bad guys inside help robbing the bank. I was looking forward to working in Mexico, a country I had never visited.

Meanwhile, there was Pajama tops. The way I got the story was the Caplan family wouldn't accept *Pajama Tops* without me. So, after a lot of wheeling and dealing, arrangements were made to fly to Miami, promote *Pajama Tops,* then return to Mexico to shoot the movie. In the meantime, the cast of *Pajama Tops* (the same cast as in Seattle) would be rehearsing without me until I returned three days before the show opened. Whew!

When I arrived in Miami to do PR, it was balmy and beautiful. They put me up in a hotel on the waterfront and told me to get ready for a cocktail party in my honor. The party was held on a magnificent yacht with the cream of local society and the Miami press corp. One of the interviews was with Larry King, a local radio host who, as we know, hit it big when Ted Turner created

HOLLYWOOD OR BUST!

CNN. I was at the Playboy Mansion in LA forty years later when Larry waltzed in and reintroduced himself. I was imressed that he remembered our interview all those years later.

The next few days were hectic as we tried to work in many promotions for *Pajama Tops* before I had to leave town and head for Mexico. It had been a fun couple of days, and I looked forward to returning.

My manager, Maurice Duke, was already in Mexico when I returned. Not only was he a childhood friend of Henry Erlich's, but he had another friend he could hang with: the famous (some would say infamous) Budd Boetticher. Budd was a film director who had recently divorced actress Deborah Paget, whom Elvis Presley thought was the most beautiful girl he had ever seen. Budd, who had directed many of the Randolph Scott westerns, was in Mexico trying to get a movie going on the life of famed bullfighter Carlos Arruza. My leading man was the Mexican film star Armando Silvestre, the director was Myron J. Gold, and the producer was Massey Cramer.

Having to speak all my lines in Spanish would prove difficult for me. Fortunately, help came from Henry Erlich's lovely daughter Gina who was just twelve. Growing up with American parents and living in Mexico, Gina was bilingual and had far more patience with me than the adults. That wonderful child would come to my hotel room each night and work with me on my lines for the next day.

The only problem with that film was the one dinner date I agreed to with my leading man, Armando Silvestre. Our director said because we were shooting our love scene the next day, Armando wanted to take me to dinner so we could discuss the scene and become comfortable with what the scene called for. Everything was fine during dinner, but when we left, I bid him goodnight, and—surprise, surprise—Armando had other ideas; he wanted to rehearse the scene for real. When I didn't go for his little ruse, Armando became belligerent and told me that my photos were far sexier than I was in person. If I remember correctly, he mentioned I had as much sex appeal as a dishrag. Thank you so much, Armando; you have proven to be another jerk. There appears to be an overabundance of them in show business.

The following day the director and producer picked me up at the hotel. They were all smiles and asked, *"Well, how did it go?"* My reply: *"We are in big trouble, gentlemen."* I told them what had occurred the night before. But, to my surprise, Armando smiled from ear to ear when we arrived at the studio. He hugged me and told me what a wonderful time he had had the night before— like what had happened didn't. Men! No wonder women have such a hard time dealing with them.

Speaking of men, when it was time to check out of the hotel, there were surprise charges on my bill I was unfamiliar with. When I questioned Duke about it, he said, *"Just pay it, June; it's a whore house."* Unbeknownst to me, Duke, Budd, and another friend had visited there frequently. Considering Duke had got me this lucrative deal, I agreed to pay his whore bills. *Grrrrrrrrrr!*

When we completed the film, Duke flew home to LA, and I flew back to Miami to rejoin the cast of *Pajama*

HOLLYWOOD OR BUST!

Tops. On the plane, I opened a gift left at the hotel desk. It was a beautiful gold charm from the actor Xavier Loya, the second male lead in the movie and a sweet man I enjoyed working with. There, you see, all men are not jerks.

Chapter 29

Robert and Marty Caplan greeted me at the Miami airport and informed me that the show had been moved to the Coconut Grove Theater. Converting their movie theatre into a legit theatre would have been a lot of work, and the Grove, a beautiful theater, became available. When I arrived, the cast was in the middle of rehearsals. Actor Brad Logan, playing my husband, yelled, *"It's about time you showed up!"* Gee, thanks, Brad; great greeting.

Opening night sold out, and it remained that way each night. What a joy it was to play packed houses every night. Marty and Robert took me to dinner after each night's performance. Dinners and more dinners. It wasn't long before I sensed that Robert was interested in me. I liked Robert, and we spent every spare moment

HOLLYWOOD OR BUST!

together by the end of the first month. I was falling in love with a man who said he loved me. I was in Miami, enjoying the warm weather, music, and tropical vegetation, looking forward to at least a six-month run, and I was in love. Everything seemed perfect.

Then, all hell broke out again.

This time, Nikita Sergeyevich Khrushchev was the First Secretary of the Communist Party of the Soviet Union from 1953 to 1964 and chairman of Russia's Council of Ministers from 1958 to 1964. Khrushchev had become buddy-buddy with Cuba's revolutionist leader Fidel Castro, paving the way for the 1962 Cuban Missile Crisis that almost caused a nuclear war. Everyone living in Miami and the surrounding area were sitting ducks from where the Soviets had begun constructing nuclear missile sites just 90 miles away in Cuba. Overnight, Miami was a ghost town. We went from selling out each performance to ninety-nine percent cancellations. We were terrified; to say the tension was high would be a June Wilkinson understatement. As everyone knows, President John Kennedy delivered a powerful television speech that let Russia and Cuba know that America would use military action to end the threat to world peace if it came to that. Thankfully, Kennedy pulled us through with a coalition of other nations supporting him. As everyone knows, the missile sites were eventually removed.

I wasn't much of a Kennedy fan because of an incident that happened during my Hollywood Studio days. I had gone to a luncheon at the Hollywood press club. Later that evening, I received a call from one of the press guys telling me he was at the Ambassador Hotel with John Kennedy and asked if I would like to meet him. Of course, I said yes. This guy, whoever he was, told me not to use the hotel's front entrance but to use the back entrance. That should have been a red flag. That's when I heard Kennedy say in the background say, *"She's not going to waste my time, is she?"*

It only took me a few seconds for that comment to hit like a category-five hurricane. I could tell from his voice the reporter was flustered by Kennedy's comment. Before the reporter could say anything more, I told him to tell Mr. Kennedy to get a hooker, and I promptly hung up. To say I was disgusted with Kennedy's arrogance is another understatement. Maurice Duke had a potty mouth, but at least he always treated me respectfully. After the Cuban Crisis, I didn't dislike Mr. Kennedy as much, but I had no desire to be in his company.

Following our run in Miami, Stan Seiden and Zev Bufman arranged to take the show on a national tour. We would fly on Mondays and remain in a city for two weeks playing in the largest theatres. We performed one show a night on Tuesdays, then added a matinee on Saturdays and Sundays. It was a lot of work, but business was fantastic. I was doing eighty percent of the promotion, but even though I've complained about the PR burden, I loved every moment of it. As a big bonus, I saw many cities, including Detroit, Chicago, St Louis, Pittsburg, and Cincinnati. And I made a decent amount of money doing it.

HOLLYWOOD OR BUST!

Chapter 30

Most Broadway shows only get a few weeks out of town to iron out the kinks before their New York opening. They would tour the country after their Broadway run (assuming they were successful). Our comedy farce show was not the kind that would generally make it to Broadway. But I was ecstatic when we got the news that we were headed to Broadway because we were doing phenomenal business on the road and outgrossing other Broadway hits touring the country.

Broadway, ready or not, here comes Baby June.

We would close at the Ford Theatre in Baltimore on May 18 and open at the Winter Garden Theater in New York on May 27. I wanted to fly my parents over to see the show, but I thought I would hedge my bets and wait until we opened, just in case we closed before the week ended. On Broadway, a bad review has always been the kiss of death, and a show could close overnight. But good or bad reviews never bothered *Pajama Tops* because, as I said, it was consistently an audience pleaser. People would often come back two or three times to see the play, as weak as I thought it was. It helped that we were blessed to have Sam Freedman working the PR for us. He was a respected New York press agent who worked hard at getting us an incredible amount of coverage. I give him much of the credit for our success.

One publicity stunt almost got me arrested. It was a hot and humid day in New York. Sam talked me into dipping, in a bikini, in the fountain in front of the New York Plaza Hotel. It wasn't long before the police showed up and told me in no uncertain terms to get out. The press got a few shots, and the photo made all the papers the next day.

Another gimmick Sam devised was very cute. As people entered the theater, the ushers handed out programs with a sexy picture of me on the cover for the men and an adorable innocent one for the ladies. After the show, I was told few programs were left on the seats or floor. People kept them as collector's items. Now and then, I will see one for sale on eBay. Glad I could help out.

I loved New York. The energy in the city was exciting and vibrant. Not only did Robert Caplan visit often, but my friend singer Johnny Ray and my business manager Sal Lazarow still lived in the city, so I visited them often. As for my parents, I didn't fly them to New York until the last week because my baby brother, John, then fourteen, would be off from school and could join my parents on the trip. They loved the show, and we had a wonderful time together.

After *Pajama Tops* closed in New York, I flew to Miami to attend the premiere of my Spanish movie, *La Rabia (The Rage)*. I was so pleased that my parents and brother could be there. At the after-party, a press member asked my dad what he thought of my reputation as a sex symbol, to which he answered, *"I think she's doing a con job on the American public."*

Thanks, Dad; I love you back.

Producer Zev Bufman decided to continue touring *Pajama Tops* and replaced everyone in the cast except Richard Vath, Don McCart, and me. This time, we would rehearse in San Francisco, a city I adore. I was friends with a wonderful Chinese family named Tsang. Three brothers, Wilfred, Willy, Wilson Tsang, and their sister Mai Tai, owned the *Rickshaw Restaurant* in Chinatown. I first met them in San Francisco while promoting the film *Macumba Love*. We have become close friends and have remained so. I was looking forward to spending time with them and saved theater seats for them on opening night.

Actor Bill Browder, who played the central character of Mou Mou, was perfect for the role. As good as Clift Halle had been, Browder took it to a new level. For reasons I don't recall, David Manley left the show several months later, and Robert Osbourne replaced him—the Robert Osbourne who became a household name hosting movies on the Turner Classic Movies cable channel.

Opening night, which should have been a wonderful

evening, was one of my life's worst. My friend, Wilson Tsang, had flown to Tahoe to spend a couple of days skiing and then was to fly back to San Francisco for the show's opening night. The plane never arrived in Tahoe. It took several days for rescue crews to find the aircraft because it had been covered with snow. Sadly, no one survived.

Unfortunately, as the saying goes, the show must go on. The play was a hit and a total sellout. Thank goodness the reviewers did not review it as if it was Shakespeare. They reviewed it as a fun, sexy French bedroom farce. They played up the fact that the audience couldn't stop laughing. Unfortunately, the laughs could not hide the hurt I felt for the terrible loss of Wilson Tsang.

On November 22, 1963, I woke up around 10 AM, called room service, ordered breakfast, and turned on the television. The press was interviewing Vice President Lyndon Johnson but called him *President* Johnson. It was several minutes before they fully recounted what had happened in Dallas, and finally, I understood that President Kennedy had been assassinated. With Jackie Kennedy at his side, Johnson was sworn in as President of the United States. Mrs. Kennedy wore the bloodstained pink suit that Oleg Cassini had designed for her. My heart bled for her. I'm not generally a conspiracy theorist, but to this day, I am not sure we know the truth about what happened in Dallas on that day in Dealey Plaza, but that's just me.

Around noon I received a call that all the theatres would be closed in memory of President Kennedy. Our final weekend before the show moved to another city, and the matinee and evening shows were sold out for both days. When people arrived at the theatre and found out that the show had been canceled and we were leaving town, the crowd turned into an angry mob, and the police were called. In a way, I didn't blame the people. They had bought tickets way ahead, and now they were screwed (excuse the expression, but I can't think of a better word!). And let's face it, not doing the show would not bring the President back.

I spent 1964 touring all over the United States with *Pajama Tops*, mostly in Shubert Theatres, and I was enjoying it more this time. In most towns, we ran for two weeks. As always, the first week was consumed with press promotions for the show. In the second week, Bill Browder and I would begin checking all the local high spots of interest the second week. That was one of the real perks of doing plays on the road; we saw sights we would never have seen otherwise and got paid for it. America, you *are* beautiful! I found it attractive in many ways, and I still do, with a few exceptions.

One of the exceptions turned out to be New Orleans. I had spent two days there without time to see any of the sights because all my time was spent promoting *Macumba Love*. I always try to stay in hotels within walking distance of the theatre. But Mike Ripps, the producer of *Macumba Love*, lived in Mobile, Alabama. Because his company did a great deal of business in New Orleans, he kept an executive apartment there. As luck would have it, no one was using it, and they offered it to me. However, it was not within walking distance of the theatre. When it was time to leave, I called for a cab to take me to the theater.

I slipped into the back seat when it arrived, but the cabbie appeared quite upset as soon as I got in. The driver began to harshly tell me he couldn't take me to the theater and told me to get out of his cab. I was confused and asked him what the problem was. He said it was because I was white and he was black. I told him I didn't care what color he was. He removed me from his cab, jumped back into the driver's seat, and told me to call a *white cab driver*. I had no idea that blacks needing a taxi had to call for a black driver, and whites had to call for a white driver. I was appalled and still am.

In England, this kind of lunacy was unheard of. I had not encountered it in New York, Los Angeles, or any other city I visited. Because of that incident, I learned that nearly every place in New Orleans was segregated, including public toilets. Boy, if I had been black, I would have gotten my ass out of the South as fast as my legs could carry me!

Bill Browder's boyfriend, Jack Cook, a professor of theatre arts in San Francisco, could only visit when the semester was over. Jack and Bill, about twenty years older than me, had been a couple since they first met in New York when they were both around nineteen. Unfortunately, in some cities in the sixties, homosexuals were actually illegal, so gays, whether men or women, had to be very discreet about their relationships. This was unbelievable to me in a country that valued its Constitution that promoted quality for all—or most, it seems, but not all.

Singly and together, Jack and Bill added so much to the art world. Together they formed the first Equity Bus

HOLLYWOOD OR BUST!

and Truck touring company. Jack became a theatre arts Professor at San Francisco State and was on the San Francisco Opera Company staff for over twenty years. Bill helped when he wasn't traveling around appearing on stage, which was his first love. These two wonderful and decent men took me under their wing, for which I will forever be grateful. I learned much more from them than I have ever learned at *The Carlyle School for Ladies*, where I learned nothing of value.

Bill was also a big help to me on stage, always keeping me on my toes and never would stand for me sleepwalking through a performance. I had to be at my best with him, and I thank him for that to this day. Bill was the organizer. He would list all the places we needed to visit in each new city. It was usually a diverse list, like going to the local museums or Filene's Basement, the department store in Boston, where one could buy designer clothes for ninety percent off. I loved visiting Filene and gladly left some of my income there with my purchases.

One sightseeing moment will stay in my heart and mind forever. While in Hawaii, Bill picked me up early on our day off and told me to wear flat shoes. We drove to Pearl Harbor and got on a boat that took us out and around the harbor, including the USS Arizona. The captain of our ship gave a short history of what happened on December 7, 1941. 1,102 Sailors and Marines were killed on the Arizona that day, and many remained below in the sunken ship. For a long moment, Bill was silent. Then told me something that gave me the chills I still get writing this. His eyes welled up, and through tears, he said softly, *"My brother is one of those sailors down there."* I got a lump in my throat, my eyes welled up, took Bill's hand in mine, and cried. I felt his brother under me and heard my father's voice in my head. I was a kid when he told me how bad it was during the war, that if the Americans had not joined the fight when they did, there would not be England as we know it today, and maybe many of us would not be alive.

Here I was, standing over the beginning of that history. The horrible event at Pearl Harbor that brought America into the war probably saved my family and me but took the life of Bill's brother. It remains one of the most emotional days of my life and always will. It took me a long time to stop imagining Bill's brother lying at the bottom of Pearl Harbor, trapped forever inside the USS Arizona. It was the only time I ever saw Bill cry, and no wonder as he was standing over where his brother was buried.

Thinking back now, I feel comforted that I had visited the new USS Enterprise before it left on its maiden voyage. I taped a *Good Night* sign-off message that was played each night for the crew before they turned in. I wished them a safe return. I didn't say it then, but I am saying it now: Thank you for your service. Thank you, America.

Chapter 31

Maurice Duke had lined up a movie for me titled *The Candidate* (1964) alongside Mamie Van Doren and Ted Night. I notified Zev Bufman, who asked me to stay on. Once he realized I had decided, he asked if I would return after I finished shooting *The Candidate,* and I agreed.

We began shooting *The Candidate*. Mamie was dating country and western singer Johnny Rivers. He rode high with hits like *Mountain of Love, Secret Agent Man, Poor Side of Town,* and *Baby*. Mamie would be on the set at the crack of dawn, knowing all her lines and ready to work. She was off to *Whiskey A Go Go* at night with Johnny until the club closed, then up at dawn. Boy, how I wish I had her stamina! Maimi was a trooper.

Ted Knight, who co-starred in *The Mary Tyler Moore*

Show, was an excellent actor to work with. But there was one particular scene that he was nervous about. Ted and I had to be naked in bed with only a sheet covering us. Dorothy, his wife, who was on set most days thought it was best if she was not present for that scene. But then, she changed her mind and showed up. While the crew was setting the lights, I could see Ted was worried that his wife was there. I asked him what was wrong. It seems he was concerned about getting aroused during the scene. *"Don't worry,"* I said; *"it's no big deal."* We couldn't stop laughing at that slip of the tongue.

Two hours later, when we were about to finish the scene, Ted said, *"June, you know what? If my life depended on it, I couldn't have gotten an erection,"* to which I replied, *"That's very flattering, Ted. Thanks a lot."* That incident was a running gag between Ted and me for several years.

On a day I wasn't shooting, my agent Sam Armstrong asked me to meet him on the set of the popular TV series *The Beverly Hillbillies*. He was meeting Max Baer Jr. for lunch and invited me to join them. A meal always seemed to be involved and kept me well-fed.

Max and I got on very well; if his dad had still been alive, his ears would be burning. I told Max Jr. about my appearance on his Dad's TV show to promote *Baby Doll*, and almost every night after that, Max Sr. and his friend, Slappy Maxie Rosenbloom, would take me out and feed me. Yet another meal!

From that lunch with Max Jr. came a life-long friendship. Max was always trying to get me into the sack (why should he be any different?). As a joke, I told him it would never happen unless the moon had my initials in big letters. One night, he called and told me to look out

HOLLYWOOD OR BUST!

the window; the moon had my initials around it. He kept that joke up for years; no, Ladies and gentlemen, boys and girls, we never had sex. Max had more lovely ladies after him than he could handle.

Everything went smoothly with the production of *The Candidate* except for one major problem. Robert Redford was starring in a political film titled *The Candidate*. The producers changed the title of our movie to *Party Girls for the Candidate*, which I detested. But you can't have two movies with identical titles, one being Redford's production—Redford gets to choose, not little old us.

And if you are still interested in how my romance was going with Robert Caplan (I was beginning not to be), I had not heard from him in months. Men, and more men!

Maurice Duke proposed recording a rock and roll record with Mamie VanDoren and me. He thought it would be great publicity for our movie. The very talented Sid Robins wrote the song. I knew Sid well as he was one of Duke's close buddies—they had dinner together at least three times a week. It's always about the food, isn't it? As I mentioned earlier in the book, Sid had written many hits (*Undecided Now* and *I Miss You So*, to name a couple). However, the song they wanted Mamie and I to record was not up to Sid's usual standard, probably because he thought rock and roll was garbage.

Sid's song was titled *Bikini with No Top on The Top*. Duke thought it would be perfect if Mamie and I recorded the song wearing only a bikini bottom while holding the sheet music in front of our bare breasts (yuk and yuk again!) while we sang, and they took pictures. You know how badly I sing if you read the chapter on my time with Spike Jones. But lucky for me, Billy Strange, my friend since I was nineteen, was well aware of my inability to carry a tune. Billy had worked with everyone who was anyone from Elvis to Frank Sinatra and produced Nancy Sinatra's hit *These Boots Are Made for Walking*. The only reason Billy took the job was as a favor to me.

When the photographers finished taking PR photos, Billy had me leave the studio, leaving Mamie alone with the band to record the song. Once that was done, they had me return and worked with me note-by-note until I got it right. Even then, it was pretty bad, but it was not all my fault. As wonderful as Sid Robins was at writing songs, this song was not bad; it was terrible! Unfortunately, Rock n Roll was not Sid's forte.

Mamie had worked professionally singing with her husband, Ray Anthony's band. She was unhappy when this awful song was included on an album titled *The Worst Singing Celebrity Album Ever*. I, on the other hand, was amused. As a joke, I gave copies to all my friends as a Christmas present. Sorry Mamie!

Months went by, and still no call from the elusive Robert Caplan. His family had stopped making excuses for him, so I knew something was up. Unless he was in a coma, there was no excuse that would be acceptable to me for his non-contact. With my work consuming my time, I didn't dwell much on Mr. Caplan.

HOLLYWOOD OR BUST!

Chapter 32

Following our stint in Kansas City, we moved to Wichita, Kansas, where we worked for Harry Peebles, fondly known as *Hap* Peebles. Hap was famous for booking concerts with the biggest and the best country artists like Elvis, Johnny Cash, and Loretta Lynn. A Broadway show was an actual departure for Hap. At the same time he was producing our show, he was producing a country music show starring Roy Clark, Johnny Western, Hank Williams Jr., and Ferlin Husky. Unfortunately, both shows were on identical schedules, so I never saw theirs.

Hap hosted a combined party for the country stars and us on closing night. The party was fabulous: great music, dancing, and, the best part, meeting all those country and western stars. I spent most of my time talking and dancing with country singer Johnny Western. He was tall and slender, with a singing voice that was strong and deep. Right off, I could tell there was an attraction between us. Johnny went his way, and I went mine, and although we kept in touch, I thought that was the end of it. As fate would have it, we were both in Boston once, beginning our romance.

Johnny has always been thoughtful and caring, and I enjoyed being with him. I honestly don't remember why we broke up. As always, spending time together was challenging because of our work schedules. I was busy with *Pajama Tops,* and he was touring with Johnny Cash, and we drifted apart, I guess. That's a hazard in show business, and probably the cause of so many failed relationships.

I had been working nonstop since my appearance at the Seattle World's Fair, and even though I loved every moment of my time working, I was tired; it was time for another break. I decided to spend Christmas in London with my parents. I thought it would be fun not to tell them I was coming and surprise them. They'd think I was still working if I sent gifts beforehand. I even considered showing up wearing a big red bow. *Nah,* I thought that would be too corny.

Zev Bufman did his best to convince me not to leave the show, but my mind was made up. He reluctantly replaced me with my British bosom buddy (excuse the tacky pun—I couldn't resist) Sabrina, whom I knew from my teenage years in London.

Christmas at home in England with the family was most memorable; a Christmas I will never forget because

HOLLYWOOD OR BUST!

of a call I received from my agent Sam Armstrong. The famous director Otto Preminger was planning to direct a movie in London and was interested in casting me for a part. Although Preminger was in Los Angeles, he arranged for me to meet some of his production staff already in London. The meeting was at eleven in the morning. When I arrived, there was a hub of activity. The only one I recognized was actor Michael Caine. Michael was a hot new property then because of his outstanding performances in the movies *Zulu* and *The Ipcress Files*, and I assumed they were interviewing him as well.

After the meeting, they invited me to lunch. I sat next to Michael Caine, and we chatted about our careers. When lunch was over, Michael offered to take me to dinner. Food and more food. I don't remember the restaurant we went to, but Michael knew everyone. Following dinner, we went to London's newest disco. Hundreds of looky-loos were hanging around the entrance with no chance to get in. They were there to get a glimpse of someone famous.

Wow, everyone who was anyone was there, including the Beatles. I was having a wonderful time, but my flight back to Los Angeles was leaving early the following day; it was bedtime for Baby June—I love my sleep time. I thanked Michael for a wonderful evening and left. Over the years, I bumped into Michael several times. Unlike many show-biz marriages, he was happily married and still is to the lovely Shakira, a former Guyanese actress and fashion model.

I had only been back in LA a few days when my

agent called and told me he had heard from Otto Preminger. Otto told him his people in London reported that I had made a good impression at my interview. Preminger wanted me to come to his office so he could interview me personally. I was well aware of Mr. Preminger's reputation with the ladies, as was everyone in the business. If I say so myself, I've always been adept at handling men whose ambition was getting me on my back on the casting couch. So, if Otto had any intentions in that area, I'd be ready for him.

Thankfully, my first meeting with Preminger went well. I found him to be quite delightful. He told me he would be in the studio on Saturday, finishing a few scenes from the John Wayne film *In Harm's Way*. He invited me to join him and said when the crew went to lunch, the projectionist would run my movie so he could see how I looked on the screen.

I watched them working on *In Harm's Way* on Saturday, which was a delight. An hour's lunch break was called; the projectionist put one of my films and left. As I said, Preminger's reputation with the ladies proceeded him, so I expected him to make a move, but, to my surprise, he didn't and remained a perfect gentleman. After viewing my film, he thought I would work well in his movie. I was, of course, thrilled. Being in a film shot in London with a cast that included Sir Laurence Olivier and Noel Coward would be a dream come true.

The next day, I got a call from Mr. Preminger. *"I'm not leaving until tonight; give me your address, and I will come over so we can talk more about your role."* Now, I know what you're thinking; How can she be so dumb? Believe me, when I hung up, I thought the same. I should have come up with an excuse like I had houseguests, or maybe we could have met at a restaurant for lunch, anywhere but my house.

When Preminger arrived, I watched him from a window climb the twenty steps up the hill to my front door. He wasn't fooling me; he wasn't here to discuss the movie. Here we go again. I told him to make himself comfortable and that I would make coffee. He said no to the coffee, sat on the couch, and patted the space beside him. I ignored his invitation to sit with him and moved to a chair. He patted the couch again, *"No, June, come sit by me,"* he said with what I thought was an uncomfortable grin. What was I supposed to do? I sat next to him, knowing full well what was coming next. His hand moved to my knee and then up my skirt, trying to get into my panties. Okay, that was enough of that. After a bit of a struggle, I pushed him away and stood. He encouraged me to sit down again. I refused. He scowled, stood up, walked to the door, turned around, and said, *"You're making a big mistake, June."* I shrugged and followed him to the door as he left. Halfway down my steps, he stopped, turned back, and said, *"You're making a big mistake. Are you sure you don't want to change your mind?"* I shook my head no. He frowned, turned, and left. It was like a bad scene from another lousy movie. It should go without saying, but I did not get a role in his film. Welcome to yet another Hollywood jerk. The casting couch lives on.

I had a standing Sunday invitation to join Maurice Duke and his cronies at Matteo's restaurant in Westwood. I called and told him I didn't feel like joining them this Sunday; he asked me why. I told him about my wrestling encounter with Preminger, and I was in no mood to go out. *"You are not going to let that fucking asshole ruin your evening, are you, June? Get your ass down here."* Reluctantly, I joined them for dinner.

Duke had filled the guys in on my encounter with Preminger. Their sympathy for me lasted all of five minutes before the teasing began. It got even worse when a well-known producer we all knew was sitting with his wife at the next table. I won't use his name; he may not appreciate seeing his comment in print. He leaned toward our table and said, *"Sorry, but I overheard your conversation. June, for Christ's sake, all you had to do was lift your top, show your breasts for two seconds, and it would have been all over, and the role would have been yours."*

Everyone laughed but me. I found nothing funny about Otto Preminger's vulgar, deplorable behavior.

HOLLYWOOD OR BUST!

Chapter 33

I was back in New York again. My friend, singer Johnnie Ray invited me to dinner at his place. He told me he had fallen in love with a wonderful lady and wanted me to meet her. I knew Johnnie was bisexual, so I wasn't sure what to expect. In the seven years I had known him, he never introduced me to any woman he was involved with. In fact, he never showed much interest in women at all. This would prove to be a very interesting evening.

I called Saul Lazarow and told him I was having dinner with Johnnie and a lady he claimed to be in love with. Saul laughed. *"What's funny, Saul?"* He laughed again. *"June, the woman in question is none other than columnist and television personality Dorothy Kilgallen."* You could have knocked me over with a feather. I'd never met Dorothy, but I had seen her on the popular television show, *What's My Line*, where she was a panelist. I also regularly read her show business columns.

Nothing could have prepared me for the scene when I arrived at Johnnie's apartment. As he always did, he greeted me with a hug. I looked past him and could not believe my eyes. Standing there in a little girl's style dress with a full but very short skirt that no one older than thirteen should be wearing was the one and only Dorothy Kilgallen. Her outfit was topped off with a big bow tied around her head. Johnny and Dorothy billed and cooed at each other through dinner like teenagers experiencing their first real love relationship. Dare I say it was nauseating? It was like watching a funny skit on a Carol Burnett show.

I stayed later than planned, trying to figure out what was happening between these two. At the end of this bizarre evening, I decided that, if nothing else, these two high-profile celebrities were genuinely infatuated with one another. If they believed it was true love, who was I to question it?

I began touring in the play *Any Wednesday*. The play had been a big hit on Broadway with the lovable Sandy Dennis in the title role. We were fortunate to have Howard Erskine, one of the producers of the Broadway production, as our director. Rehearsals went very well, and the opening night went even better; that is, until the reviews came out; the reviewers hated me, not the rest of the cast, just me, *Baby June*, everyone's darling. I never received a review that panned my performance as much. Poor Howard, who thought I was terrific in the role,

HOLLYWOOD OR BUST!

went nuts. He called a director friend of his (sorry, I have forgotten his name) to come to see the show and help us figure out what the problem was. Howard and his friend met me in the coffee shop the following day after seeing the previous night's performance. I was expecting the worst.

Howard's director friend said he thought he had the answer after seeing my performance. *"You have to get the audience to like you, June. They have to feel sorry that your character was being taken advantage of. The villain has to be the husband, not your character. There's no way the audience would feel sorry for your character if you keep wearing a robe that reveals seventy percent of your breasts,"* Ah, there was the answer. Howard had the costume lady replace the fabric they had removed from the front of my robe. The trick was to show some flesh but not to the extent we first tried to get away with. Problem solved, lesson learned, thanks to this director who knew his stuff. From then on, the reviews were good.

After a year on the road, I was ready for another break and returned home. I loved my little cottage on the Hollywood side of Laurel Canyon, hidden by all the hills and trees, and I loved being five minutes away from Sunset Blvd., where all the action was.

Billy Mize, a country singer/writer, was a friend of mine with many hit songs. One of his biggest was *You Keep Me Hanging On*, recorded by Cher, Waylon Jennings, Kitty Wells, and others. Billy called and said, *"If you're not doing anything, I'll come to pick you up. I have a friend, Ray Sanders, who's performing about half an hour out of town. I know you'll enjoy him; he's one of the best singers around*.

Billy was right. Ray was terrific and very pleasant; I accepted when Ray invited me to dinner the next day. Yet another meal led to a romance that went on for several years.

About a year into my romance with Ray, I received a call from my Mum and Dad. They said the elusive Robert Caplan and his brother Sonny had called. They were in London and wanted to drive down to Eastbourne and take them to dinner the following day. My parents were curious as I was about Robert's whereabouts, so they accepted his invitation. During dinner, Robert showed my parents a pair of diamond and emerald earrings he had purchased for me. He was flying flew to America in two days and couldn't wait to see me.

The next day, Robert called and told me about his dinner with my parents and how much he loved me and couldn't wait to see me, but not a single word about where he had been. I wanted to pull a Maurice Duke and ask Robert, *"Where the f—k have you been all these years!"* Thankfully, I held my temper. I said, *"That's wonderful, sweetheart; I can't wait to see you too."* I planned to lay into him when we were face-to-face.

Well, ladies and gentlemen, boys and girls, here it is forty-five years later, and I've never heard from Mr. Caplan again. How in the hell do you explain that? Stranger than fiction is all I can say.

Mum and I had a wonderful visit when she flew in to spend some time with me. She fell in love with my little cottage on the hill, and my friends treated her like she was a princess. Maurice Duke avoided using the *"F"* word

HOLLYWOOD OR BUST!

around her. For him, that was quite a struggle. That visit from Mum was one of my happiest. She kept reminding me how proud she was of me. I kept telling her she deserved much of the credit for my success.

My next gig was at the Candlewood theatre in Connecticut. It was the first time I had performed in summer stock. The show was *Any Wednesday* (Jane Fonda and Jason Robards Jr starred in a 1966 movie version). I knew this play backward and forwards, having toured in the play for a year on a national tour. The wonderfully funny and talented Tom Poston had top billing. I loved Tom's offbeat humor when he played the on-the-street guy on the Steve Allen TV show. I had second billing and the amazing Elaine Stritch, a star on Broadway, had third. I was a big fan of Elaine's and would have never given myself billing over her, but I was not about to bring that up to the producer. My parents didn't raise no dummy.

Everything went fine until the second day of rehearsals. We began the scene where I walked on stage wearing the too-big, low-cut negligee. I was into about five lines of my dialogue when the director jumped up and told me my interpretation was wrong: *"You are a sex symbol. You must walk out like a sex symbol, tall with your breasts held high and as far out as possible. You have to turn on every man in the—"*

He didn't get the word *audience* out before Elaine jumped up, ran out of the rehearsal hall, slammed the door, and screamed. Then silence; you could have heard a pin drop. Ten seconds later, Elaine returned as though nothing had happened and said, *"Now, where were we?"*

We went on as though nothing had happened.

When the rehearsals were over, Elaine said, *"June, I'm taking you to dinner."* Over dinner, she told me precisely what Howard Erskine's director friend had said: my character needed to gain the audience's sympathy, even though she was the mistress. And there was no way I could do that with ninety percent of my breasts prominently on display. I told Elaine it was the same problem as when I previously did the play. Her advice was, *"Then, do it your way, June, do it your way. Sorry about my scream during rehearsal. It was the only way to get the director to shut up. I think he got the message."*

Elaine and I hit it off, so she invited me to share her room at the two-story motel, inn, rooming house, or whatever it was called. It resembled the creepy motel from Psycho with Anthony Perkins more closely. I know what some of you are thinking, but you'd be wrong; Elaine is not gay; that's not why she invited me to room with her. Elaine was a people person who loved company, and she was great fun to be around. However, she had one bad habit: She was a big drinker, but it never bothered her that I wasn't. I never once saw her drinking affect her performance on stage like a few others I worked with. Elaine was a true professional dedicated to her work. She had a significant influence on me, and I learned from watching her perform

On our last night in Connecticut, I left the cast at the bar, returned to the room to get a head start on packing, then went to bed. I hadn't been sleeping long when the phone rang. It was Tom. *"Hi, June. Elaine and I are in my room, and we thought you might like to join us for a drink."* I looked at the clock. *"Tom, it's 4:30 in the morning. Are you*

HOLLYWOOD OR BUST!

crazy?"

Then the truth came out. *"After the bar closed, Elaine and I returned to my room and continued drinking. Elaine had one too many and passed out on my bed. Um, my fiancé will be here in the morning, and this won't look good. That's why I'm calling you, June."* I told Tom I would be right up. I went to Tom's room and found Elaine passed out on the bed. We had no luck getting Elaine up, so I gave Tom the key to our room, and Elaine and I would sleep in his room. The scene was turning into a Marx Brothers movie plot. Tom left, and I fell asleep next to Elaine.

Elaine and I were still sleeping when Tom's fiancé knocked on his door around nine o'clock the following morning. When I opened the door and greeted her, I explained that the cast had a few drinks after the show in Tom's room, and, unfortunately, Elaine got drunk and passed out, so Tom spent the night in my room. I called Tom to let him know his fiancé had arrived. A very hung-over Elaine woke up just in time to witness Tom embracing his fiancé, Kate. As they kissed, Elaine slowly turned to me and said, *"June, I think I'm going to be sick."*

Despite her drinking problem, Elaine Stritch was one of a kind, and I mean that in the most complimentary way. She is fun to be with, and I was fortunate to count her as a friend.

On our last night, Elaine suggested we have dinner at Joe Allen's, her favorite hangout. We got there around 9:00 PM, and it was packed with celebrities. Elaine was one of their regulars and knew just about everyone. Several movie stars were there on their way to appear in John Wayne's film *The Green Beret*.

At closing time, the owner invited his actor friends to

stay, and that's when the real party began. Unfortunately for me, David Janssen, star of the TV series *The Fugitive*, had taken a fancy to me from across the room. When Elaine got up to sing, David staggered to my table and began with the usual male song and dance about why I should accompany him back to his hotel room. Here we go again.

I told David I had no intention of going back to his hotel. He wasn't happy. The party continued until around 5:00 in the morning. David paid his bill and asked if I had changed my mind. I told him again the answer was no. He shrugged, staggered out, and caught a cab, and that was the first and only time I met David Jansen. When Elaine and I went to pay our bill, the waiter said, *"I thought David Jansen took up enough of your time, so I just added your bill to his."* We left this waiter a big tip.

The final week of *Any Wednesday* was great fun, and I was sad to see it end. I accepted an offer to continue *Any Wednesday* for two weeks at a charming theatre called *The Old Mill* in Westminster, Massachusetts. However, they could not afford the expense of bringing in the three of us, so they replaced Tom with Jeffrey Lynn and Elaine with Shirley Matson. They were both excellent actors, but I missed the old cast I had grown to love.

Chapter 34

Back in LA, I woke up in my little one-bedroom cottage and had my two-morning cups of coffee. It was a beautiful day, so I dressed and walked to explore the hilltop of the Canyon. When I left the house, I turned right and got to the junction; if I had turned left as I had for the past two years, it would have taken me down to Laurel Canyon. Instead, I turned right to reach the top of the hill. When I reached the top, the only way to go was left. Shortly, I came upon a road called Grandview Drive. What a joke! It was a dirt road no wider than a car and a half, with a gradual downslope on the left. There were a few tiny houses stuck precariously on the downslope. On the right side was a small hill you could not see over.

About a couple hundred feet later, the small hill on

the right-hand side disappeared, and suddenly a sheer drop down the mountain opened up to the most incredible view I had ever seen. The name *Grandview Drive* was an understatement. Looking down, I saw a stunning view of the Sunset Strip and could see all the way to the Los Angeles International Airport. To the right was the Pacific Ocean. The view was unbelievably spectacular! I wished I could have shared that first moment with someone, anyone. My boyfriend, Ray Sanders, was out of town touring. While Ray Locke and Ron Schnell lived just fifteen minutes from me—this was before cell phones—I couldn't call them. Then, a car approached, slowed down, and swung around me with no problem. I assumed that he lived close by because he handled the road easily.

After another ten minutes of walking, the little street widened a bit. A driveway went up a hill leading to a house with—wait for it—a *For Sale* sign. It was a single-story home with a flat roof. I made my way up this steep driveway and knocked on the door—no one answered. I peered through the window and saw that the house was empty. I could see through the back wall; all glass provided another incredible view. On the side of the house, there was a large swimming pool. It was almost as big as the community pool in my hometown of Eastbourne, England, which, at the time I lived there, was the only pool in Eastbourne.

After peaking in every window, I rushed home, called my friend and business manager, Saul Lazarow, and told him I had found a house I was in love with and wanted to buy. He told me to forget it and reminded me I already owned one home. But I was in love with the house and location, so I insisted. Saul reluctantly agreed to call the listing agent to see what deal he could make on my behalf. When he called back, he gave me fantastic news.

Saul said the owner was Louie Lomax, an African American intellectual who had written many successful books. At one time, Mr. Lomax hosted a TV program on KTTV in Los Angeles, the first African American to have done so. Mr. Lomax was going through a nasty divorce and was so disgusted that he just walked away from the house and considered leasing it. Saul made a deal where I would take over the payments, and Mr. Lomax's credit rating would stay intact.

I loved that house so much that I never envied any friends who owned Bel Aire or Beverly Hills mansions. For me, it was like living in Heaven on Earth. The wise lady I am, I did not sell my little one bedroom cottage. It would be my security blanket, just in case things went wrong, so I rented it out.

When I moved into my dream house, the first thing I bought was a round bed (they were all the rage in the sixties), and of course, I had to have satin sheets. Here's some advice from Titsalina Schwartz (the nickname bestowed on me by my close friends): Never buy a round bed unless you desire to sleep alone. One person can sleep in the middle with legs straight, but if you move out of the center, you will have to turn sideways and bend your knees so your feet won't hang over the edge. Also, satin pillows are too slippery, and you will slide off the bed unless you stay in the same position and never move. I'm restless and quickly tired of picking the pillow off the floor. I finally gave up and dragged the bed and the sheets to the garage. Goodbye, round bed.

The one good buy I made was an oversized rocking chair for two that faced the back glass wall. It was my favorite spot to have coffee in the morning and a splendid place to survey the world from my little piece of Heaven.

Johnnie Ray called. He was in town to host a show for H.E.A.R (Hearing Education through Auditory Research), a charity dear to his heart. Johnnie had enlisted a list of stars: Kay Starr, Rudy Vallee, Arlene Wells, Jose Ferrer, Michael Parks, and my buddy, Jo Anne Worley. Jonnie asked if I would do a skit with song and film stars Dan Dailey and Donald O'Connor. Of I would. Who in their right mind would turn down an opportunity to perform with two film icons? I only wished my dad had been there. He loved musicals, and seeing me doing a skit with two of his all-time favorites would have been the thrill of a lifetime for Dad.

Not long after, Marty Barth called and broke the news that Charlie Chaplin Jr. had died. I was in shock because Charlie was only forty-two years old. They said he died of a blood clot, but I knew better; it had to be the alcohol. Charlie always drank too much, even from our first date in England when I was just sixteen. At his funeral, I silently thanked Charlie for being in my life and told him I loved him. He was always there for me, as was Marty Barth, Charlie's best friend. They were many flowers. Some were from his father, Charlie Chaplin. If only he had given Charlie Jr. the love and attention when he was alive. Charlie Jr. often told me that his father was distant, often cold, and never seemed to care. How sad.

HOLLYWOOD OR BUST!

When Ray Sanders returned to town, he came to see my new palace in the sky. He was blown away by the view, as was everyone who visited. He spotted the apartment on the side and asked if he could move in, which I agreed to. After about a month of living there, he realized neither used the garage. We both parked our cars by the side of the house. So, with my permission, he put a window between the apartment wall and the garage and turned the garage into a recording studio. Clever man, that Sander's boy.

One day Ray and I were wandering around town and found a lovely pet shop. For fun, we strolled through the store, admiring the expensive breeds. Two cute puppies were in a cage at the back of the store. The store owner told us they were a mixed breed of Collie, German Shepherd, and maybe some wolf or husky mix, and they were brother and sister. Ray encouraged me to get one, but I said no. I had never had a pet growing up and wasn't crazy about getting one now. With WWII raging, food was always a problem, never mind trying to feed pets too. Besides, I had no idea how big they would grow. Ray nagged me until I gave in and bought the female. At first, I didn't name her. Everyone who saw her would say, *"She is so sweet."* So, having no particular name in mind, I called her *"She, She"* who quickly became one of my life's loves.

In 1968, my agent called and told me that the producers of the hit TV series *Batman* wanted me to join the cast in the role of Evelina. The series had a big audience following, and I said yes immediately. On the first day of shooting, I was sitting in make-up, wrapped in a cape with my hair in rollers. The makeup artist had just covered my face with the makeup base when Burt Ward and Adam West, the series stars, stopped at the open door. They had no idea I was sitting a few feet away and could hear every word. I don't remember the exact conversation, but it was classless. They talked about my appearances in Playboy and my large breasts. After they left, the makeup man, embarrassed for me, said they were both jerks and apologized for their crude behavior.

    I never gave my appearances on Batman another thought until years later when I appeared at a memorabilia convention attended by many celebrities, including Adam West and Burt Ward. My fan club president Scott Hughes and his wife, Ruth, had flown out from their home in Chicago to attend the show. While Scott was walking around checking who was there, he came upon Burt Ward's booth, introduced himself as the president of my Fan Club, and asked if he could bring me over for a photo of the two of us. Burt readily agreed. Scott then asked Adam West if we could take a picture with him. Potty mouth Adam refused. He thought it would be bad for his image since I had appeared in Playboy.

    Some people never grow up. Once a jerk, always a jerk.

Chapter 35

While my friend Tom Poston was in town for a TV interview, he stopped by to see my new house. Like everyone who visited, the view from my front window blew him away. He didn't bother to ask if he could stay with me; he simply said, *"You have a lot of room here, so I will check out of my motel and stay here."* That was my Tommy! He was only in town for a week, but he and Ray had a great time together and got in a couple of rounds of golf before Tom had to leave. I would cook for them, and we would talk and laugh evenings away. I'm pleased to report that Tom was an excellent house guest, always cleaning up after himself. I loved having him around because of his offbeat humor that kept Ray and me in stitches with his endless string of jokes.

JUNE WILKINSON

I was once a guest on Joey Bishop's late-night TV talk show. Regis Philbin was his sidekick. I don't remember why I was invited. Maybe because I had been on Regis Philbin's San Diego show several times, Regis put in a plug with the producer to have me on Bishop's show. It was easy working with Regis because he had a quick and witty sense of humor. Once Regis was on a roll, there was no stopping him.

When I appeared with Bishop, I wasn't promoting a show, so I took the opportunity to promote the heck out of my endorsement for the *Mark Eden Bust Developer*, which, as you might imagine, lent itself to lots of humor. The Joey Bishop show received so much mail from viewers after my appearance about the *Bust Developer*, so they invited me back. Believe me, when I tell you, I did *really, really, really* well with the *Bust Developer*. Unfortunately for me, fake breasts were becoming popular at that time. Plastic surgeons began inserting a jell pack under the skin, and a woman's bosom could go from a size 32A to a B thru G and beyond! So, the timing could not have been worse for Baby June and the Bust Developer. Not too long after, I was suddenly out of business! I shed many, many tears over that one.

Around this time, I was invited to a film festival in Panama. There was no reason not to go, so I accepted. I loved to travel, I had never been to Panama, and the trip would be first-class at the festival's expense. So, off I went to Panama. The first evening was a casual dinner where everyone could get to know one another. After that, we were pretty much on our own.

The following day, the organizers arranged a cruise up the Panama Canal with breakfast and lunch. At

HOLLYWOOD OR BUST!

lunch, I sat next to renowned English actor Laurence Harvey. He had recently starred with French actress Simone Signoret in *Room at the Top*, which was and remains one of my favorite films. Accompanying Harvey was Wolf Mankowitz, a famous writer who lived in England. Both men were witty, engaging, and fun to be with. Over the week we were there, we spent a lot of time together.

Harvey was married to Joan Cohn, widow of Harry Cohn, the president of Columbia Pictures. I had never worked for Columbia nor met Mr. Cohn, but like everyone in Hollywood, I knew of his reputation, which was anything but complimentary. Cohn ruled Columbia with an iron fist and treated the talent poorly. Mrs. Harvey did not accompany her husband on the trip for whatever reason. Even though he seemed to enjoy himself, I sensed Laurence was in a bad place. For starters, he was another one who drank too much. While drinking one day, he told me his life was in complete chaos. He was madly in love with a girl in England, and she was pregnant with his child. I was surprised at how candidly he was telling me this. I didn't know what to say, so I said nothing. Perhaps his heavy drinking was his way of dealing with his problems.

The festival organizers arranged for a lavish party on a small island twenty minutes away by plane from Panama City. I was to travel with General Omar Torrijos in his personal aircraft that he piloted. Torrijos and his thugs had taken over Panama in a coup d'état and instituted social reforms that sent Panama into pollical and economic turmoil.

As we entered the airport, soldiers were on both sides

of the corridor. They were armed with rifles, not by their sides but held in front of them with their fingers on the triggers, ready for action. That made me nervous. Torrijos's plane was small and could only accommodate five at the most. When we boarded, the General sat in the pilot seat, his wife beside him, and an armed guard in the back beside me. The plane took off, but the engine started stuttering while we climbed. General Torrijos started yelling and sweating profusely. His wife was as white as a ghost. Sitting stiffly as a board, I was damn afraid of what might happen next. In what seemed like forever, Torrijos had turned the plane around and safely landed back at the airport. A sign of relief was heard from all of us. Armed troops immediately surrounded the plane, and we were quickly escorted off and into the terminal.

The ground crew checked the plane to be sure it had not been tampered with. We never learned if it had been; we boarded another plane and continued as if nothing had happened. Really? How close had we come to biting the dust in that first plane? I don't want to know.

Thankfully, we arrived on the island without further drama; I had enough drama that day to last me a lifetime.

The island was stunningly beautiful, and the accommodations and the food were first-class. But I admit it took me a while before I settled down to eat and be merry following that first short flight with the President of Panama at the controls. Who wouldn't be nervous?

A footnote to history: General Torrijos died in July

HOLLYWOOD OR BUST!

1981 in, of all things, a plane crash.

I had only been back from Panama for two weeks when I got a call from Laurence Harvey's wife, Joan. They hosted a movie night with cocktails and dinner and invited their friends and me to join them. I recall she sounded a bit cool on the phone. Maybe she thought I was one of her husband's play toys, or worse, she knew about his pregnant lover and thought it might be me. Okay, that was a bit of a stretch. I did sense a coolness in her voice like maybe this was Laurence's idea, not hers.

That evening Laurence was his charming self. For whatever reason, Joan barely shook my hand when we were introduced. In a way, I felt sorry for her. Whether or not she knew about Laurence's pregnant girlfriend in England remained a mystery.

Peter Lawford was there. The man could barely stand, and he slurred his words. It was apparent Peter was high on more than just too much booze. Otherwise, it was an enjoyable evening with a friendly group of people that came off without a hitch, considering the behind-the-scenes drama with Laurence, his lover, and the impending birth of their child.

Laurence divorced his wife Joan in 1972. That December, he married Paulina Stone, the mother of his daughter, whom they named *Domino*. Laurence died in November 1973. He did not live to witness the sad, sorrowfully short life of Domino. I never met her, but everyone said she was beautiful. Domino had many different jobs. The most famous was as a bounty hunter. Unfortunately, she ran with a fast crowd, was always getting into trouble, and drugs were a constant problem.

JUNE WILKINSON

Domino died June 27, 2005. She OD'd in her bathtub on the drug Fentanyl. Director Tony Scott later made a movie about her life starring actress English Kiera Knightley.

Yet another Hollywood tragic ending.

Chapter 36

Life overlooking Sunset Blvd was wonderful. However, one little episode strikes me as funny now, but I did not find it so amusing when it happened. Ray and some musicians were recording in the apartment – garage - studio. One asked me about the round bed, which was still in the corner of the garage. He offered to buy it when I told him I did not enjoy sleeping in it. I was sick of seeing it in the garage and told him he could have it at no charge if he took it with him that day. I was happy to get rid of it.

About a week later, this guy showed up with a baby chick, a gift for giving him the round bed. I thought, okay, why not. So, I named the chick *Louisa* and let her roam in the backyard. When She She first approached Louisa, she checked her out, then, seemingly having little interest in a chicken, walked away. So, I thought, great, no problem there *She She* is not going to eat *Louisa*. I would lock Louisa in the shed at night and let her roam free during the day. I looked forward to fresh eggs sometime in the future.

As luck would have it, I was hired to do a show and wouldn't be around to take care of the little chick. What was I going to do with her? Then I got an idea. My dressmaker, Jimmy Ottobre, had two daughters, a young son, his beautiful wife, Annie, and a big fenced-in backyard. I made an appointment with Jimmy with the excuse I needed a fitting for a new dress. While Jimmy was measuring me, I told the children stories about Louisa. Then, I got around to the real reason for being there. Wouldn't it be wonderful if baby Louisa stayed with them for a couple of months? It would be *soooooo* good for the children to experience caring for a pet. With the kids' screaming, "please, please, please," Annie and Jimmy reluctantly agreed. Jimmy whispered, "*You son of a bitch, you owe me big time!*"

One down, one to go.

Ray was a semi-regular on the TV series *Hee Haw*, and most of his gigs were within driving distance, so I figured he could take care of *She She*, and if he had to go out of town for a night or two, he could take *She She*, (who loved to ride in cars) with him. So, the *She She* and Louisa problems were solved while I was away.

The show I was about to do was Neil Simon's *Come Blow Your Horn*. My leading man was Ed Byrnes, whose claim to fame was as one of the leads in the TV series *77 Sunset Strip*. Ed also had a hit record titled *Kookie Kookie*

HOLLYWOOD OR BUST!

Lend Me Your Comb. I had never met him but had seen *77 Sunset Strip* several times and thought he would be fine for the role. Sylvia Sidney was also in the cast, which thrilled me because she was a well-known and outstanding film actress.

When I arrived to begin rehearsals, a lot of commotion occurred. Mr. Byrnes discovered the billing for the show was: *Neil Simon's Come Blow Your Horn, starring June Wilkinson, Ed Byrnes & Sylvia Sidney.* Top billing was in my contract; unfortunately, I don't know if Byrnes' agents had asked for it or assumed he would get it. Maybe the agents had requested it and when told I had top billing, decided not to inform Mr. Byrnes, hoping he would not notice.

Mr. Byrnes made quite a fuss, refused second billing, and walked out minutes before I arrived. But no matter whether the contract was signed, sealed, and delivered, he must honor it. As for me, I kept out of the conflict. I would not have given up my billing unless they offered me more money. In fact, management never discussed the issue with me. The next day Byrnes was out, and Sammy Jackson, who had one of the leads in the TV series *No Time for Sergeants,* showed up to take Ed 'Kookie' Byrnes' place.

On the fourth day of rehearsals, Ray got a sit-down gig (which in show biz jargon means a job with no closing date) in Phoenix, Arizona, at *Mr. Lucky's* and was to begin the following week. He told me he had too many things to be concerned with and could not possibly take *She She* with him.

That left me with a dilemma. I was flying to a new city every two weeks. Since there was no one else I could leave her with, I had one choice; buy a large crate for *She She* to fly in alone with the luggage in the dark belly of the plane. In every city I went to, I had to hunt down a hotel that would allow big dogs, and it proved to be a challenge. Several times a day, I had to find places for her to do her business in the middle of whatever city I was in.

Sorry to say, that was the beginning and end of my romance with Ray, but not because of *She She*. Once again, it was the distance. I was in one town, and he was in another. Because I was out of town, I missed The Academy of Country Music Awards, and Ray won for his song, *Beer Drinking Music*. Long-distance romances are challenging to maintain and always seem to end.

About two months into my tour, I got a call from my dressmaker, Jimmy, that I could have done without. It seems my Louisa was not a *Louisa*, but a *Louie*, a full-fledged rooster. How the hell did we miss that? Jimmy's neighbors complained that Louie would begin crowing around 5 in the morning and keep it up until 9. The police showed up and informed Jimmy that it was against the law to have chickens in the city. Jimmy had twenty-four hours to comply, or he would be fined. I told Jimmy to put Louie in the cheapest pet store he could find, and I would pay the bill, which he did. That took care of the Louie problem, at least temporarily.

In February, we traveled to St Paul, Minnesota, for the opening of *Come Blow Your Horn*. Sylvia Sidney arrived early and promptly took the star dressing room, which was supposed to be mine since I had top billing. Nice lady that I am; I let it go since it wasn't that important to me. Sylvia loved to entertain, so the larger dressing room served her well. After each show, guests were always in her dressing room, where she served champagne and snacks. Thankfully, Sylvia and I got along well. She became my biggest booster, telling everyone how wonderful she thought I was on and off stage. Flattery is welcome; thank you very much.

I will never forget an incident that brought us the biggest laugh of any show we did. During the intermissions, I played a continuous chess game with one of the stagehands. One day, as the second act was about to start, the stagehand, whose name I'd forgotten (sorry), must not have closed the door to my dressing room. The curtain went up, and we began. A few minutes later, who should join us but *She She!* She casually walked to the center of the stage, stopped, turned, and stared at the audience. At first, we stood there in stunned silence before our lead actor said to another actor, *"I heard you've been dating dogs, but this is ridiculous."* The audience roared with laughter that went on for several minutes. That night *She She* became the show's star for one performance. She received more laughs and applause than I ever got.

Chapter 37

As I write this, it is July 18, 2014. Anyone who knows me well will tell you I am a creature of habit: I wake up, fix coffee, and turn on the TV. In the morning, I watched CBS, and in the evening, Fox News. That way, I get a diversified point of view (that's an understatement). Then I would work on this book for a while unless I had an appointment. This morning, as soon as I turned on the news, a photo of Elaine Stritch filled the screen. The commentator said she had died. My heart missed a beat; tears flooded my eyes as it sank in that Elaine was gone.

It hurts even now thinking about her. As I said, Elaine was one of a kind, and I loved her dearly. I wrote earlier about the time we worked together and what wonderful times we had as friends. But now, as I am writing, my thoughts are not about show business, but

HOLLYWOOD OR BUST!

the times Elaine and I spent together when she was in Los Angeles or I was in New York. She was never without a joke. Elaine was loud, funny, and outrageous but had a gold heart.

There was a period when we did not see much of one other. It was in the early 70s when Elaine was performing in London. In 1973 she met and married English actor John Bay. Sadly, now alone, Elaine moved back to America after her husband John died and moved to the Carlyle Hotel in New York. She called me one day to tell me she was working on a one-woman show titled *Elaine Strich at Liberty*. I looked forward to seeing it. I got to see her performance in New York, which blew me away. I'm not exaggerating when I say it was one of the most amazing one-woman shows I have ever seen.

Elaine, I am saddened to have lost you when I did; the world is too. I will forever be grateful for your friendship. You were essential to my life, and I am the better for it.

When I returned to Los Angeles (boy was *She She* happy to be home), I went to the pet shop to pick up my rooster Louie. I almost died when I got a bill for over five hundred dollars for a chicken that never gave me any eggs! I took Louie to our home on the hill, and no one complained about his crowing. His morning calls bounced over the mountains, and I'm sure no one knew it was coming from my house.

That evening, I joined Maurice Duke and the boys for dinner. I told them the story of Louisa, who was actually Louie, and I wasn't nuts about keeping him. Leave it to them to come up with a wacky idea. They suggested I run a contest on the popular Lohman and Barkley morning radio show (Duke was their manager), the number-one morning show in LA then. Duke called Lohman and Barkley and ran the idea passed them. They loved it. Louie would be presented to the winner on one of their Sunday night TV Shows. Each morning on their radio show, Lohman and Barkley joked about Louie and promoted the contest. It became the talk of the town.

Jimmy Ottobre made a unique dress for me to wear on the TV show when Louie would be presented to the winner. He stitched in a few of Louie's feathers around my neckline and on the belt. On the big day, I put Louie in *She She's* travel cage and left for the studio. When I arrived, they had put Alan Thicke in charge of Louie; the same Alan Thicke married to the singer Gloria Loring. As many will remember, Alan went on to star in the TV series *Growing Pains*.

When it was time for me to walk on stage, the stagehand took Louie out of his cage, and I held my right arm bent at the elbow, resting on my hip for support. Louie was placed on my bent arm. The winners, a middle age couple dressed in their Sunday best, were waiting to receive the newest addition to their family. Louie and I walked to center stage. Louie flapped his wings and let out a loud COCK-A-DODLE-DOOOOOOOO! The audience cheered, and I handed Louie over to his new parents. The show cut to commercials, and I returned to the green room where Peter Fonda (a guest on the show), Duke, and his buddies were eating, drinking, and shooting the breeze. Lohman and Barkley said goodbye to the audience, and

HOLLYWOOD OR BUST!

the show ended. Louie had a good home, and I didn't have to worry about him.

Wrong! There was more drama to come.

About thirty minutes later, a stagehand comes running in and announces, *"They don't want Louie. All they wanted was for their friends to see them on color TV. The damn fools left without Louie!"* Duke, Peter Fonda, and the boys thought it was hilarious. I didn't. When I went to pick up Louie and take him home, I couldn't find him. Louie and the cage were missing. To this day, I have no idea what happened to Louise, the rooster, and it still upsets me. I had nightmares about someone having Louie for dinner.

In May of 1969, I was still touring in *Come Blow Your Horn* with the same cast; however, Sammy Jackson was tired of being on the road and gave his notice. We were sorry to see him go, and we would miss him. Being the southern gentleman he was, Sammy made it his business to accompany me every night while I walked, *She She,* to ensure I was never attacked or bothered by anyone. Now, that's not a jerk; that's a gentleman.

As much as the cast and I missed Sammy Jackson's company, we were unprepared for the bombastic and ego-driven Keefe Brasselle, who replaced Sammy. I knew very little about Keefe other than he had starred in the movie *The Eddy Cantor Story,* which had received unfavorable reviews. Unfortunately for him and us, his acting in our play received even worse notices.

Keefe showed up on the first day of rehearsals with his girlfriend and took over like he was the show's producer, star, and owner. After a disastrous first day, I called Maurice Duke, who gave me the correct low down on Mr. Brasselle. In his own very elegant way, Duke said, *"He is a f-----g asshole with no talent. He's chummy with James Aubrey, head of CBS. Aubrey likes to party, and Keefe arranges for drugs and orgies."*

Duke told me that in return, Aubrey green-lit three costly CBS shows that Keefe would produce, even though Keefe had never produced a show before. The programs were *The Reporter*, *The Baileys of Balboa*, and *The Cara Williams Show*. All three ended up flops. On top of that, they allowed Keefe to host a summer variety series that the critics called a "textbook of mediocrity." Duke said Jack Benny, among others, thought Keefe was talentless, and Benny hated him with a passion. I told Duke he could add me to the list.

I'm not positive, but I don't think Keefe had ever performed in live theater. But that never stopped Mr. Ego from telling us how we should act. He even had the audacity to say he knew what was wrong with director Richard Vath's vision of the show. It would have been nice if Mr. Braselle had a quarter of Richard's talent.

I decided I couldn't put up with Keefe's bluster any longer. I gave my notice at the end of the run at the *Royal Alexander Theatre* in Toronto. It was the first time I had ever walked away from a show. Six weeks later, the show closed for good. Not because I left, but because Keefe Braselle and director Richard Vath go into a fistfight. Brasselle was an incredible talentless jerk.

A P.S. on Mr. Brasselle. In 1971, drunk in a North Hollywood bar, he got into a fight, pulled out a gun, and shot a man. He was arrested for assault with intent to commit murder. He died of cirrhosis of the liver on July

HOLLYWOOD OR BUST!

7, 1981. Guess who did not send him flowers!

Chapter 38

Even though my romance with Ray Sanders was over, we had planned to spend Christmas and New Year's together. This was in 1970 in Phoenix, Arizona. Ray still worked for Bob Sikora at the *Me and Bobby McGee Club* and I would join him there. When I boarded the plane to join Ray in Phoenix, they closed the door but opened it again a few minutes later, and an official-looking gentleman boarded. The pilot asked everyone to stay seated except for Miss June Wilkinson. He asked that I come to the front of the plane. What now, I thought? The airline official who boarded took me aside and broke the news as gently as possible. My family contacted the airline and informed them that my father had died. I was so overcome with grief that I only vaguely remember all that occurred next.

HOLLYWOOD OR BUST!

The airline was extremely helpful. A flight about to leave for London was held up, so I could quickly board it and be on my way to London. For the entire flight, I sat alone and cried. Thoughts of my childhood with my dad filled me with hundreds of memories: me by a river watching my dad rowing, cheering him on, willing him, and wanting him to go faster and win the race. There was the time he drove to London after reading some rude reporters' comments in a newspaper about me cleaning up my act. He had a newspaper take a picture of him washing the glass window frame I used on stage and was quoted as saying, *"That's better; the window is clean now. The audience can appreciate my daughter's beautiful body."* He spent all those hours playing the piano with me as a child; even though he knew I was tone-deaf, I loved to sing while he played.

When we arrived in London, I rented a car, drove straight to the church in my hometown of Eastbourne, and found the funeral had begun. They ushered me to my Mum's side. She was sitting with my brothers on either side of her. Robin moved over to make room for me. I hugged her, held her hand without saying a word, and wept. Mum turned to me and told me Dad had died from a cold that turned into pneumonia. Life is often unfair, and I felt this was one of those times.

In 1970, John Kenley hired me to work at the Kenley Theatre in Warren, Ohio. John was known for his extensive theatre knowledge and outrageous behavior. He had been involved with show business all his life, beginning with his church's choir when he was only four. He left school at fifteen to choreograph a burlesque show, and even though he was a hermaphrodite, he served in the Navy. After his stint in the Navy, his career was off and running. He worked for Broadway producer Lee Shubert as Lee's right-hand man for ten years. John's dream was to open his own theater, and he did so in Warren, Ohio, and it became a huge success. The format was nothing short of clever for a theater in the middle of Ohio. John would bring in stars from the stage, movies, and television like Ethel Merman, Rock Hudson, Merv Griffin, Bobby Rydell, Tab Hunter, Emogene Cocoa, and Jayne Mansfield. Audiences flocked to the theater.

John dressed as a man for the theatre season. When the season was over, he moved to Florida as a woman. I enjoyed his company very much because he was warm and exciting to be around.

The play John hired me for was *Marriage Go Round*. I was thrilled to hear I would perform with Vivian Blaine, well known for her outstanding film and stage performances. When they told me the suave French actor Louis Jourdan had agreed to play the husband, I was in seventh heaven.

Allow me to digress again.

Speaking of Frenchmen, in the early sixties, Paramount Studios hired me several years before to be in an additional scene for an already completed movie starring Maurice Chevalier. Maurice pushed me all day on a swing while he sang to me. He was Mr. Charming and a pleasure to work with. At the end of the day, he kissed my hand and told me how beautiful and wonderful I was to work with. He left me feeling like a million dollars—or euros— although the French currency was francs then. So, given my one experience with Maurice Chevalier and a little research, I read about how much Grace Kelly enjoyed working with Louis Jourdan and what a great kisser he was. If he was good enough for Grace, Jourdan was more than good enough for me.

On the first day, I met Louis in the lobby while we waited for our car to take us to the rehearsal hall. It was me, Jourdan, Vivian Blaine, and actor Donald Buka. The production manager apologized and told us our ride was delayed and would be thirty minutes late. Louis approached Vivian and me (not Buka, for some reason). *"Would you ladies like to join me for coffee in the restaurant?"* Vivian and I accepted. To our surprise—or should I say, to our embarrassment—Louis instructed the waiter to bring three separate checks. Vivian and I looked at each other. *"I'll get it,"* I said. *"Okay, I'll leave a tip,"* Vivian quickly added.

Now, this was back in 1970 when a cup of coffee was less than a buck. We couldn't believe that this suave Frenchman wanted to split the check. What made it even worse was Mr. Jourdan was paid ten thousand a week to appear in the play. Go figure.

Working with Louis was nice because he showed up perfectly at rehearsal. The bad thing was he never changed the way he said his lines, from the first day of rehearsals to closing night. No matter how we interpreted a line, Louis would consistently deliver his lines the same way every time, down to the slightest nuance.

I was worried I was having trouble pronouncing the one and the only line I had to say in French. I went to

Louis, sitting doing nothing, and asked him if he would help me with the correct pronunciation of that one line since he was the only one there who spoke French. Unsmiling, he said no, it wasn't his job to be the dialogue coach. He was sitting on his ass contemplating his navel, doing nothing! I couldn't believe my ears!

I wasn't the only one having trouble with Louis' snotty French attitude. One night, Vivian and I were having dinner after the show when she asked me what I thought of his kissing. I told her, *"Vivian, it's like kissing a block of wood. He kept his mouth as tightly closed as possible as if he was afraid he would catch some disease or I would try and stick my tongue down his damn French throat."* Vivian laughed, *"Oh, thank God; I thought it was just me."*

My kissing scene with him was a bit more involved than Vivian's. We had to end the scene with a kiss that required us to lock lips on lips for several minutes. Jourdan acted like having to kiss me was so disdainful he struggled to keep from vomiting. No exaggeration. During the scene, his lips would stay on mine; his mouth closed shut, pressing so hard that I couldn't move them. That is, except for one night. He opened his mouth so wide he took in my entire mouth and ninety percent of my nose. It was difficult to catch a breath from the small amount of my nostril that was still free. I'm not exaggerating. When the scene was over, he didn't say a word. He left the stage as if everything was normal. I never mentioned it to Leslie Cutler, the director; I thought I would wait and see if Louis did it again. Thankfully, he didn't.

A few weeks into the show, Louis' wife came to visit. Vivian and I were expecting a real bitch. Boy, were we wrong! The lady was beautiful and charming and would join us for drinks, something her husband never did. Mr. Jourdan's only drink with us was in that coffee shop, and Vivian and I *paid for it*.

Vivian married Stuart Clark, who was not in show business. They moved close to me in Los Angeles, and I saw them frequently. As for Louis, what can I say? He was great to work with (except for that kiss) and is one tight-ass *Frenchman*.

Chapter 39

In 1972, I received a desperate call from the Alhambra Dinner Theatre in Jacksonville, Florida. They had opened *Pajama Tops* with Joy Lansing in the lead, but Joy had become sick and had to take leave. I knew Joy, but only slightly. We had met at a few functions, and once I was seated next to her at a private dinner party. The few times we were together, I found Joy a delightful and interesting lady.

Joy's tests confirmed she had cancer and had to undergo immediate surgery. The theater management knew I had toured with *Pajama Tops* and had performed in the role on Broadway. They expressed a script to me with a few changes from the Broadway show. I agreed to take over for Joy. When I arrived, I had only one day to work on the blocking before the show opened.

HOLLYWOOD OR BUST!

When Joy returned to Los Angeles, she underwent major surgery. Unfortunately, the surgery could not save her, and her cancer recurred. Sadly, Joy died on August 7, 1972. If you are ever in Hollywood and walking by 6259 Hollywood Boulevard, please look down, and you will see Joy's star on the Hollywood Walk of Fame. She is not forgotten.

As for the show, it went very well. Ted Johnson, the theater's owner, was great to work for. And considering we only had one day to rehearse, the director, George Ballis, did a fantastic job getting the show up and running again.

When *Pajama Tops* closed in Jacksonville, I fell into my usual Sunday night routine in LA: the Playboy mansion or dinner at Matteo's Restaurant with Maurice Duke and the boys. I had been working nonstop for months and needed another break to recoup. It's not the show that saps your strength; as I said, it's the endless promotion with the press, radio, and television. The rule is and remains; if you want a full house, you keep promoting; there's no getting around it, so I do what is required with a smile. Whatever crazy idea the press agents thought up, I'll do it.

There was one hectic promotion I clearly remember, and that was the Phil Donahue Show. Back then, Phil's TV show broadcast live from Dayton, Ohio, and enjoyed a loyal following. So, when Phil invited me to be a guest, I accepted—I'd be crazy not to. Like I said before, my parents didn't raise no dummy.

Unfortunately, there was a distance problem. Phil was in Dayton, and I was performing on stage in Cleveland. Phil's answer to the problem was to send a helicopter to pick me up and take me back. I tried not to act frightened, but it was my first time in a helicopter. I don't like to fly unless I have to, let alone a helicopter. I have known too many people who have died in helicopters. But trooper that I am, I always do what needs to be done, like it or not. I did Phil's show, and they flew me back to Cleveland in that scary helicopter.

My business manager Saul Lazarow invited a new client and me for dinner. The client was not your usual show business hotshot. He was a professor at Yale and Harvard Universities. He had written a screenplay, and to his good fortune, Paramount Studios optioned it. But first, Paramount wanted him to turn it into a novel, which, if successful, would be an excellent promotional tool for the eventual release of the movie version. Boy, were they ever right! The book, *Love Story*, became the number one bestseller in the United States and was translated into twenty-five languages worldwide. Saul's new client was non-other than Professor Erich Segal.

I expected to meet a middle-aged egghead, bald with dark-framed glasses. That turned out not to be the case by a country mile. Erich was a handsome young man and an accomplished athlete who ran in each Boston marathon between 1955 and 1975. After our dinner, Erich asked to see me again the next day, and the next, and the next. It seems he was captivated by little Baby June. Saul told me that when they were together, he quickly tired of Erich always talking about me; I thought that was very sweet.

One thing I enjoyed about Erich was his zest for life. However, he would act like a kid if he happened to spot someone famous. It surprised me how star-struck he

HOLLYWOOD OR BUST!

was, especially since he had written the script *Yellow Submarine* for the Beatles, who was number one in the world then. There was something very endearing about someone so intelligent and, suddenly, in the rich and famous category. But he still got a thrill from meeting or seeing someone he admired.

As I sit here writing, I'm smiling, thinking about a phone call I got from our mutual business manager Saul. He had just finished meeting with Erich about his upcoming promotional tour in Japan to promote *Love Story*. Erich wanted them to postpone the trip for a month so he could learn enough of the language so he could do his interviews in Japanese. That was Erich, ever the intellectual.

Although I was on the road again for most of that year, Erich and I spoke on the phone regularly. A few times, he surprised me by showing up with the excuse he was there for a meeting or on a book lecture tour. One time I surprised him. I was opening in Boston at the Shubert Theater, and Erich was running in the Boston marathon. I arrived about an hour after the race had begun. Thank goodness I had a warm coat on because it was freezing. I did my best to be incognito, but with all the press there, before long, I was recognized.

I don't recall how long it took Eric to finish. His best time had been in 1964, at two hours, fifty-eight minutes, and thirty seconds. It was inspiring and emotional when the first few runners appeared on the horizon. The crowd went wild, but Erich wasn't among the runners. He showed up about an hour later with a larger group. I moved closer to the finish line so Erich would see. When he did, he moved toward me as he neared the finish line.

He crossed the line, then dramatically fell in my arms like the end of a mediocre *B* movie.

I loved it, and the press loved it!

Erich sent me an excerpt from an interview he did for a newspaper. It read: *"I have been incredibly busy the last two years. I have been teaching full-time at Harvard. During the same time, I've written a musical comedy with Richard Rodgers that has gone through eighteen drafts to date. I wrote Yellow Submarine for the Beatles. I wrote Love Story, both the novel and the screenplay. I wrote R.P.M. for director Stanley Kramer. I also wrote two scholarly books and a four 400-page translation ... and dated June Wilkinson."*

My show was doing very well, and I had finished most of the press promotions by the end of my first week. So, when Erich invited me to one of his lectures at Harvard, I accepted. When I arrived, the place was packed. I had expected the lecture would take place in a classroom. Wrong again! It was a theatre with almost as many seats as where I was performing, except our theater had regular comfortable theatre seats; these were the wooden stackable chairs. I found a seat at the back. Erich came onto the stage. His so-called lecture was like nothing I'd ever seen before. Erich was performing, not lecturing. He was all over the stage, running and jumping up and down, sitting on the edge with unbelievable energy and passion as he spoke. What a great show—I mean, lecture.

I read an article by Doonesbury cartoonist Gary Trudeau about the so-called lecture. Trudeau described Erich perfectly; *"Erich Segal, renowned for his lectures, prowled the stage brimming with excitement and erudition. All that and a sharp brain too. The students and everyone else there*

HOLLYWOOD OR BUST!

loved him."

Not to shift gears, but to shift gears, Eric Segal's brain reminds me that I haven't talked about my baby brother John. When John was five, I left home to work in the Windmill Theatre. Three years later, I left for America. While I was gone, John grew tall and slender, but his most significant development was his brain. John was always the brainy one in the family. He was the head of his class, and his teachers loved him. They were thrilled to have a student in public school who they felt would get a full scholarship to college.

Remember, England was still recovering from the war in the fifties, and very few scholarships were awarded. My Dad thought all this fuss about getting John into college was a waste of time. *"Only the rich went to college,"* he argued. Dad also believed that the upper and lower classes never mixed. What made Dad happy was John played in the school band. His instrument was the cello, but Dad thought the cello was only for the upper class—John proved him wrong. And, bless his heart, my baby brother John received a full scholarship to Cambridge University.

Chapter 40

Following my stint in Boston, I flew to New York at the invitation of Alexander Cohen, one of Broadway's most successful producers. Alexander produced *Hellzapoppin*, starring comedian *Soupy Sales,* and plans were in the works to produce it as a TV special. Alexander inquired whether I would be interested in appearing in skits with the comics. It was to be shot in Los Angeles. Yes, I was thrilled and told him I would!

I was anticipating my return to Los Angeles and my little piece of heaven in the Hollywood Hills. *She She* was pleased to be home, also. She must have peed a hundred times on the grass and ran free up and down the enclosed hillside below my property.

I was getting ready to start rehearsals for *Hellzapoppin* when I received a call from the production staff. They asked me to come for a meeting the day before rehearsals were to start. When I arrived, I was sent into a room with girls who looked like they belonged to the chorus. A heavyset lady entered the room, approached me, and introduced herself (I don't remember her name). She told me in an off-handed way, *"Miss Wilkinson, I know Mr. Cohen would like you to be in the show, but I'm not sure we can use you. We need someone who can dance."* My lips curled into a grin, *"No problem,"* I told her, *"I am a dancer."* She added, somewhat arrogantly, *"Well, you must be able to tap dance."* I gave her a look, stood up, did the time step, then the double time step and the triple, and sat down. She stared at me momentarily, didn't say anything, and turned and left. She was clearly trying to find a way to get rid of me, but for what reason, I had no idea. When I returned home, I called Alexander Cohen's office in New York and told them what had happened. The lady I was speaking to told me to hold on. A few minutes later, she was back on. *"Miss Wilkinson, rehearsals start tomorrow, and we absolutely want you there."*

That settled that.

On the first day of rehearsals, I felt like I was back at the Windmill Theatre. The stage was busy with stagehands and crew setting things up. I was told it would be forty minutes before they were ready for the cast, and I should take a seat out front. The seats were empty except for one person sitting and sipping a cup of coffee. He introduced himself as Marc Richards, then excused himself and said he would be back. He returned with a cup of coffee and handed it to me. Every morning, Marc would greet me with a hot coffee. That was the start of another wonderful lifelong friendship. There, you see, there is more than one gentleman in the world.

Marc was the writer of the New York revival of *Hellzapoppin*. He and I were the only ones hired by Alexander Cohen. That may have accounted for the unfriendly attitude we both had received from the California office. Marc was a great writer, and although he was on the payroll, they never once asked for his input. It was their loss.

I enjoyed working with everyone in the cast, especially Jack Cassidy and Ronnie Schell. Their roles were to mirror Rowan and Martin from laugh-In. Although Jack Cassidy was more of a leading man, he had a good singing voice, a good sense of humor, was charming, and was a bit of a rogue. Lynn Redgrave, also in the show, was a member of an English family I was very familiar with. Her father, actor Michael Redgrave, was knighted, *Sir Michael Redgrave*. Her sister Vanessa is one of the all-time great actresses and was nominated at least five times for an Oscar and won for her role in the movie *Julia*.

Lou Wills, one of Maurice Duke's buddies, was also cast in the show. He had appeared in *Hellzapoppin* in New York in 1943 and was a great entertainer from the old school. Later, Lou became a producer, and we worked on several films together. Small world indeed.

On the third day of shooting, I noticed a young boy about eleven years old following me around. He was working hard at not being noticed. I turned around fast and said, *"boooooo!"* He jumped back a step and grinned from ear to ear. It was Michael Jackson. He and his brothers were also appearing in the show. *"Are you following me?"* I asked. His face stretched into a wide grin, and he sheepishly said, *"You have the biggest boobs I've ever seen."* All I could do was laugh, and so did Michael. He hugged me around my waist and ran away. How could I get mad at him? He was so adorable.

The brothers were billed as *Michael Jackson and the Jackson Five*. Boy, what incredible talent! There was something magical about Michael that the whole world would come to know. He was mesmerizing when singing and dancing; you couldn't take your eyes off him. Yet, as the world would discover, Michael's life was tragically sad in many ways. The day he died, all I could think of was the first time I saw that adorable, fun-loving little face following me around on the set of *Hellzapoppin*.

When I think I'm hot stuff, I remember the talented Lyle Waggoner, who was also in the show. Lyle and I didn't share any direct interaction. As everyone knows, Lyle would hit his stride as a cast member in the hugely successful *Carol Burnett Show*. Years later, I bumped into Lyle with my then-husband, Dan Pastorini, and he didn't remember me. I told him we were in *Hellzapoppin* together. He said the only thing he remembered about the show was a skit that he thought was so funny he couldn't stop laughing. A girl, he said (me), with large breasts, played the accordion. She pretended the accordion squashed her breasts, then screamed and ran off stage. Huh, so much for my talent! Maybe Lyle didn't recognize me because bust implants were popular in the late 70s, and some were so big they made me look like Twiggy. Well, not quite, but almost.

Like many men in the business, Jack Cassidy was a bit

of a womanizer. But he was a loveable rogue with a great sense of humor. Once he realized he wouldn't get me into the sack, we became good friends. Jack was married to the very talented and beautiful actress Shirley Jones, but at that time, they had separated, so I gave him a pass for his passes.

Unfortunately, despite all the outstanding talent who appeared in the show, it received only so-so reviews when it aired. But there were negotiations to pick it up as a weekly show. However, only three of us were chosen for the new version: Ronnie Schell, Jack Cassidy, and me, Baby June.

As I said, Jack was a bit of a rogue and had a keen eye for the ladies. He had moved into a lovely house in a gated area of Hidden Hills and invited me to dinner to see the place. Following dinner, we sat around telling stories. I had been there long after I had planned to leave when the doorbell rang. Jack's face slackened, and his eyes went wide. He glanced at his watch and sheepishly apologized to me. He had arranged for two party girls to spend the late hours with him, presumably after I left. *"Don't worry about it, Jack; my fault for not being a party girl."* I quietly slipped out the back door. That wasn't the only time. I was at Jack's house for lunch one fine day when another lady showed up. It was Yvonne Craig, the actress from the television series *Batman*. My, Jack did keep himself busy.

As for the proposed *Hellzapoppin* series, Ronnie, Jack, and I finally got the bad news: the network decided not to pick it up as a series. To say I was disappointed is a considerable understatement, but life and show business stop for no one.

HOLLYWOOD OR BUST!

Chapter 41

Producer Zev Bufman called my agent and offered me the role of Mary in the stage play *Norman Is That You*. I received an offer to rent my house while I was gone, which I had never done. Saul, my business manager, was all for it. So, I rented it to Gene Shiverly and Fred Mitchell, both in the record business and very nice guys. Their friend, Tom Owens, wanted to rent my tiny guest house, which was fine with me. Tom suggested I let the pool man and gardener go; he would prefer to do the work himself. Not having to pay for a pool man or gardener saved me a lot, but more importantly, I always felt safe leaving Tom in charge.

Norman Is That You, written by Ron Clark and Sam Bobrick, was about a Jewish couple struggling to accept their son as a homosexual. The play opened on

Broadway in 1970 and was directed and produced by George Abbott. The cast included Maureen Stapleton, an actress I adored. It only ran for nineteen performances on Broadway, but when I read it, I loved it. It might have failed on Broadway because it was the first time Broadway tackled homosexuality.

The production would star Milton Berle. I knew Milton; he was one of Maurice Duke's cronies and occasionally would join the boys at Matteo's. The Director was Danny Simon, the brother of writer Neil Simon. According to Danny, he, not Neil, was the one who came up with the idea for the Broadway hit, *The Odd Couple*. The idea came to him during his divorce when he moved in with one of his buddies. According to Danny, he wrote the first act and then gave it to his brother Neil to finish. The rest, as they say, is show business history.

On the first day of rehearsals, Milton made sure everyone knew he was the star and in charge. It wasn't his ego. It was his professionalism; he wanted it perfect. There was one scene where Milton demanded precise timing. It was the scene where the parents found out that their son was gay. Milton was right because it was one of the show's best moments with one of the funniest lines. Milton drove the Director and me crazy working on the timing. We must have spent two days on that one scene.

The stage was split into two rooms. A front door stage left opened into a living room that took up three-quarters of the stage. At the back of the set was the bedroom door that opened into the living room. A wall came to the edge of the stage, dividing the bedroom

HOLLYWOOD OR BUST!

from the living room, giving the audience a full view of both rooms. Unknown to the parents, their son rented out the spare room to a stunningly beautiful and sexy female, played by none other than—you guessed it—me! Okay, so I got a lot of help from makeup and lighting, but you get the picture.

The scene starts when Milton and his wife come to the front door, find it unlocked, push it open, and slowly walk in. At that moment, I'm getting out of bed dressed in a baby doll nightgown, and I'm supposed to walk into the living room where Milton looks at me and thinks I'm his son who has had a sex change. With a look of horror, Milton says, *"Norman, is that you!?"*

After two full days of perfecting our timing, Milton walks in, and instead of looking around the room while I slowly get out of bed, he starts the line just as I begin to stretch. I hear Milton begin to say, "Norman, is—?" I rush out of bed and haul ass to the door before Milton finishes the line. The cast could not stop laughing when the curtain came down, although Milton didn't find it funny. After all our rehearsing, Milton—known for his impeccable comedic timing—had screwed up big time.

Back in Los Angeles at Matteo's, Uncle Milties' buddies wanted to know how the show went. I told them it went just fine, but I never revealed Milton's goof because they would have driven him nuts, never letting him forget it.

I never tired of getting back into the Los Angeles social scene. Johnnie Ray had moved from New York with his new boyfriend, Bill Franklyn, who had become his manager. They rented a beautiful place on Malibu

Beach but gave it up when they toured Europe with the great Judy Garland. When Johnny returned, he rented a house just down the hill from me off Queen Street off Sunset Blvd. Bill remained his manager, but Bill decided to no longer live together as lovers. I never learned why, and I didn't ask. However, whenever Johnnie needed to show up someplace with a hot female date, I was it.

From when I first met Johnnie in England—remember, I was just sixteen—I've always had a plutonic soft spot in my heart for him; we were like brother and sister. I wish the public could have known Johnnie the way I did. He was one of a kind and the sweetest man I knew. He was such a great entertainer; when he was performing, I'd get goosebumps; he was that good. Of course, there were times when he wasn't at his best for whatever reason, but we won't talk about that. Everyone has their off days.

My friend Wilfred Tsang called from San Francisco. He was invited to a party at comedian Buddy Hackett's Malibu beach house and wanted me to join him. On the day of the party, it was sweltering. Hot pants were in, as was the bra-less look. My dressmaker, Jimmy, had just made me a pair of cotton hot pants with an opaque top with the same print as the pants. The top was backless and looked like a scarf tied behind the neck that draped over and down, covering my breasts. It fit perfectly to my body unless I did a handstand, which meant my breasts would have been on full display. God forbid!

When we arrived at the Hackett's, the guests were dressed in fancy jeans, swimsuits, and bikinis, so I felt my outfit was perfect for the occasion. There were many celebrities in attendance. As we entered the living room, a short, stocky, loud-mouthed lady sitting at the end looked at me and screamed at the top of her lungs: *"Everyone, look at that broad. Oh boy, I'm so lucky. I had that exact outfit on, but at the last second, I decided to change."* It was non-other than the wonderful comedienne Totie Fields. She didn't say it to be mean but to get a laugh, and she did.

Buddy Hackett, standing beside me, took the end of the scarf and lifted it, exposing my breasts. I stepped back and pulled my top down, but not before Buddy's wife, Sherry, snapped a picture. She introduced herself and thanked me for being such a good sport; everyone laughed and applauded.

The day following the party at the Hackett's, I got a call from non-other than Secretary of State Henry Kissinger, who had been at Hackett's party along with his date, actress Jill St. John. *"How did you get my number, Mr. Kissinger? It's not listed."* Henry replied in his deep voice, *"Miss Wilkinson, there is no such thing as an unlisted phone number if you work in the White House."*

Duh, June, you dummy, did you happen to forget the man works for the President of the United States?

Henry asked if he could take me to dinner, and, of course, I was flattered, so I accepted. When Henry arrived to pick me up, two bodyguards accompanied him; they remained outside my front door. We enjoyed a glass of wine and chit-chatted for about forty minutes. I'm not sure what I expected, but Henry was engaging with a good sense of humor—neither of which I was expecting. He asked if there was any particular restaurant I had in mind for dinner. I did not. He suggested we drive along the Sunset Strip and pick one we liked. Then he remembered one he had visited, a trendy place that guaranteed a long line waiting. *"Not to worry, we'll go there,"* Henry casually said.

When we arrived, as expected, there was a long line. A man was standing at the door with a clipboard and pen. He recognized Henry, and, to my surprise, he ushered us past the line. I can only imagine what those in line were thinking. The restaurant was full; there wasn't an empty table. All eyes turned to us, or more precisely, to Henry. He requested two tables, one for us and one for the secret service agents required to sit near him. In a matter of seconds, waitpersons showed up with two tables and placed them down in front. Henry leaned to me and whispered in his distinct voice, *"When I am no longer in office, I must remember not to come back to these restaurants. I will miss not getting this fine service when I am a civilian."*

Dinner that evening was pleasant, and I enjoyed Henry's company. He was easy to talk to, just another delightful human whose company I enjoyed. We made another dinner date, but Henry had to break it when he and President Nixon traveled to China. As for me, I was off on another road trip to Texas.

Chapter 42

I played theatres across Texas, beginning in Houston, then Dallas and Fort Worth, in theaters operated by the Windmill Dinner Theatre chain. It was the first time I performed in a dinner theatre. I knew I would have to tone down my volume, not use a natural voice like in a movie, and not be as loud as in a large auditorium. I was looking forward to this new challenge, as I do all new challenges.

Finally, it was opening night, and we had an oversold house. Management was going crazy trying to find places to add chairs. I could hear everything said on the stage because all the dressing rooms had speakers. Before the show began, the manager stood on the stage, spoke to the audience about the show, and then announced that Dan Pastorini, the quarterback for the

Houston Oilers, was in the audience. The crowd went wild! I turned to my dresser and asked what a quarterback was. He looked at me like maybe I was stupid before patiently explaining that the quarterback was the team's captain. Ah, I got it.

Little did I know Dan Pastorini, the famous quarterback, was about to enter my world, and my life would change forever, and not necessarily for the better.

Thankfully, the show was going well. After the opening night performance, management hosted a party for the press and special guests. Mr. Pastorini, *The Quarterback*, was in attendance. He was quite handsome and looked about my age; I was 32 then. Good looks were never the most important thing to me because Hollywood was full of handsome jerks, but Dan had a unique look about him—at least, that was how I saw him.

Mr. Pastorini had come to the show with a local female sports reporter. It was apparent to me that she had the hots for him. Someone introduced me to Dan, and we talked for about ten minutes before the press encouraged us to dance together for a photo op. Rule number one; never miss a photo op. Rule number two; never miss a photo op. Dan and I danced and made small talk as a photographer shot away.

The party was in full swing, but I was tired. I snuck out with Bill Browder, who took me back to my hotel. An hour later, I got a call from the lobby—it was Dan Pastorini, *The Quarterback*. He wanted to come up and visit. I was about to say *no*, that it was too late. Bill had the room next to me with a connecting door that was ajar. Bill was gay, in case you all have forgotten, and wanted to know who was calling. I whispered that it was

HOLLYWOOD OR BUST!

Dan Pastorini asking if he could come up. Bill grinned. *"Then let him, girl; he's a big shot quarterback. I'm just next door if there's a problem."*

Dan walked into my room with a cup of coffee in each hand. There were two beds; I sat on one, and Dan sat on the other. Before we knew it, daylight began to filter into the room. Dan only had a few hours before he was due at practice and asked to lie down. We both fell asleep with our clothes on, he on one bed, me on the other. When I finally woke up, the handsome quarterback from the Houston Oilers was gone.

To cut right to the chase, we had both felt a strong attraction that night, and Dan and I were together almost every day from then on. A strong attraction is not to be denied. After each show, he was waiting to take me to dinner. Before long, as expected, the news leaked out, and the press had a field day with our budding romance.

I visited Dan at his house. Now, I admit I'm not a great cook, but I've gotten pretty good over the years. Back then, I had a breakfast recipe that one of Johnnie Ray's friends gave me after finding only orange juice and a bottle of Champagne in my frig.

The recipe was for Italian eggs, guaranteed to impress whomever I made it for. Luckily, I had the recipe in my address book. So, looking in Dan's refrigerator, I found all the ingredients I needed and made Italian eggs for him. The eggs turned out fabulous. Dan, the Italian quarterback, loved them. The way to a man's heart is over his taste buds to his stomach. A year passed before he realized it was the only recipe I could cook.

Halfway through my time in Houston, I got a call

that gave me chills. I don't know where they got their information, but the police told me they had received a tip that a woman was Dan Pastorini's girlfriend and threatened to kill me if I didn't stop seeing her boyfriend. The police contacted Dan about who he had dated and if it could be one of them. It bothered him so much that he hired a bodyguard for me. But after about a month and nothing had happened, I told Dan not to waste his money. I preferred to take my chances. They never did find out who the lady might have been. If whoever she was had confronted me, I would have strangled her for the inconvenience she caused us.

Bill Cosby, who I knew, was in town and invited me to join him and his friends after the show. I told him I had a date with Dan Pastorini but suggested they join us. *"No, but thank you, June,"* Bill said, *"I have to give that poor boy a chance to complete one pass this season."* I thought that was hilarious, but I didn't think Dan would appreciate the joke, so I never told him.

My time in Houston was coming to an end. Three days before I was to leave, Dan and I were eating at the International House of Pancakes. Houston was one of the bigger cities in Texas, but after 10 PM, the only places open were fast food restaurants. Believe it or not, Dan proposed to me in the House of Pancakes. Certainly not the most romantic setting, but I heard myself saying, "Yes." Mr. Quarterback must have been damn sure of himself because he had an engagement/wedding ring specially made for me that he designed. The ring was stunningly beautiful.

Our engagement was the talk of the town, and it made all the papers and TV news. But, as fate would

HOLLYWOOD OR BUST!

have it, getting married was difficult.

A week after our official engagement, Dan got an emergency call from his family. His father had suffered a heart attack, and the family didn't know if he would make it. Bud Adams, the Oilers owner, loaned Dan his private jet. Dan flew out and was home within hours, only to learn there was nothing wrong with his father. It seems Mr. Pastorini received a call from a friend who told him Dan's fiancé I appeared in Playboy Magazine several times and women were only featured in Playboy if they slept with Hugh Hefner. Nothing could have been more outrageous. I was, at the time, the most photographed pin-up in the world, so in Dan's father's eyes, I had to be a slut who slept with Hefner.

When Dan returned, he told me what had happened. He was furious. He couldn't forgive his father for faking a heart attack to get him home so his father could dump that ridiculous rumor on him. We decided then and there *to hell with family*; we would go on a cruise and get married on board a ship as soon as my contract was up. The show moved to Dallas, but we both had Mondays off, and I was in close driving range to Houston, so we got to spend time together.

I have to tell you of an incident I thought was hilarious. Unfortunately, Dan failed to appreciate the humor.

Whenever Dan flew, he was always the last one off the plane. I never did know why. After the last season game, just before the Christmas holidays, Dan flew to Dallas to be with me. It was snowing and very cold. I wore thigh-high white boots, 6-inch heels, and sexy white lace panties. Otherwise, I was naked under a white fur coat. A bundled-up he descended the stairs of the plane alone. When he reached the bottom, he saw me in the distance. I opened my coat, gave him a quick flash of my semi-naked body, and said, *"Welcome home, Baby."*

The boy was not amused.

Our first Christmas together was picture-perfect. It was snowing, and we spent Christmas Day with Craig Morton, an alternate quarterback for the Cowboys, and several other players, their wives, and girlfriends. A big pot of chili was simmering, sent by a friend of Dan's who owned one of the more popular restaurants in town.

After Dallas, the next theatre was the Windmill in Fort Worth, so Dan and I got to see a lot of each other on our days off. Next, we moved to a theatre in Scottsdale, Arizona, so being together suddenly wasn't as easy. Dan flew in to stay for a couple of weeks when the football season was over. The weather was beautiful, and I remember we had a wonderful time together during those weeks.

Although we had not told them, someone snitched, and Dan's parents learned we were planning to get married at sea. They begged Dan not to since they wanted to attend the wedding. However, he was still upset over his father's false heart attack and was ready to say no to them, but he gave in. So, with trepidation and thoughts of my mother, who would be thrilled to be at my wedding too, I agreed the cruise was off. It was more my wanting my mother to be with us than it was to accommodate Dan's parents.

The next day, while we were sunbathing by the pool and looking up at the mountains, we both had the same thought; the mountain would be a beautiful spot to get

HOLLYWOOD OR BUST!

married. So, on my day off, we drove as far as we could up the mountain, then hiked up into the area we thought was the most beautiful, which it was, but it was freezing up there. We looked at each other without saying a word, turned around, and headed back to the car, joking about getting married on a lump of ice. I remembered telling Dan, *"What, tell your parents it would be great to be married on the mountain, except everyone would be frozen stiff before I said 'I do.'"*

Scottsdale was the end of my contract. Management wanted to add six months, but I declined; getting married was number one on my list. Although I wasn't crazy about the idea, we agreed to spend a couple of weeks at Dan's parents' home in San Jose, California. They had owned a small restaurant but were now retired. I called my Mum and broke the news that I was getting married. I told her I would fly her to America for the wedding as soon as we had confirmed the date. She was so thrilled.

While visiting Dan's parents, we spent a day walking around Carmel. We saw a beautiful inn overlooking the ocean and decided to have lunch there. Later, as we continued walking around, we came across a tiny chapel connected to the hotel. Once again, great minds think alike; This chapel in this setting was the perfect place to get married and was within driving distance of most of Dan's relatives. Those I would invite lived in San Francisco or Los Angeles within easy driving distance. Dan and I set a date for the wedding, and I began making the arrangements.

Although I was not Catholic, Dan's family was, so I agreed to a Catholic ceremony to please them; it would help my shaky relationship with my future in-laws. I asked Bill Browder to walk me down the aisle. I invited his then-partner, Jack Cook, Ray Locke, Ronny Schnell, Johnnie Ray, Maurice Duke, his buddies, Kenny Rogers, his wife, and others. Neither Dan nor I wanted a big fancy wedding; we just wanted to get married. When Johnnie Ray heard there was a piano in the chapel, he offered to play and sing as guests arrived for the ceremony.

My Mum flew in from England, and we found her a dress for the wedding. I was thrilled to have her there with me and would have been heartbroken if she had not. God love him; Dan designed a wedding dress for me that I had made by a dressmaker who did an excellent job. Dan declined to wear a tux, much to his parent's disapproval. Instead, he had made a unique white lace shirt with large wide sleeves, a white vest, and white pants. His parents, as I suspected they would be, were horrified! Stubborn Dan stood fast and wore what he wanted.

Then, as if we didn't have enough interruption in our plans, all hell broke loose.

Dan's parents received a call from a couple whose young son idolized Dan. Dan had made an appearance at a youth football camp and was very gracious to their son. When they found out he was getting married to June Wilkinson, they felt obligated to tell Dan and his parents the bride-to-be was, in fact, a prostitute. What? Where the hell did they hear that? Whoever this friend was claimed to know who my pimp was; it was none other than Marty Barth. *Marty Barth?* My God!

The only Marty Barth I knew was Charlie Chaplin

HOLLYWOOD OR BUST!

Junior's best friend, who was so kind to me in my teens. The same Marty Barth that took me wherever I needed to go when I needed a ride. This was insane! Who were these people, and where did they get such vile and hurtful information? I told Bill Browder what had happened. He agreed that it was best to postpone the wedding until it was all straightened out. Dan was livid that his parents would believe such an outrageous story.

I was desperately trying to find Marty Barth, but none of the old numbers were still good, and since Charlie Chaplin Jr. had died, I couldn't find anyone who knew Marty. After a week of going slightly insane, I remembered Marty had a brother who worked for the LA police department. I called and asked if they had a Mr. Barth working there. I hit the jackpot! Marty's brother was second in command! When they put me through, he confirmed he was Marty's brother but told me Marty had passed away a few years back. I explained who I was and why I was calling. He laughed and said, *"Excuse me for laughing, June, but this is hilarious. Considering who you are, if my brother had been your pimp, he would have been driving a Rolls Royce, not the beat-up old clunkers he drove. Give me Dan's parent's number, and I'll straighten them out. I'll also find out who called Dan's father and put the fear of God in whoever it is for passing along this unsubstantiated and vile rumor."*

It must have worked because Dan's parents never mentioned it again. Shame on them for believing such an outrageous story in the first place.

Bill Browder would give me away, and George Webster was Dan's best man. Sadly, Johnnie Ray was scheduled to be out of the country for our chosen date and couldn't be with us. I was heartbroken. We decided to have some fun with the music. Dan and I picked the songs: *Wedding Bells Are Breaking Up That Old Gang of Mine, Get Me to The Church on Time, June Is Busting Out All Over, You Gotta Be a Football Hero.* You must admit we at least kept our sense of humor.

Maurice Duke called. He didn't want to make the journey in case our date changed again but promised to throw us a party when we returned to Los Angeles. Then, a day later, Duke called again. He was upset and yelling so loud everyone could hear him. Duke was furious that I had turned down an engagement with the theater folks in Texas because I was busy arranging our wedding. Duke made it clear he was upset with us, Dan, his parents, and me. *"I can't believe you turned down big dollars for that f—king asshole."*

That pissed me off because Dan's parents were in the room. I wanted to get Duke off the phone and told him I'd call him back. Dan's father, never to be outdone, wanted to know why I had turned down that much money. I didn't think it was any of his damn business, but that should have been confirmation I was not marrying Dan for his money.

About four days before the wedding day, I got a call from Dan's family priest, who said he wanted to speak with me. Dan went with me. This holier-than-thou priest informed Dan we couldn't get married until I went through six months of counseling on all the church's rules. Huh? Was he nuts? I put up enough of a fuss that he changed his tune. We could go ahead with the wedding if I had not previously been married, which I wasn't. I had to agree to bring up any children we had together as Catholics. I had it with this guy, stood up, and told Dan the meeting was over, and I was leaving. Dan was as upset as I over what had just come out of this priest's mouth. I've wondered if that priest was in cahoots with Dan's parents. I was livid; I told Dan that any ceremony *but Catholic* would do just fine.

I spent the night before the wedding at the Highlands Inn. Dan spent his final night as a bachelor with his buddies and close friend Martha Locke, who had flown in from Houston to attend the wedding. As we women always try to stick together, Martha shared with me that some jerk in the family had made the stupid statement that I would never have children because I wouldn't want to ruin my body. Does it never end with these jerks?

The ceremony went off without a hitch, and I was happy my mother was there to share it with us. We celebrated with lunch in a private room, and everyone seemed to get along. Poor Kenny Rogers and his wife arrived several hours late because they had gotten lost. As a consolation, the four of us had dinner that night. Then Dan and I went to our suite at the Highlands Inn as man and wife. Whew, we had finally got it done.

The following morning when we awoke, I turned on the TV. The host of the program was talking about our wedding. Once again, we had made the news. We ordered breakfast. Dan opened the door when it arrived, and a smiling waiter and a waitress walked in. Kenny Rogers followed them, singing a love song and strumming his guitar. Bless him; I could not think of a more romantic way to start married life! Thank you, Kenny, my friend.

Chapter 43

As the saying goes, the bad things that happen in life are sometimes for the best. I begrudgingly admit that has proven to be mostly true in my life. For example, if everything had gone as planned with the wedding, my Mum would have flown in, attended the wedding, and returned to England after a few weeks. Because of the delay of two months, she met many of my friends who fell in love with her. Mum was the best mother ever. She did everything she could to make my dreams come true. I've said it before, and I can never say it enough.

When Bill Browder told me Mum had mentioned she would love to live in America, we went to work, making it happen with the help of Maurice Duke and his lawyer buddy. They cut through the red tape and did it much faster than if I had tried to do it alone. Mum got her

HOLLYWOOD OR BUST!

green card. I had to agree to be responsible for her financially. I received my green card because I had a contract with Ray Stark, Elliot Hyman, and Paramount Studios, and I would be financially secure and able to work in America.

Dan had rented an apartment for us at the Houston complex he stayed in when he signed on with the Oilers. Here's one that should make you laugh but almost got us evicted.

It was a hot, humid day, and the parking lot at Dan's place—now our place—was in view of the crowded swimming pool. One day, we parked in the lot next to the house and prepared to go inside. I opened the car door, and *She She*, who spotted the pool, jumped out, ran, and belly-flopped into the crowded swimming pool. The people there cheered her on, but management didn't think it was funny and raised a fuss. If it happened again, they warned, we would have to move. That's when Dan and I began looking for an inexpensive place to buy. We finally settled on a small two-story townhouse on Sandpiper Avenue.

The head coach for the Oilers was Bill Peterson, who the Oilers hired away from Florida State. Under Peterson, Florida State held the best college record during his ten years as head coach. Unfortunately, Peterson's first season for the Houston Oilers proved disastrous; the team finished winning one in thirteen. I admit I didn't know much about football, but basic sense made me question many of Peterson's play choices, as Dan did. There was one play Peterson called that ticked

Dan off big time.

The game was not going well. Peterson's solution was to tell Dan about a dream he had the night before, where Dan won the game at the last second by throwing a *Hail Mary* pass, hoping one of the receivers would catch it and make a touchdown. Dan thought it was way too risky to call a pass. Peterson insisted. Dan followed orders and throw a pass, and guess what? It was intercepted! To say Dan was one pissed-off quarterback is an understatement.

Peterson was out, replaced by Sid Gillman, a cranky older man who complained a lot.

The day following a game, like clockwork, the phone would ring early in the morning, usually before we were awake. It was always Coach Gillman. *"Good morning, June; sorry to wake you, but I need to talk to Dan."* He could not wait to talk to Dan the day after every game to evaluate what went right or wrong. The last person Dan wanted to hear from was his Coach. Not only was Dan not mentally ready for these conversations early in the morning following a game, but he was also in extreme pain after every game. As it turned out, halfway through the 1975 season, Gillman decided to retire, and Bum Phillips took over as head coach. Dan and Bum hit it off right from the start.

Let me back up a bit. Once we returned to Houston after the wedding and the football season started, I noticed a gradual change in Dan. The man I fell in love with, the man who wanted to spend every second with me when I wasn't on stage, was now gone. He would leave most nights to hang out with the boys and come home in the wee hours of the morning. I called Bill

HOLLYWOOD OR BUST!

Browder in San Francisco, seeking his advice. Bill thought that maybe the stress of playing and having a losing season was the problem. Maybe Dan was depressed, and his going out was a way to deal with it. If that were true, Dan wasn't discussing it with me, and I resented that.

One of the best things that benefitted the team was when they made a deal with the Baltimore Colts to add Bill Curry to their roster. Curry's close confidant and Baltimore Colts legend, Johnny Unitas, was unceremoniously benched in 1972, and many responsible for the franchise's success in years past were shipped out of Baltimore, Bill Curry among them. Dan believed Curry would be a great addition to the Oiler's rooster.

When Bill and his family moved to Houston, Dan thought we should take them to dinner to welcome them. Since I was not a great cook, it seemed like a good idea to sign up for cooking classes, and if all went well, we would have dinner at our house. *"Don't take them out to dinner,"* I told Dan. *"Whatever I learn in today's class, I'll make for them later tonight at home."* With more than a bit of hesitation, Dan agreed. Oh boy, big mistake.

When I arrived for the class, I discovered it was about making a gourmet meal. I thought it was going to be an introductory cooking class. I had no idea we would jump right into the hard stuff. Okay, no panic; what the heck, all I had to do was to write it down step by step and get all the right ingredients. When the Currys arrived, I had everything under control—so I thought. After a few mouthfuls, Bill threw down his knife and fork and yelled, *"Dan, you son of a bitch. You took us to*

Kentucky Fried Chicken and told us to eat up because your wife can't cook! This dinner is so damn delicious, and I'm full of fried chicken and—"

That was as far as Bill got. Dan started laughing, and the Currys joined in. It's a good thing I saw the humor in Bill's joke, which I'm sure Dan put him up to. By the way, I never made that dish again.

During a brief stint with the 1973 flagging Houston Oilers, Bill Curry suffered a catastrophic leg injury when he took a hit in the back of a leg by Ram's great, Merlin Olsen. Though he did not retire until August 1975, the injury essentially ended his playing career.

HOLLYWOOD OR BUST!

Chapter 44

I signed on to appear in *Mr. & Mrs.* at the Showboat Dinner Theatre in Clearwater, Florida. I was looking forward to the show because Sherwood Schwartz, the creator of *Gilligan's Island* and *The Brady Bunch,* wrote it. Jackie Coogan, who had befriended me in Atlantic City during my first visit to America, would be my leading man. As many will remember, Jackie played Uncle Fester in the smash TV hit *The Addams Family.* Our director was the ever-capable Richard Vath, whom I first worked with at the Los Angeles Grand Theatre in Hollywood when I was nineteen, then again when I appeared on Broadway and the following road tour.

Dan flew to Clearwater to visit but didn't show much interest in the show or, for that matter, keeping me company in the dressing room. While I was on stage, he was out drinking and wouldn't return till one or two in the morning.

I remember back when Dan went to training camp in Kerrville after we married. He missed me and begged me to visit him on my day off. So, after my Sunday show with just a few hours of sleep, I drove to his hotel in Kerrville. When I arrived, Dan wasn't in his room. I found him in the coffee shop. He was thrilled to see me, left money on the table, grabbed my hand, and rushed me to his room for you know what.

Unfortunately, Dan's bad behavior would get worse. Stay tuned.

In 1974 I got a call from Massey Cramer, the co-producer of *Las Rabia*, the movie I had shot years before in Mexico. He sent me a screenplay he wanted me to read and thought I was perfect for the female lead. The story was titled *Weed* (1975), and on my first read, I loved it. I called Massey and told him I would do it. Massey told me the script's co-writer, Bob Emery, would be directing. I loved what Massey and Bob had written. It was a solid story with great characters and a lot of action. The entire film would be shot in the Florida Everglades, where I had never been.

About three weeks later, I received a call from Massey telling me he ran into a problem with his original money guys, but thankfully, a new moneyman stepped in, and the film was still a go. The new money guy, a wealthy St. Petersburg attorney, was football crazy. I've always believed that Dan's involvement in the production convinced this attorney to put up the money. So, with some trepidation on my part—it would be Dan first motion picture—we would play opposite of one another in the two title roles.

The Florida Everglades location was like a magical movie studio backlot for us, with 5,000 square miles of low-lying marsh, waterways, hidden coves, and wildlife. It was a beautiful location but in the middle of nowhere. The entire production company was housed at a beautiful nearby Everglades resort. Many locations were in and around the resort or not too far away, which was perfect because we never had to travel that far.

When we arrived, Massey introduced us to Writer/Director Bob Emery and Mister Money Man, whose name I have forgotten, nor do I care to remember. He was an ego-driven lawyer prone to loud outbursts of laughter, often for no good reason. All Mr. Money Man wanted was to sit around and chat with Dan, boring him endlessly with football talk. To Dan's credit, he was polite and listened, but I could tell he was bored with this guy.

Massey gave me a revised script that he explained had been modified by the Money Man's friend, Bill Whitlock. As it turned out, Mr. Whitlock was a private investigator who worked from time to time for Mr. Money Man's law firm and fancied himself a writer. As you will see, that turned out to be yet another disaster.

They cast Otis Sistrunk as one of the bad guys. Otis was a well-known defensive lineman for the Oakland Raiders. One evening over dinner with Otis and his wife, Otis took pleasure in reminding Dan that when Oakland played Houston, he had the pleasure of setting Dan down on the turf a few times. They both laughed about that. Otis was a sweet guy and a great player but a pretty shy person.

Anyway, back to our dinner with Massey, the director, and Mr. Money Man. After a few hours, I excused myself and went to our room. I was tired and anxious to read the revised script before I fell asleep. Unfortunately, this new version bore no resemblance to the original script Massey had sent me. This revised screenplay was terrible, obviously written by a would-be hack writer. I had to speak with Massey immediately. I got him on the phone and started in on him. I was so upset I could hardly talk. Massey politely asked me to calm down and promised we would discuss it over breakfast.

In the morning, we met alone in the dining room. Massey explained that he, too, was unhappy with the revisions. But all contracts had been signed, and the only way he could honor them was to agree to the terms set by the new Mr. Money Man, and one of them was this new writer. Mr. Money Man had never produced or been involved in any area of show business, and this was his big chance to be a movie producer. Massey's hands were tied, and he no longer had control over his production.

I met with director Bob Emery who confided in me that he told Massey that he wouldn't shoot Whitlock's mangled version of the script. Massey told Bob to shoot the film the way he wanted, hopefully fixing what would have been a terrible screenplay. I don't know how he pulled it, but Massey kept Whitlock off the set.

We started filming, Bob quietly made the necessary changes, and no one was the wiser. Mr. Money Bags hung out with Dan and Otis, mostly with Dan, when

HOLLYWOOD OR BUST!

they weren't filming. I have to give Dan credit. To keep the peace, he was very patient with Mr. Money Man.

When we would leave for a location—remember, we're in the heart of the Everglades—they would shuttle us out into the swamp in large airboats powered by a propeller mounted on the rear that resembled a colossal house fan. Once out there, all we could see were miles and miles of marsh and occasional alligators—very beautiful but dangerous. Gale DeCamp, the production manager, instructed us not to wander off the beaten path. He didn't have to tell us twice because exotic animals were everywhere, and some could prove deadly. The alligators were the most significant menace. They would wade just below the surface looking harmless while spying on animals walking along the bank. We saw one snatch a small animal into the water and devour them in seconds. Thank goodness I didn't bring *She She* with me!

Bob Emery was a lifesaver on that film. He always showed up prepared and knew exactly what he wanted. Knowing Dan wasn't an accomplished actor, he would take plenty of time with him. Bob also brought in solid character actors Bill Thurman, Frank Logan, Edward Faulkner, and Doug Vance.

That's not where the story ends; the drama continues. Mr. Money Man wrote over $80,000.00 of bad checks on the last week of the production. The film was about to sink into the marshes of the Everglades National Park, never to be seen by an audience. Bob Emery's lawyer came to the rescue. His attorney had written into Bob's agreement that he would hold a lean on the movie until he received his final payment. That meant that Bob was now the owner of the film. His lawyer arranged for other investors to step in, buy out Bob's lean, finish the production, and arrange for its distribution to movie theaters.

The new backers and the distributor changed the picture's name from *Weed* to *The Florida Connection*. Everybody thinks they're a producer in Hollywood, Florida, and elsewhere.

I worked with Bob Emery again in 2001. Bob was preparing to shoot the movie *Swimming Upstream* and wanted me to join him as a co-producer on location in Bristol, Rhode Island. The film starred two-time Emmy Award recipient Michael Moriarty, supported by Matt Czuchry, Kelly Rutherford, Elisabeth Harnois, and Ben Savage, all seasoned film and TV performers. I would be working alongside producer Tom Busch. With my extensive acting background, Bob asked me to also function as the dialogue coach, which I gladly did. We spent five lovely weeks shooting in this quaint New England seaside town, where I made many new friends. Later, the film won the best dramatic motion picture award at the Los Angeles Angel City Film Festival, which I attended with Bob, who accepted. Following its theatrical release, the movie made its TV debut on the Lifetime Movie Network.

Mr. Emery wasn't finished with me yet. In 1993, Bob created, produced, directed, and edited a series for the Starz/Encore Network titled *The Directors*. Each episode featured a single motion picture director, along with many of the stars that appeared in their films. What began as a thirteen-episode series kept getting renewed

HOLLYWOOD OR BUST!

by the network. Ultimately, Bob and his company produced 91 one-hour shows, and the series played in over 75 countries.

It was late in 2000 when Bob called and told me that producing, directing, editing the series and delivering shows on time to the network consumed his time back in the office. He could no longer continue traveling to Los Angeles or New York to oversee the taping of the shows. He hired a producer in New York City, and since I knew my way around the production process, he asked if I would take over as producer in Los Angeles. I agreed and worked on the series for five years until the last episode was delivered to the network.

I'm pleased to say that since we first met in the Florida Everglades, Bob Emery and his wife Susanne have remained close friends, and we remain in regular touch.

Chapter 45

Dan and *She She* loved to travel in a car. Dan enjoyed driving, so we would take short road trips to get away. She She loved to sit by the window with her head hanging out, letting the wind blow in her face while taking in all the scenery. We stopped in all the little out-of-the-way motels and restaurants to catch sleep and food. Those are some of the good memories.

Dan's contract with the Oilers was up. His manager, Tommy Vance, was negotiating a new contract, but it wasn't going well. My house renter, Tom Owens, had a friend with a connection to the new World Football League, and his friend had the rights to the Los Angeles franchise. The World Football League was in trouble and hanging on by a thread about to break. So, they

HOLLYWOOD OR BUST!

were delighted to do what they could to help Tommy's friend and put the screws to the NFL.

They advised Tommy to inform the Oilers the deal they were offering was not good enough. Dan was now negotiating with the Los Angeles franchise of the World Football League. When Tommy Vance told the Oiler's management, they laughed and said that the World Football League didn't have the rights to Dan, which was true.

Surprise, surprise, within hours, the rights had transferred to Los Angeles (how convenient). When the Oilers' owners discovered what was happening, they got damn nervous. We thought they might sue. But, within a very short time, Tommy made a deal for Dan with the Oilers that was the highest ever for a quarterback up until then. But, considering what players make today, Dan's contract was a joke.

After we married, Dan's big concern was always my work schedule. So, I agreed I wouldn't work during the football season, but I would begin again when the season was over, which solved that problem. There were others to come that we couldn't solve.

Two years into our marriage, Dan bought a small house in Houston about a mile from Yorktown on Sandpiper Road. During that time, Dan became very friendly with Don Ragland and his wife, Susan. Don was in the oil business and had an entire floor in a high-rise with one office he had never used. So, after a while, Don let Dan use the office and his secretary whenever needed.

The football season had just finished, and Dan was invited to play in a celebrity tennis tournament in

Canada. We thought it would be great fun, so he accepted. They would take us there and back on a private plane. When we were about to leave, I was on the phone trying to get hold of my doctor. Dan interrupted and reminded me it was time to go. I told him I was out of birth control pills and was trying to reach the doctor. He said, *"Don't you want a child?* I answered, *"Yes, of course, in which case I don't need the pills, do I?"*

The private plane that was to take us home was filled with celebrities. Jack Gilardi, a big-time theatrical agent, married to Annette Funicello, was by himself, as was actor/director Rob Reiner who was married to actress/director Penny Marshall. Bill Cosby was there with a lady who was not his wife. Once in the air, a young lady took off all her clothes and ran down the aisle, throwing her arms around a stunned Rob Reiner, standing and talking with someone seated. Rob laughed and made a joke of it. I couldn't tell if he was happy or embarrassed about what was happening. He had no idea who this young lady was, but she was making a silly fool of herself. The other ladies onboard didn't think it was funny. The stewardess took her back to her seat and told her to get dressed and remain seated for the rest of the flight, or she'd be in big trouble when we landed. We never found out why this girl did what she did. Maybe she had too much to drink or was high on some drugs.

We were only home for a week before we were off to Oklahoma for a celebrity golf tournament. At the end of the tournament, they held a black-tie dinner with entertainment and dancing to Les Brown Jr.'s band. I

HOLLYWOOD OR BUST!

knew Les and had not seen him in several years, and looking forward to catching up.

The tournament was first-class all the way. I tried to get Dan to pack a tux, knowing that the dinner would be black-tie, but, stubborn as he is, he refused. Everyone was dressed to the nines at dinner except Mr. Quarterback, who wore old worn-out jeans and a washed-out T-shirt.

When we returned to Houston, I had three days before I was off to appear at the Alhambra Theatre in Jacksonville, Florida. Dan was supposed to go with me since the football season was over.

Then the crap hit the fan.

Out of the blue, Dan informed me he wasn't happy. He wasn't sure he wanted to be married anymore. What? Is this not the guy who asked me about having a baby? I called Bill Browder, who was in San Francisco, and told him what had happened. Bill arranged for me to get to Jacksonville the next day, where I would be performing. He flew in early and met me at the airport. This gave me a couple of days to think about my situation and calm down before rehearsals began. Dealing with the pressure of the show and the press helped me not to dwell on the deteriorating situation at home.

Well, ladies and gentlemen, when it rains, it pours.

I had never missed my period before, and here I was, five weeks into the show, and my period was six weeks late. Bill found a clinic where appointments were not required. I wore no make-up and had on very loose clothes. At the clinic, you paid in advance, signed in, and waited until it was your turn. I signed in using a fake name. I met with the doctor and was told to return to the waiting room and wait for the test results. When the results were in, a nurse called out my fake name and said, *"Congratulations, you are positive."* You could have knocked me over with a feather! I was pregnant, with six more weeks left before closing night.

The crew and cast were all waiting when Bill and I walked backstage that night. In unison, they yelled out, *"Congratulations!"* Unbeknownst to me, the wife of the theater's cook was also in the doctor's waiting room, overheard the nurse tell me I was positive, and told everyone back at the theater. They all thought it was a happy moment, but only Bill and I knew the truth.

As the weeks passed, I would carefully check to see if my baby bump was showing. I have never had a problem with weight. I naturally tend to gain a little when I am happy and lose when I am unhappy. I wasn't just unhappy; I was miserable and hardly gained a pound. There was no sign of my pregnancy, and I never suffered a day of morning sickness.

Four days before closing night, Dan called. He apologized and begged me to return. When I told him I was pregnant, he whooped and said he was overjoyed. Thank God for small favors.

Over dinner that night, Bill Browder put on a cheerful face when I told him of Dan's call, but I could tell he was not that confident. He said, *"Leopards don't change their spots, June. Watch your back."* That thought also ran through my head; was Dan truthful with me? There was also the other side of the issue, and having a child brought me a sense of joy, no matter what might happen between Dan and me. I was in seventh heaven,

HOLLYWOOD OR BUST!

even allowing myself to dream of our becoming the perfect family and living happily ever after.

My feelings of utopia didn't last long. Within a couple of months, Dan was back to staying out until the wee hours of the morning. He always had some excuse when I asked where he was, what he was doing, and with whom? What was going on? I kept a positive attitude, concentrated on having a baby, and read books on pregnancy. I decided to have natural childbirth as it was much less drama for the baby. Despite finding a doctor I liked and trusted, I was depressed again because Dan was out almost every night and often didn't return until 4 or 5 most mornings.

Thinking of something I could do while I was pregnant that would make me feel better, I decided to have my under-arm hair permanently removed—silly me. I found a hair-remover salon run by five lovely young ladies. I told them I was pregnant and feeling ugly, and the only thing I could think of to improve my disposition was to permanently remove the hair under my armpits. That and some of the Houston Oilers wives who threw me a baby shower were the only happy moments I can think of during my pregnancy. Browder would often call to cheer me up, and although he never mentioned Dan, I knew he was disgusted with him. My Houston girlfriends made no effort to disguise their disgust with Dan. Who could blame them?

Chapter 46

I had never dropped by Don Ragland's office, even after Dan began using it. One day I decided to go in for an unannounced visit. As I walked in and talked to the secretary, I could hear Dan talking on the phone in his office with the door open. He was leaving to go to New York the next day, and it sounded like he was making a date with a female that was more than just a friend. His excuse for going to New York was to attend a meeting about a TV commercial deal and would be staying with his buddy, Roy Shuman, who was in the athletic shoe business.

When I shared my suspicions with Ragland's wife, Susan, she agreed; it did not bode well for Dan. Her husband, also out of town, kept spare keys at the house. She would pick me up at midnight and let me into the

HOLLYWOOD OR BUST!

office. I could nose around Dan's notes and phone calls to discover what he might be up to.

At midnight, Susan picked me up with a bunch of keys. Getting into the main building was no problem. But, when we tried to get into the office, none of the keys worked. We must have wasted a half-hour trying but with no luck. Then, when we were about to give up, I remembered how I had seen plastic credit cards used to open locked doors in films. I took out my credit card and slipped it into the space between the door; thank you, Mumma; the door opened. Once inside, we found all sorts of incriminating information about his activities with women that were more than just friends, including the one in New York. I gathered all the information I needed, and we left.

When I returned home, I called Browder and asked him to call the girl in New York and ask to speak to Dan. Bill agreed to call but would hang up if Dan answered. Minutes later, Bill called me back and said, *"Sorry, June, but a girl answered. Dan came on the phone when I asked for him, and I hung up without saying a word."*

I thanked Bill and immediately called the girl back. When she answered, I told her I was Dan's wife and to tell Dan not to bother coming home. To this day, I have never told Dan how Susan and I broke into the office and learned of his activities. So, I'm sure he'll be quite surprised if and when he reads this.

For me, it was a time of reflection; what had I done to cause Dan to act this way? I had been there for him day and night. I could only conclude that boys, especially good-looking, famous NFL quarterbacks, have difficulty keeping it in their pants.

Although I told his girlfriend to tell Dan not to bother coming home, two days later, he showed up. We had a long and heated discussion, with most of the heat coming from me. He apologized profusely. Once we talked it out, we decided it would be best not to say anything to anyone fearing the press would have a field day with the story, and the scandals would begin. It wasn't the best solution by any means because I wanted him out, but we did what we thought best for the moment. So, it would remain our secret until I finished the show I'd signed to do in Houston and the baby was born. For appearance's sake, we would stay together in the house. But I told Dan I decided to return to California after the baby was born, and the doctor thought it would be okay for the baby to travel. I would live in my home in California, and Dan would keep the house in Houston. I still wanted to do the Lamaze method, and Dan offered to help with the baby's birth. I was angry with myself for being in this situation and could not help but wonder what had happened to the wonderful man I had fallen in love with, who couldn't stand being away from me for a second. And now, before our child was even born, we were breaking up. It was like living a bad dream that repeated itself over and over.

On March 8, I awoke with what I thought was the beginning of my labor pains. It was 6 AM. Dan had not arrived home yet, which was not uncommon behavior for him since the beginning of my pregnancy. Thankfully, I had a doctor's appointment at ten that morning. I took a shower, dressed, and sat on the doorstep reading a book, waiting for Dan to arrive. I couldn't concentrate; my mind kept returning to the beginning of our relationship. Dan was so in love with me that he couldn't wait to rush to my side whenever he had a free moment. What went wrong?

My thoughts drifted to all the legal and illegal drugs the players were accustomed to getting. Could that be the problem? Dan would be hurting bad mornings after a game. He would visit the trainer and return home feeling just fine. I never thought much about it then, but as I write this, I think, *"Was this the reason for all the drug problems in sports?"* Although I can't prove it, the trainers must have been shooting Dan up with powerful stuff. It was probably the same for many other players, too, although Dan was the one who got the most pounding on the field during a game. Sports fans may recall that it was Dan who came up with the idea of wearing a flak jacket under his shirt for protection.

I was still sitting on the doorstep, dealing with a developing backache, when Dan arrived for the doctor's appointment. During the final two months before the baby was born, I must have read at least a dozen books on natural childbirth. Not one mentioned it was common to get a backache when your due date was nearing. At my appointment, the doctor confirmed it was common in the later stages of labor, but although I was beginning my labor, he did not expect the delivery until later that night. He sent me home to get whatever I needed and to return to the hospital by 4 that afternoon.

Dan's parents prayed for a boy, but I only wished for a healthy baby. I knew I would have to name him Dante if it was a boy. I knew Dan's parents would be disappointed if it wasn't a boy, but not my mother and me. This baby proved stubborn and refused to make a timely appearance. It must have known what a lousy situation it was about to be born into.

It had just turned midnight in the early hours of March 9. The baby didn't seem to want to make an appearance. I could hear my doctor talking to another doctor who suggested a cesarean delivery, but my doctor wanted to give the baby thirty more minutes. I didn't think I could take another ten minutes, let alone thirty! When I told my doctor, he ignored me and walked out without saying anything. My pain was getting intense. I forced myself to think of something else. For reasons I have never understood, my brain flashed a picture of a portrait I had once seen of a lady identified as Brahna. I recall how that picture had taken my breath away. The lady was beautiful and had the most incredible blue eyes.

My doctor returned and apologized for walking out on me. He said he was sure I could handle another half-hour without pain pills. He needed the baby to cooperate and fight its way out; drugs could make the baby lethargic and possibly force a cesarean.

The Doctor was right because a beautiful pink baby girl entered the world in less than an hour. I felt an incredible sense of overpowering love. I stroked my baby gently and whispered, *"Welcome to the world—"* I paused and thought for a moment, then heard myself say, *"Welcome to the world, Brahna."*

Dan went to the waiting room to let the gang know it was a girl and we were both doing fine. I heard cheering and the champagne cork popping in the nearby waiting area. After hating every minute of being pregnant, I had just given birth to my daughter, who instantly became

HOLLYWOOD OR BUST!

the love of my life. But here I was with a beautiful newborn daughter, and it looked like my marriage was ending.

Chapter 47

So, here we were with a new child, and our marriage was up in the air with no clear resolution in sight. But we agreed we would put on a happy face as far as our friends and the public were concerned, at least for the time being. What would happen in the weeks and months to come remained unknown.

Before Brahna was born, Dan's new interest was boat racing, and he was good at it. Several weeks following Brahna's birth, we took her for her first outing to Lake Mizzel in Liberty, Texas, where Dan was racing. Dan loved his boat, *The Quarterback Sneak,* and thought he could win this race. When the race was about to start, Brahna and I settled into seats at the back of the crowd, high enough for me to have a good view but remain

HOLLYWOOD OR BUST!

unnoticed. Right after the starting gun went off, Dan's boat took the lead, and he kept it. As he crossed the finish line, something went tragically wrong.

The boat went out of control, lifted into the air, and veered left onto the shore toward the crowd. I couldn't see Dan because of the position of the boat. It all happened so fast that I didn't know if he was still in the boat or had fallen into the water. Dale Johnson, who had been wading in the water close to the bank, was instantly killed when struck by Dan's out-of-control boat. Sherry Gaskins, a beautiful ten-year-old, was hit in the head as the boat passed over her with Dan still inside.

It remains one of the worst days of my life, one I will never be able to forget. Here I sat with my baby daughter in my arms, and the Gaskins' baby girl was gone in a second. Later, there were rumors that Dan had been drunk, but I can attest there was zero truth to that rumor. A Liberty County grand jury later ruled that criminal responsibility was not involved and it was an accident.

We did not go to Dale Johnson's funeral. If I remember correctly, only family members were invited. We did go to Sherry Gaskins' funeral. Seeing their beautiful little girl lying there was heartbreaking; the terrible moment will stay in my heart forever.

There was no problem getting into my clothes. I had only gained a few pounds. It was also difficult dealing with the press and pretending Dan, Brahna, and I was one big happy family, nor could I get the boat accident out of my mind.

When the show at the Windmill ended, I decided to take Brahna and return to Los Angeles. I could no longer maintain the pretense that we were a happy family. I said goodbye to our neighbors, Jo and Chester. Since they both knew what was happening, they were openly disgusted with Dan. The Argovitz and the Raglands were the only others who knew what was happening, and they would keep our secret for now.

Back in Los Angeles, my friends went out of their way to make me feel loved and wanted. My Mum, on the other hand, was heartbroken. She believed Dan was still very much in love with me. When Dan's parents found out, they wanted the details and wanted to hear them from me. I knew they were dying to see Brahna, so I agreed to travel to San Jose, California, for a visit. They seemed thrilled to see Brahna even though I knew they, more specifically Dante Sr., had wanted a boy.

One of the most painful conversations I have ever had was explaining to Dan's parents why he and I had split up, and it was painful for them to hear. I told them that Dan had to take responsibility for his actions, and if they wanted the details of his side, they would have to hear directly from him. We let it go at that. I was never privy to what Dan might have told them.

Luckily for me, Brahna was a very happy and content baby. While pregnant, the books I read during and after pregnancy recommended breastfeeding. Wanting to give Brahna every advantage, I breastfed her. I was never comfortable feeding her in front of anyone. And that reminds me of a funny story.

Dan's mother, Dorothy, Brahna, and I visited a café for a coffee when Brahna started to fuss a bit. I looked at my watch; it was past her feeding time. So, I excused myself and went to the restroom to feed Brahna. I sat in

HOLLYWOOD OR BUST!

the cubical with the door closed. Suddenly, Dorothy's head appeared from under the door. When I asked her what was wrong, she admitted with a guilty look that she didn't believe I was breastfeeding because I always excused myself and left when I needed to feed Brahna. Oh, for God's sake, give me a break.

Another memory of a moment when Dorothy had stayed with me. When she visited us, we went shopping, and I bumped into a friend. I introduced Dorothy as my ex-mother-in-law. In a loud voice, Dorothy grimaced and said, *"I'm not your ex-mother-in-law. I have not divorced you!"* Of all Dan's six wives (yes, six wives), I was the only one ever invited to visit and join his parent's family events.

As I write this, I'm almost too embarrassed to admit what I agreed to next. Once we parted and I was back living in LA, Dan began calling, insisting he wanted me back, that he loved me, missed Brahna and me, and had made terrible mistakes, and I would always be his love. Guess what? I still loved the oaf and returned to his side —so sue me. The next dumb move was letting Dan talk me into selling my house that overlooked Sunset. He insisted we begin a new life together; we would wipe away the bad memories. As for selling my home, his argument was since he had to be in Houston most of the time, it made more sense for me to sell my house, and he would sell the Houston house. We would buy a bigger residence in Houston for our growing family. Because I desperately wanted Brahna, Dan, and I to be a real family, I agreed. I called Saul Lazarow, and within a week, because of a misunderstanding between us, he not only sold Grandview but my little one-bedroom cottage, which I had not wanted to sell.

I will spare you the ugly details, but Dan's old behavior returned before I knew it. Why, I thought, what compels him to act this way? I couldn't take being on this maddening merry-go-round anymore and packed up once and for all, and Brahna and I headed back to Los Angeles. Mum had moved into a little apartment in the valley, and we stayed with her while I house-hunted. It was like I was beginning life all over again, and it was brutally painful.

I began my hunt for a new house, but within a week, I was depressed. Nothing was even close to my home overlooking Sunset Blvd. One day, while searching for a new place, I was close to where my friends Marc and Grace Richard lived and visited them. When Marc answered, I burst into tears and blurted, *"I can't find a place to live."* Grace joined us and put her arm around me, but Marc looked at me disgustedly. *"You've put up with all that shit from your asshole of a husband, and just because you can't find a place to live now, you're crying—give me a break, June!"* He was right. He made me realize I had to get on with my life without delay.

By then, I knew I'd never find another dream house like the Sunset house, so I stopped trying. Instead, I found a row of brand-new townhomes in Sherman Oaks across from a beautiful park with tennis courts, a kiddie playground, a swimming pool, and a Jacuzzi. I bought one of the townhomes and moved in, determined to put the past behind me and move on.

HOLLYWOOD OR BUST!

Chapter 48

*B*efore long, I was back on the road performing again in *Ninety-Day Mistress*. When the show arrived in Dallas, Dan, who was in Houston, called. It was my day off, and I was having dinner with some cast members. My live-in lady traveled with me to help with Brahna while I worked. She answered the phone. She was not a fan of Dan's, having worked for us at the house in Houston, and fully aware of his bad behavior—like bringing females into our home when I was not in town. She took great delight in telling Dan I had a 'hot date' and had flown to Vegas for the night. Dan called our friend Pootie. She told him I had gone to Vegas for dinner with one of the Dallas Cowboys. When Dan reached me, he started ranting about my going out with one of the Cowboys. With venom in my voice, I said, *"If I'm out* there, it's because you put me there, and Mr. Pastorini, who I go out with, is none of your damn business."

I hung up. From that day on, I began dating whenever an offer came my way.

About six months into my tour, I had a week off before we had to fly on to the next stop, Jacksonville, Florida. The lovely lady traveling and helping with Brahna decided she wanted to spend more time with her family. I would miss her, but I understood. I called the agency, hired another lady, and arranged for her to meet me at the airport, ready to fly to Jacksonville. Well, she never showed up, and I went crazy. In desperation, I called my Mum, explained the situation, and asked if she would consider joining me in Jacksonville if I arranged an airline ticket. She was thrilled and arrived the very next day. When I picked her up at the airport, her first words were, *"Don't you dare hire anyone. I want the job of looking after my granddaughter!"*

I happily gave my Mum the job; I don't know why I hadn't thought of it before. It was the start of a wonderful new time in our lives. Mum, bless her heart, was in seventh heaven, spending all her time with her granddaughter.

In two weeks, I was to begin my next gig with Windmill Dinner Theater in Scottsdale, Arizona, which, I am pleased to say, went really well. On the last week of the tour, I got a call from Maynard Sloate. Maynard produced the shows for the main room at the Union Plaza Hotel and Casino in Las Vegas. He and Frank Scott, one of the Union Plaza owners, wanted to fly

HOLLYWOOD OR BUST!

down, catch my show, and meet with me afterward. They did not tell me why, but I was intrigued, and they had my full attention. They planned to fly back after the show that night. We were sold out, but the manager, who knew how important it was to me to meet with them, arranged for two of the best seats in the house.

After the show, Maynard and Frank came backstage and said it was perfect for their casino and asked if I would be interested in performing it there. I was beside myself; appearing in Las Vegas was *The Big Time*. My Mother was excited too. She never dreamed her daughter would headline in Las Vegas, where Frank Sinatra, Dean Martin, Liberace, and many other top performers appeared. Vegas was the number one entertainment destination in the country. I felt like I had hit the big time, more significant than when I starred on Broadway. My name would be on the Union Plaza's big marquee, more prominent than on Broadway. I wished my dad was alive to have seen it.

I reminisced about how I had taken this play from the tiny little Los Angeles Grand Theatre in Hollywood to the Seattle World's Fair to the highest-grossing show on the road, thanks to all the wonderfully talented people I was privileged to have worked with. Now I would be playing in the biggest playground in the country, and boy, was I ever ready.

Baby June had hit the big time, and I would make the most of it.

Playing in Vegas was unlike playing in Ohio (sorry, Ohio). Everyone wants to visit when you're headlining a show in Vegas. Friends visited me from as far away as New York and even London. On my day off, I would get a sitter for Brahna and take my Mum to a show at one of the other casinos. Mum never dreamed she would be living this kind of life, and I was so pleased that I could provide it.

Business was fabulous, and the show kept getting held over. Even Dan's parents came to see the show. They had never seen me perform and were genuinely impressed with the show and my performance. Although, I admit I was a bit nervous that they were in the audience. They were also impressed with how big my name appeared on the marquee. —smile, smile! And to top it off, they loved the show and my performance.

There was one incident that would come back to haunt me. I agreed to a local TV interview, and Bill Browder went with me. The young lady, who had won the Miss Photogenic contest, finished her interview ahead of us and walked by. Bill whispered, *"She must be photogenic because she's nothing in person."* I turned to check her out. She was thin with a flat chest and an okay face, but I thought nothing and brushed it off.

Little did I realize then this lady would be someone Brahna and I would come to hate.

After Vegas, I began touring in a new show, so I let Tim Rossovich and his longtime girlfriend, Cis Rundle, stay at my townhouse. I had become friends with both of them when Tim played for the Houston Oilers with Dan. Tim was no longer playing football. He was filming a movie with the English Actor Albert Finney titled *Looker in Los Angeles*. Hugh Hefner had invited Cis to his Sunday night movie at the Mansion. When she told him she was staying at my townhouse, he told her I was to come by when I got back.

HOLLYWOOD OR BUST!

So, on my first Sunday in town, I went with Cis to the Mansion. We arrived around six that evening. The place was already abuzz with a crowd. There were, of course, beautiful girls, but it was the crowd that blew me away. It was an incredibly diversified collection of famous to infamous from all walks of life. Soft music played throughout the grounds. In the gardens out back, beautiful peacocks roamed freely. Hef greeted me, and we chatted. We enjoyed a fantastic buffet dinner and then watched a first-run movie.

Following the movie, everyone mingled with more drinks and finger food. Hef told me how happy he was to see me and invited me to come up any Sunday; my name would always be on the list at the gate. The only bummer was Sundays were the nights I looked forward to having dinner with my manager, Maurice Duke, and his cronies at Matteo's. When I told Duke my dilemma, he yelled at me in his usual sweet way. *"Shmuck, of course, you go to the Mansion, socialize and have dinner. You sneak out and join us for coffee if it's a bad movie. Now, did I manage that well for you?"* I often took his advice.

Chapter 49

Moving to the Sherman Oaks townhouse was great for Brahna and *She She*. As I mentioned, across the street was a vast park where *She She* loved playing and making friends with the other dogs. Brahna had great fun with all the little kiddy stuff, like swings, slides, and sand pits.

When Brahna was old enough to attend kindergarten, Lily looked after her and *She She* when I was working out of town. Dan showed up for Brahna's kindergarten graduation, the first time we had seen him in a long time.

Brahna loved sports, so I enrolled her in the Bee Hive soccer team for five-year-olds. It was a bit of a joke. At that age, all the kids except Brahna seemed afraid of the ball and would jump if it came near them. Brahna was the only one who would run up and kick the ball.

HOLLYWOOD OR BUST!

So, they won every game without much interference from anyone. There was also a huge swimming pool in the park where Brahna learned to swim. When she was older, she trained as a lifeguard; fortunately, she never had to save anyone.

The next show I did at Union Plaza in Vegas was *90-Day Mistress*. School was out for the summer, so Brahna and Mum joined me. Both the reviews and business were good. After the first show at eight o'clock, I would take Mum and Brahna downtown for dinner. In those days (not anymore), you could go to almost any downtown hotel and get a great meal for four dollars. Mum, of course, was in seventh heaven. In England, few people could afford or get a steak, even after the war's end. Guess what Mum ate almost every night?

The second show was at midnight. When we finished, most of the cast and I would go out for breakfast, then home around five. On one sweltering night, on the spur of the moment, we decided to go to Lake Mead for a swim. That became our regular routine.

Although Brahna and Mum were enjoying their time in Vegas, school would begin soon, and they had to return to Los Angeles.

A month after they left, I was tired after a midnight show, so I skipped breakfast with the gang and went to bed. I don't recall how long I had slept when a noise woke me up. A masked man with a flashlight had a gun to the side of my head. In a low, raspy voice, he said he wanted my engagement-wedding ring that Dan had designed and that I still wore. I had the blanket up to my shoulders, trying to remain still. My arms were under the blanket. Slowly, I slipped the ring from my finger and under my left thigh and told him all my jewelry was in the hotel vault. He climbed onto the bed, straddled me, and placed the gun between my eyes. I could see the anger in his eyes as he said, *"Don't lie to me; I watched you come in with it, so you have a choice. Either we do this the easy way or the hard way?"*

Fearing for my safety, I pulled the ring from under me and handed it to him. I feared he would pistol whip me for trying to hide the ring if I didn't. He ordered me out of bed and to remove whatever I was wearing; he wanted to see the body everyone talked about. I don't know what it is, but I get very calm whenever confronted with something scary.

As I stood naked with my eyes locked on his masked face, he took his gun and began moving it around my breasts and up and down my body for what seemed an eternity. Then he abruptly snapped out of his trance and told me to stay in the closet for ten minutes. In the dark closet, the gears in my head were turning a mile a minute. I slowly opened the closet door, waiting for what seemed like yet another eternity (probably no more than three or four minutes). The room was empty. I rushed to the corridor. It was also empty. Thinking he must have gone down the stairs, I called the front desk and told them what had happened. The police were up in my room within minutes, but there was no sign of the thief, nor did they ever catch him. The police thought it might have been an inside job by someone familiar with the building.

I refused to let the robbery get the better of me. I

HOLLYWOOD OR BUST!

forced myself to do the show the next night even though the management suggested I take a few days off. Looking at the bright side, being unable to wear or look at that ring again probably helped me get over Dan much sooner. When he heard what happened, he flew into town to ensure I was alright, which I thought was quite nice of him.

Being a dancer, I exercised regularly and, in the eighties, switched to aerobics when it fast-tracked as the new fad popular. I woke early every morning and attended a class about fifteen minutes from home. Aerobic exercise was done to music that encouraged you to move and was popular with both men and women. Aerobics works all your muscles with not much stress. It was fun, and I enjoyed it, and it was a great way to start my day.

One day, two new gentlemen joined the class. When we took a short break, they introduced themselves to me as Tommy Bennett and Ron Williamson. They were from Toronto, Canada, and were hooked on the American aerobics craze. They complimented me on being in great shape and doing the exercises well. They explained how they planned to open a studio in Toronto and wanted to discuss a business opportunity that might interest me.

After the class, the three of us went for coffee. Tom and Ron told me they had this space in mid-town Toronto, Canada, where they would open an aerobics studio. If I were interested in joining them, the studio would be called *June Wilkinson's Aerobics Studio and Health Centre*. I would not have to live in Toronto, but they would make an apartment available whenever I was there. My job would be to choose the other teachers and do radio and TV promotions, but only when my schedule allowed me to be in Toronto. Now, who in their right mind would turn down such an offer? Not me, I assure you. It was a great way to stay in shape and get paid. It was a winning venture all the way around.

The next day I flew to Toronto with my new partners. We discussed the game plan for the promotions and how I would handle my first aerobics class. The only competition back then was from Jane Fonda, who successfully did her thing in Los Angeles. We were off and running in Canada with what turned out to be a very successful venture.

A couple moved into the townhouse next to ours with their two daughters, Tandy and Kelly. Kelly, it turned out, was an excellent tennis player. She and her coach would practice on the tennis courts across the street almost daily. Brahna began watching them, which was the beginning of her interest in tennis, and she begged me for lessons—I agreed.

She had several coaches, but the two that made a big difference were Jerry Rush and Gene Malin. With their coaching, Brahna started competing. She began winning almost every tournament she entered and, before long, was the number one junior player in Los Angeles.

One lazy day with nothing important on my schedule, I took a stroll and window-shopped along Sunset Plaza between Laurel Canyon and Beverly Hills. Someone tapped my shoulder as I was looking in a dress shop window. When I turned around, a vaguely familiar lady said, *"Excuse me, but I know you from somewhere."* She introduced herself as Sherry Hackett. Ah, yes, comedian Buddy Hackett's wife. I reminded her that my date, Wilfred Tsang, and I had attended a party at her house. *"Right, Now I remember."* She spoke. *"It's good to see you again. Say, if you have time, lunch is on me."*

That, ladies and gentlemen, boys and girls, was the beginning of a beautiful friendship. It has endured all these years and enriched my life in so many ways, which I'm grateful for. Sherry was fearless, always coming up with crazy and sometimes fabulous ideas. Early in our friendship, she mentioned she had many friends who weren't married and thought playing matchmaker would be fun. She would throw a singles party at her Beverly Hills home that might lead to wedding bells for some. Buddy Hackett, bless his heart, always went along with whatever crazy idea Sherry had. Always the funnyman, he said, *"I'm already married, so when you toss this party, I'll watch TV in my study in the back of the house. If a couple does fall in love and wants to get married, they can have the wedding in our backyard at no charge. That'll be my contribution."*

Sherry held a couple of parties, but no new romances developed, as far as I recall.

Chapter 50

The Union Plaza Hotel in Vegas brought me back to do *The 90-Day Mistress* again. Brahna was on school vacation, so she and Mum would be coming with me, and they were looking forward to it. The last time I was there, I appeared on World Sports TV. For fun, I was on the show and made a few football predictions, and, would you believe, they came up as winners. They talked me into doing the show every week. The big betters began coming to the hotel, hoping to catch me in the Casino to see what I might be predicting. This time, the hotel asked me in advance if I would agree to go on the nationally televised *Las Vegas Sports Line*, and I agreed; it was fun and great for business.

I performed two shows a night, one at eight and a second at midnight. Halfway through the run, the cast decided to relax one night, swim in Lake Mead, and watch the sunrise. They found a spot where the water was not deep but warm and beautiful. The next night we went again, and I took Brahna with us. We swam and had fun for a couple of hours, then went back and picked up Mum for breakfast before I was off for some sleep. To this day, Brahna and I love having coffee in the morning and watching sunrises.

The Windmill Dinner Theatre in Houston hired me to do a show titled *Wally's Café*, which had flopped on Broadway. It was written by Ron Clark and Sam Bobrick and had an excellent cast that included James Coco, Rita Moreno, and Sally Struthers. But for whatever reason, the show did not do well even with that fine cast. Even though it failed on Broadway, the Windmill wanted to try it. They cast me along with Avery Schreiber and Cindy Wood. I played a girl on her way to Hollywood, convinced she could become a star. Avery and Cindy played a married couple who got conned into buying a small Café in the desert with nothing around for miles. My character had thumbed a ride with a guy who would take her as far as Las Vegas but instead dumped her in the middle of nowhere. After walking a few miles, she comes across Wally's Café and takes a job as their waitress.

The show went well enough that Howard Pechet of a Canadian dinner theater chain was interested in bringing the show to Canada. Our first show was in Edmonton, Alberta. My Mum, Brahna, Avery, Cindy, and I flew into Edmonton and stayed at the Mayfield Inn, which also housed the theatre on the first floor. The

Pechet's were kind enough to enroll Brahna in the Mayfield school, and she began attending the following day.

The theater's press agent loved Avery, Cindy, and me because we were up for almost any promotion, no matter how crazy an idea he conjured up, and some were crazy. Canada had a daily newspaper in every city called the Sun, and each day they would have a pinup photo of a local girl with the caption "Sunshine Girl." Most of the girls were photographed in a bikini or one-piece swimsuit, and their ages were posted next to their photo; they were usually between 18 and 20. The press agent thought it would be fun if I posed as the Sunshine Girl, and the newspaper was all for it. As I've said, if you want big crowds at the show, you must get as much press as possible. When my pin-up photo came out, my age was listed as 42. Many people visited the theatre to see if I looked like the photo. I won't bore you with the great reviews for the show. Just know we did great business all across Canada.

A month after we returned to Los Angeles, I got a call from Myron Gold, the film producer, who was still living in Mexico. He was preparing to shoot a movie, *Frankenstein's Great Aunt Tilly* (1984), starring the outstanding English Actor Donald Pleasence. I had never met Donald, but I was a big fan. Zsa Zsa Gabor was also in the cast. More on Zsa Zsa below.

I loved Myron's family (remember his daughter spent hours helping me with my bad Spanish in her dad's movie *Los Rabia*). I was worried about leaving Brahna and Mum with my being so far away. But I got lucky.

HOLLYWOOD OR BUST!

My friend Willy Tsang moved to China after the plane crash that killed his brother, becoming a well-respected psychic. But after living there for several years, he returned to America. When I learned he had not found a place to live, I asked if he would like to stay at my house while I was out of the country. He agreed. I felt better knowing Lily and Brahna would be in good hands with Willy there.

Filming *Frankenstein's Great Aunt Tilly* was fun. Everyone, actors, crew, and make-up artists, were great, and we got along well. Donald Pleasence arrived with an English lady friend on his arm. She never visited the set, but I would see them going out for dinner every night, always elegantly dressed. Actor Aldo Ray, also in the film, was a sweet guy and good to work with, but he drank too much. I didn't spend too much time with him because of his drinking.

I had two days off, but the crew worked for those two days on the scene with Donald Pleasence in bed with Zsa Zsa. I heard from the crew that it was hell. Zsa Zsa treated everyone like dirt and complained about everything. The only thing she liked was the very expensive, sexy nightgown she wore in the scene, which she managed to take with her when she left town. I knew and liked Zsa Zsa's sisters Magda and Eva. They had always been nice to me. But Zsa Zsa... *not so much.*

I hardly had any time back home before I had to begin rehearsals at the Plaza in Las Vegas for *What the Butler Saw*, written by Joe Orton, an Englishman. Joe was born in 1933 and bludgeoned to death in 1969 by his long-time lover, Kenneth Halliwell. Halliwell then committed suicide. I'd never seen the play performed. The reviews and business turned out well for us, but in retrospect, it was my least favorite play I'd done at the Plaza—sorry, Mr. Orton.

I think it was the second week of the play when Donald Pleasence showed up and surprised me with a visit. I was delighted to see him. Each evening following my first show, he took me to dinner and always at one of the posh dining rooms in the hotel. I hope the reader is ready for what happened next because I wasn't.

One evening at dinner, he told me the real reason he had come to Vegas. He had fallen in love with me and wanted me to return to London with him after my show closed. Well, ladies and gentlemen, boys and girls, I was stunned into silence; I didn't know what to say. Donald had never told me his feelings while filming in Mexico, nor would it have mattered. I had always thought of us as just good friends. I had to tell him I was genuinely flattered in the most delicate way, but I did not have the same feelings for him. Donald jumped up from his seat and left. That was it; he just left. He never gave me his address or phone number or contacted me again. Men. Besides the obvious, why do we need them?

Dan and I were not yet divorced. He showed up in Vegas for some function. With Brahna in school in Sherman Oaks, I had no reason to see him. The real shock was when I received a call from a gentleman who introduced himself as the husband of a lady Dan was meeting in Vegas. He found out his wife had been leaving their son at the hotel pool while she went in and did the nasty with Dan. I felt very sorry for her husband.

HOLLYWOOD OR BUST!

On second thought, the husband was lucky to have gotten rid of her, and Dan's bad luck was that he married her. Of all of Dan's six wives, she was the worst. Remember I said we would come to dislike the lady I had seen at my TV interview? Right, that was Beverly, Dan's newest wife. Brahna hated her with a passion.

After Dan and Beverly married, he invited Brahna to visit them. She was his daughter; he had every right to see her, so I agreed. I was working, so when Brahna returned home, Mum picked her up at the airport. When they returned, Mum walked into my dressing room with a strange young boy. "Where's Brahna, Mum?" The child looked at me and said, "Mum, it's me, Brahna." I looked again, and sure enough, it was Brahna dressed in jeans and a t-shirt. Her beautiful long hair that had been down to her waist was gone. It was chopped off as short as a boy's crew cut. I was in shock. *"Brahna, what in the world did you do?"* She was practically in tears. *"I didn't do anything, Mom. Beverly and Dad were drinking and decided to comb my hair. It had too many tangles, so they cut it."*

If words could kill, I would have called them. Brahna and I still hate that woman with a passion to this day!

Dan's next wife, Dena, I did like. She treated Brahna well, and that was most important to me. When Dena learned how well Brahna played tennis, she encouraged her to play in area tournaments. I am proud to say that Brahna was undefeated the entire time she spent with them in Houston.

I don't know what happened, but Dan's marriage to Dena did not endure, and before he knew it, he was onto the next wife, Wendy Akin. I met Wendy once when she and Dan were in California and spent a day with Brahna. Brahna said Wendy was kind and respectful to her, which was all I cared about. Dan married three times after that. Since I was long over him, I stopped caring.

HOLLYWOOD OR BUST!

Chapter 51

Several years passed before I saw Dan again, but very briefly. Brahna, Mum, and I remained on good terms with his parents. They were grateful I never denied them access to Brahna.

On Feb 27, 1991, Dan's father, Dante Pastorini Sr., died. I flew to San Jose alone; Brahna had school and a scheduled tournament, so she and Lily could not go. When I arrived at the memorial, the room was empty except for Dan, sitting alone. I greeted him and kissed him on the cheek. He was happy to see someone he knew. He wasn't married or living with anyone and had not visited his family. He stayed by my side like glue all day, asked a lot about Brahna, and gave me updates on our friends in Houston. He talked about a new little house he had just brought and invited me to visit. Dan can be charming when he wants to be, but I knew getting involved again would be a big mistake. I thanked him for the invitation but declined. On many emotional levels, I was sad when I left San Jose.

As they say, I was playing the field and didn't have a steady boyfriend. When a friend found out I was going to San Francisco for a few days, he wanted me to meet up with a friend of his who lived there. I was never big on blind dates, but I figured why not since I wasn't dating anyone. The man's name was Steven Kay, an attorney. It was a nice change of pace to meet anyone, not in show business or connected to football (Later, he would become a partner in a team, but I never held that against him. Just kidding).

Steven met me at the airport, and the evening went well. He asked me to join him and his parents for dinner the following evening. Again, it was a pleasant evening, and his parents proved delightful.

If you've read this book carefully, you know what's coming next. Although we lived in different cities, Steven and I started dating regularly. He never questioned what I did when I wasn't with him, and I never asked him what he did while I was not around. I also made it clear there would never be any hanky-panky if Brahna were with me. Dating someone who never pressured me and cared about my daughter was a plus. Steven and I dated for several years. The distance between us took its usual toll. But I'm happy to say we are still good friends and keep in touch. He was the kind of friend I wish everyone were fortunate to have.

1992 was one of, if not the worst, of my life. My

HOLLYWOOD OR BUST!

Mum, whom I don't remember ever being seriously sick, was helping me set the dinner when she fainted and fell to the floor. Brahna and I lifted her to a chair. She regained consciousness quickly and tried to fluff it off. But Brahna and I suspected something was wrong and decided she had to be examined. We arranged for her to visit a doctor who ordered a battery of tests. When the test results returned, the doctor told us Mum had stage 4 colon cancer and didn't think they could save her. At first, I didn't know how to act or what to say. Finally, I told the doctor to try everything they could, and the medical process began.

I was delighted when Mum said she wished to stay in America after my wedding. But, as I said, the only way we could get her a green card was to swear under oath that I would be financially responsible for her and that she would never become a ward of the court. I was able to get her on my insurance, but before long, the co-pays and out-of-pocket expenses began to snowball. When her coverage reached its max and insurance stopped, I needed to return to work to cover the mounting bills. My brothers took turns flying in and looking after Mum, Robin from England, and John from Germany. When college began, John had to return to Germany, and eventually, Robin needed to return home too.

Brahna insisted she could care for her grandmother and pestered me until I agreed. Since I was desperate, I took a chance and left Brahna in charge. God love that child; she was a remarkable caregiver. Brahna's school was only ten minutes walking distance from the house. She would dash home during recess and care for whatever her grandma needed. They'd watch TV together every night with our feline *Cutie Pie*, who would sit on Mum's lap. Brahna would clean the house after feeding Mum and put her to bed. I could not have been prouder of my amazing daughter.

Difficult as it was to leave Mum, I needed income to help pay the bills. So, back to Canada I went appearing in a play I had never done before. It was an English farce called *Keys for Two*. My leading man was Robert Pine, a lovely actor to work with who had just finished appearing in the successful television series *Chips* with Eric Estrada. Robert said he loved the thrill of performing before a live audience. However, he would be with us only for the first city. He had committed to a special in Hollywood, but he wanted to return and rejoin after that. The producers didn't think that would be fair to whoever his replacement would be. We were sad to see Robert leave, but that's how it sometimes works.

The show's press agent came up with a wonderful idea. We would run a contest called *Win a date with June Wilkinson*. To everyone's surprise, it quickly became the talk of the town. Radio, TV, and the newspapers all had a field day anticipating the potential winner and how the date would go. For the love of me, I don't remember how the winner was chosen. The entry letters ran the gamut from funny, sad, and clever, and a few were in terrible taste, as was expected. The winner was Gene Prokop, and, lucky for me, he turned out to be very friendly and tolerant of the paparazzi, who could be a little much, to put it mildly. I had much fun on the date, and I hope Gene did too.

Gene, wherever you are, here's hoping you enjoyed our evening together, have since found a wonderful woman, and are living the life of your dreams. Thank you for the fun time and for being such a good sport.

It was 1985. After a month off and spending time with Mum and Brahna, I flew into Beaumont, Texas, to begin shooting a movie produced by Bob Burge titled *Texas Godfather*. The story centered around a New York City attorney secretly running a cocaine-smuggling ring in Texas. When the mob tries to move in on his operation, he goes to Texas to try to stop them. The cast included Vince Edwards, Paul Smith, and comedian Phil Foster. Yours truly was cast as the female lead. Maurice Duke's daughter, now a grown woman, also had a role. By the time the shoot was over, I had made at least five new lifelong friends, including actor Paul Smith (*Bluto* in the film *Popeye* with Robin Williams) and his wife, Eve.

One evening while visiting Paul and Eve back in Los Angles, they introduced me to an attractive, beautiful lady who became the notorious Mandy Rice-Davies. Many will remember that Mandy and Christine Keeler nearly brought down the British government together over a sex scandal. Many in the government were caught up in the scandal, like John Profumo, England's Minister of Defense, who was forced to resign.

Mandy was nothing like what I expected. She was attractive, classy, and beautifully dressed, and the evening, to say the least, turned out to be quite interesting. Mandy had moved to Israel and married Rafi Shauli. She and her husband opened a disco appropriately called *Mandy's Disco,* which was very successful. While in Israel, Mandy fell in love with a man who lived in Europe. She neglected to tell her husband she was leaving with her new lover; she just up and left. As you might imagine, our evening together was pretty fascinating. And that, ladies and gentlemen, boys and girls, is putting it mildly.

Mum was steadily getting worse. She never spoke of it or how she dealt with it, but I think she knew she didn't have much time left. She wished to return to England to see everyone one last time, which I arranged. Unfortunately, she was only back home for two months before returning to the hospital and, finally, to a nursing home. With the help of my brothers, at least Mum was receiving proper care. Brahna and I immediately arranged to fly to England to be at her side. In a month, Brahna and I had to be in Chicago for the wedding of my friend, Richard Spoley, who was like family to us. Richard had no real family of his own. Brahna and I would be the only guests he considered family at his side. It was challenging since I didn't want to leave Mum. But she also knew Richard well and insisted we attend his wedding. We hugged and kissed Mum; it would sadly be the last time we saw her. It broke our hearts, for no one on this earth could have had a better mother or grandmother, and Brahna and I miss her every day; she is never out of our thoughts.

Chapter 52

It was January 17, 1994, at our Sherman Oaks Townhouse. Me, Brahna, and two of her young friends, Nicole and Talia Turner, were sleeping. Talia and Nicole were in the spare bedroom. At 4:39 AM, the house started shaking; windows cracked, glass flew everywhere, and the roof and walls crumbled. The 1994 Northridge earthquake had struck. It went on for what felt like an eternity. Not knowing what was happening, we were petrified. It took me a minute to realize it was an earthquake. As soon as it stopped, I jumped out of bed and checked on everyone; everyone was okay except Brahna. Most of the ceiling and the fan over her head had fallen on her. The bed and furniture had slid to the door, blocking it so no one could get in. When the fire department showed up, two firefighters made their way through the debris and rescued Brahna. Fortunately, she was only bruised but badly shaken up.

As bad a shape as the house was in, it was nothing compared to what was happening elsewhere. At Brahna's school, the supervisor always arrived early to check everything before the children arrived. As was his routine, he began with the covered parking area. As he walked through, the earthquake started. The roof of the covered area collapsed and killed him.

In our Sherman Oaks complex, my townhouse was the most damaged. The roof was ripped off; no glass was left in any of the windows, and debris was everywhere. My living room floor cracked and rose in the middle three feet. We counted our blessings that none of us was seriously hurt. What upset Brahna the most was our cat *Cutie Pie* was missing.

For several days we searched the neighborhood, posted notices, went to shelters, and hunted the nearby park. After ten days, we gave up. Then, one day when the girls were sitting out front, a skinny, dirty animal slivered across the street, looking scared to death. Halfway across the street, we realized it was *Cutie Pie*. Brahna screamed, "*Cutie Pie*"! Our cat stopped, frozen in place, still looking very scared. Brahna rushed over, picked her up, caressed her, took her into the kitchen, and fed her milk. *Cutie Pie* had always been *Miss Social*, and in days of old, she would walk along the front wall every morning after breakfast. It took her about a month before she would go outside and another month before she acted like her old self again.

I hope we never again go through the trauma of another significant earthquake like that one. It was

HOLLYWOOD OR BUST!

awful.

Brahna won almost every tennis tournament she entered. Then, out of the blue, she was invited to attend Nick Bollettieri's Tennis Academy in Florida for two weeks as his guest. She loved Bollettieri, and Nick loved her and her extraordinary tennis abilities. They asked if she could stay an extra two weeks, which she did. Then, they offered her a full tennis scholarship. But, while she was there, her schooling was independent of tennis; I would have had to pay for that. As I write this, I still feel guilty. Mum's medical bills had used up most of our money, and I didn't have enough to pay for private schooling. I know Brahna was very disappointed, but she never complained.

One door closed, and another opened. Loyola Marymount University in Los Angeles offered Brahna a full athletic scholarship; food, lodging, and classes were all included. But she needed pocket money and didn't want to ask me. With the help of my friend, comedian Mort Saul, who had a connection at Johnny Rockets fast-food restaurant, she got a job as a waitress. Six months later, she got a second job at California Pizza Kitchen. She worked at both restaurants the entire time she was at Loyola. Thank goodness for Brahna's excellent work ethic. Did I not say my daughter was amazing?

However, all was not well in paradise, and problems popped up between her and me in her third year of college. She seemed angry all the time; nothing I did was right. Finally, I had to bring it to a head. I took her to dinner and asked her what was wrong. She hesitated, then, with tears in her eyes, she told me she was gay and worried sick about how I would react. My daughter had always been a tomboy, but I had never suspected she was gay. She always had male friends madly in love with her, but I don't remember Brahna ever reciprocating.

Brahna's first actual date was when she was around eleven or twelve. One night, I was at Playboy Mansion, and Hef, Mort Saul, and I sat around talking about our kids. Mort said his son, Mort Jr., was beginning to show interest in girls, but the boy had never been out on a date. As a joke, Hef said, *"June's daughter is about his age, so we should fix them up."* Well, you know how we parents are about our kids, always sticking our noses in their lives. Yes, we three evil parents thought it was a fun idea. We would arrange a date between Brahna and Mort Saul's son.

We arranged for them to meet at the mall. Mort Saul would drop Mort Jr. off on the lower level in front of a store, where there was a bench. I would bring Brahna in, and they would meet up, go for dinner at one of the restaurants by themselves and be back on the bench at a pre-arranged time.

I made my way to the second floor to meet up with Mort, and, like giggly teenagers, we spied on the kids from there. Aren't parents wonderfully evil?

Mort and I grabbed a cup of coffee and waited. When the kids left the nearby restaurant, they were smiling and laughing like they had enjoyed each other's company. We let them sit on the bench talking for about another 10 minutes before Mort and I went down different stairways. When we reached the kids, Mort and I pretended we had just bumped into each other. Okay, so we lied; sue us.

HOLLYWOOD OR BUST!

For Brahna and Mort Jr., it was a beginning of a great friendship. Mort Jr. was always lovely to be with and up for anything we invited him to, no matter what. I had been given seats to the ballet, for example. Now, most young boys would have no interest in ballet. But when Brahna asked Mort Jr. to join us, he surprised us and accepted.

Sadly, there was trouble on the horizon for young Mort. In his teens things began going wrong. He may have gotten involved with the wrong crowd and got hooked on drugs.

Mort Sr's comedy routine always had a political bent. He was a clever comedian, and he was always controversial. That was his stage persona. In truth, he was moral, kind, and one of the most honest men I had ever met. I never heard Mort cuss or say anything nasty about anyone. But, with Mort Jr's drug addiction, Mort was dealt a heartbreaking blow. He had to help his son get clean, which would take money, so he had to go on the road again. Who would look after his son while he was gone? Since I would be in town for a few months, Mort asked if I would look after his son, which I was more than happy to do.

I forget the year, but one day, Mort Jr. asked Brahna to take him to downtown Los Angeles for business. When they returned, Brahna was screaming at him. Unbeknownst to Brahna, Mort's appointment was to pick up his drugs. It was too late; they were there, Mort Jr. made the deal, and Brahna could do nothing to stop it. They drove home in silence; Brahna was fuming. I made him empty his pockets, and there were the drugs. When his dad returned to town, I had no choice but to tell him the truth. Mort Sr. went ballistic. He immediately enrolled his son in a rehab facility.

Following rehab, Mort Jr. stayed clean for a while, but, whatever his reasons, he failed to stay clean, and one day OD'd and died. As I write this, I feel deeply sad for Mort Sr, who loved his son so much. Mort Jr. was one of the sweetest young men, but like so many, he was caught up in something he couldn't control.

On October 26, 2021, my friend Mort Saul Sr. died at 94. He will be forever remembered for his bold social commentary on current events and scathing stand-up routines targeting political heavyweights without regard for who they were, from presidents on down.

Wherever my friend Mort is, I want him to know that Brahna and I loved him and his son and will never forget that Mort was a wonderful friend and father who did everything he could for his son.

The Union Plaza in Las Vegas opened at 1 Main Street in July 1971. It was downtown's largest hotel-casino at the time, with a 22-story 500-room tower. It cost a whopping $20 million to build and was managed by a group of downtown casino operators, Jackie Gaughan. In 1990 Gaughan acquired the hotel/casino for an undisclosed sum and changed the name to *The Plaza* and their entertainment format. Stage shows were out.

I was sad about the change because I loved working there. Everyone, from the owners to the servers and dealers, was terrific, and I would miss them. Brahna and my mother loved being there too. It was Mum's favorite place, and I'm so grateful she could spend the time she

HOLLYWOOD OR BUST!

did there.

I want to close out this chapter with one of my films that stands out in my memory. It was Robert Burge's 1986 production of *Vasectomy, a Delicate Matter*. I enjoyed making it because the fantastic cast was endless fun to work with. There was Abe Vigoda, Lorne Green, Paul Savino, and one of the best dancers ever, Suzanne Charney. She was director Bob Fossie's lead dancer in his 1969 film *Sweet Charity*, starring Shirley MacLaine. Lucky for us, Suzanne was branching out into acting and racked up an incredible film and TV credits list. Check her out on IMDB.com. I'm happy that Suzanne is another of my lifelong friends.

JUNE WILKINSON

Chapter 53

I can't think of a more exciting way to end this book of my life and travels than my trip around the world with my friend Sherry Hackett. Sherry had her mind set on embarking on an adventure around the world. She and Buddy had been to India, but Sherry was eager to see more of the country and other places she had never visited. Buddy had seen as much of India as he cared and was not anxious to visit again. So, Buddy made me an offer I couldn't refuse. He offered to pay all my expenses if I was Sherry's traveling companion. Like I said several times, my parents didn't raise no dummy. I couldn't say yes fast enough.

Sherry knew my younger brother John and his wife Annemie were teaching in Berlin and arranged for our adventure to start there. Did I mention Sherry was a

HOLLYWOOD OR BUST!

camera nut? Most of the time, there was a camera around her neck. I not only have memories but plenty of photos too. After we visited John and his wife, we flew from Berlin to New Delhi, where we spent several lovely days there.

Sherry brought along lots of luggage. It wasn't until she unpacked in New Delhi that I realized most of it was clothes she brought along for the poor, which she handed out whenever she saw someone in need. That was Sherry, a lady with a heart of gold.

As we walked around, I got used to Sherry passing out clothes to someone she thought was in need. But, one day, we were walking along a crowded street and passed a young girl who looked to be about nine. She was unwashed, had no shoes, and was dressed in an old torn cotton dress that was supposed to close at the back but was missing buttons. The girl was just standing there, looking sad and watching people pass. With her clothes bag slung over her shoulder, Sherry approached the young girl and spoke to her, but the girl didn't seem to understand. Sherry opened the bag, rifled through the clothes, and handed her a few things Sherry thought might fit her. The look on that young girl's face when she realized what Sherry had given her was priceless. That scene was repeated several times during our trip, but I will never forget that little girl's look.

A couple of days later, we moved on to the Taj Mahal. Now, driving in India is very scary. Like England, they drive on the left. However, if the left side is blocked or going too slow, drivers move from one lane to another anytime they like causing many near accidents. One accident did happen on our drive to the

Taj Mahal. The two young boys in front of us lost their lives because they kept moving from one side of the road to the other and were struck head-on by a large truck.

When Sherry and I arrived at the entrance to the Taj Mahal and looked down the long walkway, it was so beautiful that it took my breath away. From our guidebook, we learned the Mughal Emperor Shah Jahan built the Taj Mahal in honor of the Persian princess Mumtaz Mahal, his beloved third wife. She died in 1632 while bearing their fourteenth child, and Shah Jahan never recovered from the loss. Soon after the Taj Mahal's completion, Shah Jahan was deposed by his son Aurangzeb and put under house arrest at nearby Agra Fort, where he could see the Taj Mahal from his cell window. Aurangzeb buried him in the mausoleum beside his wife after Shah Jahan's death. In the 18th century, the Jat rulers of Bharatpur invaded Agra and attacked the Taj Mahal. They took away the two chandeliers, one of agate and another of silver, which hung over the main cenotaph; they also took the gold and silver screen. Kanebo, a Mughal historian, said the gold shield which covered the 4.6-meter-high (15 ft) finial at the top of the central dome was also removed during the Jat despoliation. A sad ending to one of the world's most beautiful structures built by a man who loved his wife.

We were invited to be guests at the Tata Tea Plantation. We saw a narrow road lined with bushes on both sides when we arrived at the entrance. We drove down the road, which seemed to continue forever in diminishing circles. There were no buildings in sight, just bushes and more bushes. We learned later that the bushes grew the tea leaves.

Our drive ended at a magnificent mansion where we would stay for four days. On our last night, a formal goodbye party was held for the guests. Sherry and I traveled light—no fancy clothes on this trip because we did not expect to attend black-tie affairs. Somehow, we managed to look presentable for what was a formal affair.

Our adventure took us across India to Bombay, Singapore, Katmandu, and the Tiger Tops animal preserve in the Himalayan Mountains. There we rode elephants, but there was no running water or electricity. Staying in the preserve and living by candlelight after dark turned the night incredibly beautiful.

Our next stop was Bali, which was so beautiful, but oh so humid. I don't know what the facilities are like now, but even fancy hotels did not have air conditioning back then. Let us hope that has changed. We cruised through the Indonesian Islands, then onto Komodo Island, famous for its dragons. We ended our trip in China.

I will never forget that once-in-a-lifetime journey, thanks to Sherry and Buddy Hackett.

The second question one asks when writing their memoir is how to end their trip down memory lane. Sorry, nothing fancy here, just that I am grateful for everything I was privileged to experience and all the wonderfully talented people I was blessed to work with and befriend. I treasure my friends in and out of show business. And the two most significant joys of my life, my mother for all she did for me and my one and only precious daughter, Brahna.

I hope you were able to keep pace with my never-ending memories and that you enjoyed accompanying me on my trip. Be well, everyone, be well.

About the Author

June Wilkinson was born on 27 March 1940 in Eastbourne, England. She started as a stage performer at 12 and became the youngest topless dancer at 15 at the Windmill Theatre in London from 1957 to 1958. During a promotional tour in the United States, she was discovered by Hugh Hefner. Her first appearance in *Playboy* in September 1958 was titled "The Bosom." She was a brunette in those days but a blonde in later shoots.

Wilkinson's second *Playboy* appearance was photographed by Russ Meyer. Meyer was an independent photographer, filming his ground-breaking *The Immoral Mr. Teas* (1959). Because she was under contract to Seven Arts at the time, Wilkinson could not officially appear in Meyer's film. However, as an uncredited and unpaid favor to the director, Wilkinson's breasts can be seen through a window in one scene.

Wilkinson appeared in *Playboy* again in August 1959 in a spread titled "The Bosom in Hollywood." During this period, she appeared with Spike Jones' band and actor Billy Barty. Recalling this period in her career, Wilkinson later remembered Barty with affection but commented that Jones had no sense of humor off-stage. In 1960, Wilkinson was featured in *Playboy* five times, in June, July, August, October, and again in November. Her feature in the November issue was titled "The Bosom Revisits Playboy." Wilkinson appeared in the 1960 voodoo film *Macumba Love*, which promoted her measurements as "44-20-36". At times reported as up to "45-22-35", in 1963, Wilkinson stated that her measurements were actually "40-22-35".

In 1961 Wilkinson made several stage appearances on the U.S. West Coast with performers such as Louis Jourdan in *The Marriage-Go-Round*, Sylvia Sidney in *Come Blow Your Horn*, and Milton Berle in *Norman, Is That You?* She had a brief role in John Cassavetes' 1962 film, *Too Late Blues*.

In December 1962, Wilkinson made her final appearance in *Playboy*, though her photos continued to appear in the magazine in anniversary and retrospective features. Though she was never an official Playboy Playmate, she was featured in the magazine on seven occasions and was one of the magazine's most popular photo subjects. She appeared in more than fifty other men's magazines and newspapers from 1958 to 1970, making her one of the most-photographed models of the era.

Wilkinson was the star of director Myron Gold's 1963 film *La Rabia* or *The Rage*. Directed in Mexico City, the film has Wilkinson as a stripper with a gigolo boyfriend. She met Dan Pastorini, NFL quarterback for the Houston Oilers and Oakland Raiders, in 1972, and they were married in 1973. They co-starred in the 1974 film

Florida Connection (also known as *Weed*) for the producer of *Rage*. The couple divorced in 1982, and Wilkinson never remarried. She has a daughter, Brahna, by Pastorini.

In the 1970s-1980s, Wilkinson starred in a series of sex comedy teasers, such as "Three in a Bedroom," "The Ninety-Day Mistress," and "Will Success Spoil Rock Hunter?"

In 1997, in her late 50s, June returned for another nude shoot in *The Best of Glamour Girls: Then and Now* vol. 2 (Winter 1997). In 1999 when *Playboy* published its list of the "100 Sexiest Stars of the Century", June came in at #30. She hosted *The Directors*, a Stars/Encore series where she interviewed filmmakers.

Filmography

Thunder in the Sun (1959 - (uncredited)—*Mr. Tease and His Playthings* (uncredited)—*Grand Jury* (1960 - uncredited)—*The Private Lives of Adam and Eve* (1960)—*Career Girl* (1960)—*Macumba Love* (1960)—*77 Sunset Strip* (1961)—*Too Late Blues* (1961) (uncredited)—*The Continental Twist* (1961)—*Lover Come Back* (1961) as Sigrid Freud, Stripper on Standee—*The Bellboy and the Playgirls* (1962) as Madame Wimpepoole—*The Rage* (1962)—*Who's Got the Action?* (1962) as Bride—*The Candidate* (1964)—*Batman* (1968)—*The Doris Day Show* (1971)—*The ABC Comedy Hour* (1972)—*The Mack* (1973)—*The Florida Connection* (1975)—*Frankenstein's Great Aunt Tillie (1984)*—*Texas Godfather* (1985)—*Vasectomy: A Delicate Matter* (1986)—*Talking Walls* (1987)—*Medium Rare* (1987)—*Keaton's Cop* (1990)—*Three Bad Men* (2005).

Stage Performances:
(Not in chronological order)

Pajama Tops—Keys for Two—Come Blow Your Horn—Any Wednesday—Will Success Spoil Rock Hunter—Fanny—Marriage-Go-Round—90-Day Mistress—Wally's Café—What the Butler Saw—Babes in the Woods—Baby Doll—Norman is that You—Mr. & Mrs.

www.ingramcontent.com/pod-product-compliance
Lightning Source LLC
Chambersburg PA
CBHW071228070526
44583CB00017B/2093